LORD LUCAN

James Ruddick

75p

HEADLINE

First published in 1994
by HEADLINE BOOK PUBLISHING

First published in paperback in 1995
by HEADLINE BOOK PUBLISHING

10 9 8 7 6 5 4 3 2 1

ISBN 0 7472 4677 7

Typeset by
Letterpart Limited, Reigate, Surrey

Printed and bound in Great Britain by
Cox & Wyman Ltd, Reading, Berks

HEADLINE BOOK PUBLISHING
A division of Hodder Headline PLC
338 Euston Road
London NW1 3BH

In memory of Frances Luckett
1969–88
My dearest friend

Contents

PART THREE: THE QUESTIONS 167

Acknowledgements

I am indebted to many people who agreed to see me for interviews and discussions about John Lucan and the murder at Lower Belgrave Street. In particular, I must thank Veronica, the Countess of Lucan; former Detective Chief Inspector David Gerring; the Press Office at Scotland Yard; the staff of the British Newspaper Library, Colindale; Dennis Gilson, a trustee of the Lucan estate; and all those who consented to talk about Lucan on the condition that their names would not be revealed. In addition I must also thank Bill Jones and Ian McBride of Granada Television.

For the history of the Lucan family, I have consulted Cecil Woodham-Smith's book *The Reason Why*, researched in 1953 with access to the family papers. For details of the social milieu of the time, I have drawn on contemporary press reports and on the chronicle *Gossip* by Andrew Barrow. I have also drawn on biographies of the central characters and these are credited, with their authors, whenever used. All other material has come from interviews with the author and from Lucan's own letters and papers.

J.R.
London, 1994

Introduction

On the night of November 7th, 1974, a particularly brutal murder took place at a house in London's Lower Belgrave Street. The victim was a 29-year-old nanny from Basingstoke, Sandra Rivett, who was bludgeoned to death in the basement of the house. At the same time, the 37-year-old Countess of Lucan, who lived in the house with her three children, was also attacked, but she managed to escape and to raise the alarm.

Almost immediately, the police began a manhunt for Lady Lucan's estranged husband, Richard John Bingham, whom she identified as her attacker. The hunt for Lucan, which eventually stretched to France, South Africa and Australia, became a British *cause célèbre*, preoccupying the press both at home and abroad for many months. At the same time, an inquest was held into the death of the nanny, which gradually fermented into a trial without the accused. Lady Lucan gave evidence of how she had been brutally assaulted in the darkened hallway of her house. It was revealed in court that Mrs Rivett was identical in height to Lady Lucan, and should have been out of the house on the murder night. The jury were left with the clear implication that Lord Lucan, lying in wait to murder his wife, had killed the wrong woman in the darkness, and then, discovering his mistake, had waited until Lady Lucan appeared before launching a second attack. They subsequently took just thirty-one minutes to deliver a verdict naming him as guilty of Mrs Rivett's murder.

But the Lucan case was never as conclusive as the popular press suggested. And in due course it was to acquire all the resonance of a classic unsolved murder.

The story functioned on several levels. First, there was the problem of his disappearance, which haunted the police and intrigued the public. Lucan's abandoned car had been found in Newhaven, close to the harbour and the ferry terminal, and this suggested that he had committed suicide in the sea within a few hours of the murder. But the reporting of constant 'sightings' of the missing Earl became a national sport, to the embarrassment of the police, and the popular wisdom was that he remained at large, possibly shielded by his friends, anonymous in plastic surgery.

Secondly, there was the central question of what had actually happened that night. The police maintained that it was a simple case of mistaken identity. But Lucan himself had carefully described before his disappearance how he had surprised an intruder at the house, and how he feared that Lady Lucan would blame him for the murder. Despite the apparent certainty over his guilt, which his vanishing trick cemented, the doubts and the controversy continued to echo on.

But the Lucan case aroused interest for another, more pragmatic reason: the curious tensions that existed between Lord and Lady Lucan, which surfaced at the Coroner's inquest, and which were so powerful that even the Coroner commented on them. The marriage of the Lucans became a disputed terrain. The most popular view was that Lucan himself was a personable and well-liked man who had been tortured by an impossible wife. His friends spoke of his civility, his warmth, his immense social grace, and talked of how universally disliked Lady Lucan had become. Her detractors circulated stories of her anti-social behaviour, her anxiety and her shocking outbursts in public. She had indeed been treated by a psychiatrist and was acknowledged to be a difficult woman. People popularly supposed therefore that Lucan was someone to be sympathized with, admired even, for his ability to cope with an increasingly hostile and poisonous domestic situation.

But the murder revealed a more complex view than this. Lucan had come from a grand and distinguished line. His great-great-grandfather had ordered the Charge of the Light Brigade. His great-grandfather had assisted at the Coronation of King Edward VII. His grandfather had been a lord-in-waiting to King George V when Lucan was born. Lucan found that his title opened all doors, and he exploited his social position to gain entry to a select group of rich people, many of whose existence revolved around the smart gentlemen's clubs of London.

In due course, Lucan became a full-time gambler, and spent his days turning the pursuit of pleasure into a professional occupation. He gambled and lost; gambled and lost; gambled and lost. In these trying circumstances, Lady Lucan, who was considerably more sensitive and intelligent than her husband, began to suffer with depression. Always highly strung, she found Lucan's addiction to gambling almost impossible to cope with.

In addition to this, Lucan himself was something of a throwback. He disliked the levelling culture of London in the 1960s and shut himself away in the insular and aloof clubs of Mayfair. Here, entrenched 19th-century values prevailed. There was a common spirit of reaction and suspicion. The gamblers yearned for more rigorous days and seemed, to external observers, to be increasingly out of touch with the outside world. Lucan would not talk to people who did not have proper shoelaces. He could not understand why young people wanted to grow their hair long or to speak with red-brick accents. He himself retreated into the military culture of his ancestors and fretted about the state of the country. In a time of national crisis, some of his friends had joined private armies. They talked of military coups and of rescuing England from the hands of foreign powers. In the meantime, they contented themselves with lamb cutlets and with trying to flip a Chemmy Nine.

After his disappearance, it was this world, a world of easy living, underpinned by the confidence of wealth, that came so vividly to life.

But it was the mystery itself that proved to have the greater longevity. In due course, the puzzle of his disappearance assumed the attraction of a common parlour game, with cranks, armchair detectives and mercenaries all claiming to have unearthed a solution, while the aspect of an unsolved murder, with all the enigmatic possibilities of injustice and false accusation, attracted the more serious investigators.

In the late 1980s, while working as a freelance journalist for a television company, I took up the threads of the story and began a quest for the solution. For seven months, as the research developed, I tracked down surviving witnesses, reread the documentation and reportage, and generally revived the questions and puzzles that had engaged the original investigators in 1974. I conducted many interviews and had access to Lucan's own personal files and papers. There came a point where I reluctantly had to break off the work because of the need to complete a script for filming. But the trail, I felt, could lead on, into previously uncharted areas, and I was anxious to go on pursuing it. For the moment, however, I was committed to other projects.

The subsequent interval lasted four years. This was much longer than I had intended but it brought certain advantages. Other investigators published the results of their findings, all of them drawing different conclusions, and the way remained open for a definitive account. There were further ripples of controversy in the national press. But there was never anything to bring the enigma to a conclusion, and indeed it gradually assumed the status, with age, of being a permanently intractable mystery, which would thwart even the most diligent eye.

Then, in 1994, I was recruited to the production team of a programme that was being made to mark the twentieth anniversary of Lucan's disappearance. It was then that I found all the old curiosities and obsessions coming to life again. I exhumed my notebooks and began to pore over all the familiar points. The interval had been useful, too, I found, in gaining a fresh perspective of the affair, and particularly in addressing the crucial forensic evidence. The trail opened up again and I began to meander down once more, now determined to complete what I had first started almost a decade earlier. Although I had been absent from the case for almost four years, this had been in the sense of actual activity, and as far as watching new developments went I had always kept it within arm's reach. Friends and fellow journalists would habitually send me cuttings through the post, aware that my interest in the case had become a quiet, perennial obsession, or would ring me up with gossip and news to add to the files.

As the publishing deadline approached I gathered my material around me and began to write at speed. The characters were all there, sprawled out over my desk, their life histories, their idiosyncrasies, and they sprang to life at the merest touch. I swotted up on the scientific notes I had acquired, making conclusions where possible, leaving questions unanswered if there was no hard and fast evidence. The aim was to produce the definitive account, in the absence of the Earl of Lucan, and to chronicle a powerful moment of British social history, which could be found in contemporary reports but which had never been enshrined in a single published account.

★ ★ ★

The first and second parts of the book are a straightforward, linear narrative. They deal with the events that led to the murder, the hunt for Lucan, and the climax of the story in the Coroner's Court. The third part of the book is about the search for an answer. It covers the decade of on-off research that I undertook, the occasional breakthroughs that I made, the distractions and diversions, and the final possibilities that we are left with. Sometimes, probably inevitably, the three threads intertwine.

In setting out on this task, my aim was not to produce the last word. The case is too notorious and too attractive for that. My aim was to complete a sufficient amount of research, and study the known facts with an imaginative eye, in order to produce a verdict that the reader can feel confident with, and that might, in the vacuum of permanent uncertainty, be considered as close to final as we can presently achieve.

Prologue

On the night of November 7th, 1974, two policemen were patrolling through Belgravia, in south-west London, in their police van. They had been expecting a quiet night, according to what they later told reporters, but at ten o'clock a call came through on their radio alerting them to an incident in a public house in Lower Belgrave Street. The call said simply that there had been an assault and that assistance was required. Swinging the van round, the two officers drove off in the general direction of Belgrave Square.

Fifteen minutes earlier a handful of customers had been sitting quietly in the bar of the Plumbers Arms, which lies on the southern tip of Lower Belgrave Street, close to the junction with Grosvenor Place. The cold weather had apparently kept many regulars at home and the landlord, Arthur Whitehouse, counted only nine customers in his bar. A little before 9.45 p.m., however, the peace of the pub was broken by the door bursting open and a woman covered in blood staggering towards the bar. She was not wearing a night-dress, as was later reported, but her clothes were drenched in dried blood and she continued to bleed from a series of severe head wounds in the centre of her forehead.

The landlord came out from behind the bar and helped the woman on to a banquette. She was apparently hysterical and was screaming about escaping from a murderer. In court, seven months later, Mr Whitehouse would tell the jury that she had cried, 'Help me! Help me! I've just escaped from a murderer. He's still in the house. My children, my children.' Instead of setting out to rescue these children, Mr Whitehouse and his customers settled themselves around the semi-conscious woman and tried to ascertain what had happened. Mrs Whitehouse rang for the police and tended to the woman's injuries with a bar cloth.

By the time the police van pulled up outside it had been established that the woman's name was Veronica Bingham, that she was the 37-year-old Countess of Lucan, and that she had run in her blood-soaked clothes from the Lucan family's large Georgian mansion, thirty yards up the street.

Police Sergeant Donald Baker, the driver of the van, made sure that an ambulance was on its way and then, with his partner, Police Constable Phillip Beddick, walked up Lower Belgrave Street to the door of the Lucan house, number 46. The door was locked. The house was in darkness. Seeking another way in, Baker opened the wrought iron gate that led from the street down the short flight of steps to the basement below, where there was a wooden door used for putting out the rubbish and the milk bottles at night. That door was locked, too. Baker peered in through the basement window but could see nothing for the venetian blinds. Coming back up the steps, he and Beddick decided to force open the front door. They did this not violently, using shoulder power, but by inserting a small strip of plastic, which unhinged the latch.

Inside, the long hallway was in darkness. Baker tried a light switch but nothing happened. The bulb apparently had burned out some weeks earlier and had not been replaced. (This was to be a familiar story in other parts of the house.)

Baker sent PC Beddick back down the street for a powerful police torch. Then he began slowly to advance down the hallway towards the stairs at the back of the house. On his left hand side a doorway opened out into a darkened living room, which was densely furnished with ancestral portraits and family heirlooms. Further along, on the left, another door led into a dining room, where there was a magnificent mahogany dining table, six gilded chairs, and a crystal chandelier. On the right, a staircase led up to the remaining five floors.

As he neared the end of the hallway, Baker saw a faint trace of light coming from a little cloakroom. He pulled back the curtains of the cloakroom and saw a shaving striplight on over a washbasin mirror. The light also revealed faint traces of blood in the sink, on the magnolia walls and on some of the woodwork. Turning away from the cloakroom, Baker noticed traces of blood on a lampshade, on a small hall table and across both walls of the hall. On the ceiling he could see more traces of blood, both smears and direct sprays and splashes. At his feet he noticed a small white object which he momentarily took to be a doll's leg.

Without waiting for PC Beddick, Baker went through the basement doorway and peered down into the gloom below. He tried the light switch here, too, but there was nothing. He began to advance down the stairs of the basement, sensing that this had been the main site of attack. At the foot of the stairs there was a tray of broken crockery. The street light came in through the venetian blinds and revealed a scene of utter catastrophe. There was blood across the furniture and across the walls and ceiling, and on the parquet floor there were two huge pools of it, one directly at the bottom of the stairs, the other leading into the kitchen. Behind him, at the rear of the basement, there were three or four large footprints in blood, apparently leading to the back door.

Sergeant Baker walked through the basement, mindful of the blood, and tried the door. It was open. He went out into the windswept garden and looked for any sign of an intruder's escape. He could see nothing. He went back into the house and closed the door. He looked around the basement again and then went up the basement steps back into the hallway.

PC Beddick had still not returned with the torch, so Baker continued his search of the house alone. He went up the stairs on to the second floor. This was also in complete darkness, apart from a little bedside light burning in the main bedroom. The sheets of the bed were ruffled here, and Baker noticed that there was a blood-stained towel draped over the pillows. He left the room and went up to the next floor. Here, in two bedrooms, he found the three Lucan children. The heir, Lord George Bingham, aged seven, was asleep in his room at the front of the house. His younger sister, Camilla, aged three, was asleep in the room she shared with her elder sister, Frances, aged ten. Frances was not asleep. She was standing by her sister's bed, wide awake and anxious to know what had become of her mother and her nanny.

At that moment, PC Beddick reappeared with the torch. Baker left Beddick in charge of the three children and went back to the basement. This time he was equipped with a proper light and was able to carry out a more thorough search.

The light yielded several gruesome discoveries. Firstly, the little object in the hall which Baker had thought was a doll's leg was no such thing. It was a short piece of lead piping, about nine inches long, and wrapped in surgical tape. Earlier, in the neon streetlight coming down the hall, Baker had thought the object was white; but his torchlight now revealed it to be covered in human blood. It was also 'grossly distorted'. The carpet around the piping was also covered in blood and the light revealed more sprays of blood over the walls. In the basement, Baker found a lightbulb lying on a cushioned chair. The ceiling socket was empty, he noticed. So he replaced the bulb and turned on the switch.

Now, for the first time, Baker noticed a large canvas mailbag in the kitchen doorway. The bag was drenched in blood. The top of the bag was folded over but the cord wasn't drawn tight. Lifting the flap, Baker saw part of a human thigh in black tights.

'I took out an arm,' he said, later. 'It was very white. I could feel no pulse.'

This was the body of Sandra Rivett, the Lucans' nanny. She had been beaten to death.

Sandra Eleanor Rivett was just twenty-nine years old. She had one small son who lived with her parents in Basingstoke. She had been working for Lord and Lady Lucan only six weeks when she died.

The death of Sandra Rivett was to open up one of the greatest *causes célèbres* of modern times. It would be fair to say, in fact, that nothing quite so devastating had disrupted the leisured world of the British aristocracy in recent memory. In the 1920s, it is true, a young socialite had shot dead her lover in a mews house in Chelsea, and during the war there had been the sensational murder of Josslyn Hay, the 22nd Earl of Erroll, in Kenya, which had ruthlessly exposed the dissipated lifestyles of the early settlers. Later, in 1946, there had been a shooting at the war-time home of the King of Greece, in Chester Square, Belgravia, where the housekeeper had been found slumped on the floor with a bullet in her head.

But these scandals were in the colonial past, more than a generation ago, and they had worn thin with constant examination. Nothing comparable had occurred in more recent times that any working journalist or policeman could recall, and in this sense what followed in Belgravia that night was a ground-breaking investigation. It had legal repercussions, too, and when it eventually came to court, seven months later, there were to be far reaching changes in the criminal justice system as a direct result.

For those involved, the unfolding drama of November 7th had an illusory quality about it. In hindsight one can find a pattern to the events, take up the linking thread and run the sequence together. But at the time, things must have seemed hopelessly fragmented. All that contemporary witnesses recalled, in the early hours of the drama, was a common sense of foreboding. Sandra Rivett's death had opened up a faultline in the very foundations of the English ruling class, and that faultline would continue to echo on down the years.

In due course, as news of the murder spread around London, a flotilla of police officers arrived in Lower Belgrave Street. Journalists and reporters were dispatched to the scene, and a number of television and radio crews arrived, apparently to the irritation of the residents. Belgravia is the aristocratic village of London, and its aesthetic grandeur reflects the intensely private, insular presumptions of its occupants.

At 10.20 p.m., after Lady Lucan had been conveyed to St George's Hospital, a detective sergeant arrived. He was the first CID officer on the scene. His name was Graham Forsyth and he was stationed at Gerald Road police station, just around the corner. Sergeant Forsyth had been told that Lady Lucan had been violently assaulted, that her children's nanny was dead and that the Lucans' eldest daughter, Lady Frances Bingham, had said that, although her parents were separated and Lord Lucan lived in a flat nearby, her father had actually been in the house earlier that night. While she was watching TV, at about 9 p.m., her mother and father had walked into the bedroom, Lady Lucan crying and already covered in blood. Her father had turned off the TV set and her mother had sent her up to bed.

Understandably, this raised Forsyth's suspicions and he immediately set about looking for Lucan's address. He discovered that Lucan owned a mews cottage in Eaton Row, directly behind number 46, but received no reply at the door.

He found a ladder and broke in through a top window, but the house was empty.

On his return to number 46, Forsyth was confronted by another significant development. A tall, elderly lady had pushed past the uniformed officers guarding the house and had announced herself to Sergeant Baker as Lord Lucan's mother. 'I've come here to collect the children,' she said. 'My son telephoned me a short while ago and asked me to pick them up and take them back to my flat.'

Forsyth then took up the cudgels. He told the Dowager Countess of Lucan that her daughter-in-law had been badly injured and that her grandchildren's nanny had been killed. She said she was not surprised by this. Her son had told her that there had been a terrible accident at the house and that Veronica, Lady Lucan, was injured. 'He said to me, "I want you to get the children out as soon as possible." ' The phone call had come just after 10.30 p.m., she said, as she was returning to her flat in North London. She was a widow and lived alone. Her son had sounded extremely shocked: 'almost incoherent with shock'. He had told her that he had been passing the house when he had seen a struggle going on in the basement between his wife and an intruder. He had intervened, the intruder had escaped, and his wife had then blamed him for the whole thing. The scene in the basement had been 'ghastly', he had said, 'with blood and mess everywhere'.

Forsyth asked what relations were like between Lucan and his wife. The Dowager said that her daughter-in-law had been diagnosed as a manic depressive and that there had been a court case for the custody of the children. Lady Lucan was not diagnosed as violent, except verbally, but in the original case it was thought she might be a danger to the children. This was clearly intended to throw doubt on the obvious supposition from events, but Sergeant Forsyth pressed on. He needed to trace Lord Lucan immediately, he said, for questioning. He asked the Dowager what kind of car he drove and where he lived. She told him that he had a blue Mercedes and that he owned a flat in Elizabeth Street, about a hundred yards away. Forsyth then allowed her to go upstairs and collect the children. He told PC Beddick to accompany the Dowager back to her flat in case Lord Lucan should contact her again.

A little after 11 p.m., Forsyth rang his immediate superior, Detective Chief Inspector David Gerring, who was in charge of Gerald Road police station. Gerring was already in bed, though not yet asleep, when the call came. He told Forsyth that he was on his way and would be in Belgravia within the hour. 'I told my wife I'd be gone for a couple of hours,' Gerring said to me later. 'In fact she didn't see me for another four days.' On the way, Gerring picked up his own superior, Detective Chief Superintendent Roy Ranson, who was based at Cannon Row. The two men were something of a partnership in the Metropolitan Police. Although they came from widely differing backgrounds, each had a number of commendations, and they had both earned reputations as skilful handlers of potentially sensitive cases. Ranson had worked on the missing tax papers of Harold Wilson. Gerring had investigated the shooting attempt on Princess Anne.

On their arrival in Belgravia both officers went straight to 46 Lower Belgrave Street and, having examined the scene of the crime, moved on to Lucan's flat in Elizabeth Street. They found the Mercedes outside with a flat battery and decided to authorize the forcing of the front door in order to search the building. It was an extravagant, meticulously kept apartment, with five bedrooms and a large dining room. Ranson went into the main bedroom, where a light was switched on, and looked around. 'It was so curious,' he said. 'It looked as though it was waiting for its owner to return from the bathroom. On the bed, there was his suit and shirt, and on the bedside table there was his wallet, car keys, change, cheque book and driving licence – all the things a man

14

usually carries around in his pockets.' Ranson sat on the bed and opened the bedside drawer. Here he found Lucan's passport and address book. The address book, he said, 'was filled with the names of people that most of us only read about in newspapers. I realized then that we were about to break into a different world and that there might be problems.' The inhabitants of Lucan's world were mainly people like himself: patrician, upper class, hypercivilized. The address book included John Aspinall, the doyen of London gambling, the tycoon Jimmy Goldsmith, and Dominick Elwes, the painter. Yet it was one of the more curious aspects of the case that the wealth which appeared to surround the Lucans was in reality an illusion. The flat was rented. The house belonged to a family trust. The car was on HP. Later, the police would discover that Lucan had lost his vast inheritance at the gaming tables and had recently been forced to raise the family silver for auction.

Later that night, Ranson and Gerring went to St George's Hospital and interviewed Lady Lucan. It was an informal interview because she was in a debilitated condition after her assault. But she had no doubts about what had happened at the house that night, or about who had attacked her. She told Ranson and Gerring that it should have been Sandra's night off but that she had changed at the last minute. She had also offered to make Lady Lucan's customary cup of tea at 9 p.m., too, which was another alteration to the established routine. And she was the same height as Lady Lucan. When Sandra had not returned from making the tea, Lady Lucan had gone down to the basement to look for her. She had not got as far as the basement, however, because she had been attacked on the ground floor. She had fended off the assault by grabbing her attacker's testicles and squeezing until he desisted. She recognized her attacker as her husband, she said. He had intended to murder her and had lain in wait in the basement, having removed the lightbulb. When Sandra had appeared he had attacked her by mistake, thinking it was

15

the Countess. When Lady Lucan had then appeared he had had no choice but to attack her, too. Lady Lucan said she had calmed her husband and persuaded him to take her upstairs to look at her wounds. Frances had been sent to bed. The TV had been switched off. But when Lucan had gone into the bathroom for a face flannel, Lady Veronica had seized her chance and fled from the house, running down the street to the Plumbers Arms.

'She was a highly convincing witness,' said Gerring, later. 'She never once wavered,' added Ranson, 'no matter how much we questioned her.'

In due course, the officers decided to issue a red alert for Lucan's arrest.

Meanwhile, as Lady Lucan was speaking out against her husband, and the police in London were searching for him, Lucan himself was driving along the A27 into Sussex, to a small, parochial town, about fifteen miles from the coast, called Uckfield. Uckfield is a catchment area for retired businessmen or for commuters with the stamina for the hour-long journey to central London. It is a town of considerable wealth. It is also extremely quiet.

Church Street, to the north, is one of the more luxurious roads of the town. At the top of the street is a rambling Victorian rectory, with a long, looped drive and a spread of thick ivy across the red-brick frontage.

The building did not belong to a rector, however, but to a professional gambler, a cousin of the Duke of Norfolk, named Ian Maxwell-Scott, who lived there with his wife Susan, a barrister. Susan had been called to the Bar in the 1960s but had never practised. The Maxwell-Scotts had seven children and lived in considerable luxury.

On the night of November 7th, Ian had decided to stay in London. He was a director of the Clermont, a gambling club in Berkeley Square, and had apparently had one drink too many during a backgammon match and decided not to risk the drive home. Consequently, Susan was alone in the house with her children and her large German Shepherd dogs. She was already in bed and asleep when the front doorbell rang. She got out of bed and crossed to the bathroom window and peered down. She saw Lord Lucan standing below in the doorway. Lucan was an old friend of her husband's. She pushed open the window and called down. Lucan said, 'Hello, Susie, I'm sorry to bother you so late . . .' Before he had finished, Mrs Maxwell-Scott said, 'Hang on, John, I'll come down and let you in.'

Her first thought, she said later, was that Ian had attempted the drive home after all and had had an accident. 'Shows how selfish you can be,' she said. But Lucan had not come with news about Ian; he had come to *see* Ian, he said. 'He said to me, "Hello, Susie, sorry it's so late, is Ian around?" I told him that Ian was staying in London and then invited him in. I didn't have to be clairvoyant to know that something was wrong.' Lucan's hair was awry, Mrs Maxwell-Scott recalled later, and he looked a little untidy. 'Dishevelled is too strong a word,' she said, 'but normally he looked rather spruced.' She also noticed a 'wet patch' on the hip of his trousers. She led him through into the drawing room and poured him a scotch. Lucan sat down in a gold wicker chair by the french windows.

'I must tell you,' he apparently said, 'I've been through the most nightmarish experience. It's so incredible I don't know whether you or anyone else will believe it. But I'll tell you anyway.'

Lucan then elaborated on the story he had earlier told his mother over the telephone. He said that he had been walking past his wife's house in Lower Belgrave Street, on his way home to change for dinner, when he had glanced down into the basement and seen a struggle going on between his wife and an intruder. 'He said that it was incredible that he should be passing at that precise moment,' Mrs Maxwell-Scott said, 'and I replied that it wasn't that incredible. I know he

17

frequently did go past the house to check that everything was all right. He said that he did do that quite often, yes.' Having a front-door key, Lucan rushed in and ran down into the basement. As he reached the bottom of the basement steps he slipped and fell into a pool of blood. That accounted for the patch on his trousers. The man he had seen attacking his wife ran off, apparently up the basement stairs. Lucan got up and went to the aid of his wife.

'I can't tell you how awful the basement was,' he said. 'There was blood everywhere. Veronica was covered in blood and she was hysterical. She pointed to a sack in the corner and accused *me* of having hired this man to kill her.' Later, in court, Mrs Maxwell-Scott would allege that Lucan told her that this was 'something Lady Lucan frequently accused him of. He claimed that she got the idea from an American TV movie.'

Mrs Maxwell-Scott asked if Lucan had got a proper look at the attacker and Lucan said that he had not. He described the man as 'large'. She did not ask which way the man fled and Lucan didn't volunteer the information. But when she said that it might have been someone wanting to kill the nanny, Lucan apparently replied, 'No, not that. Sandra was a good girl.'

Eventually, Lucan said, he had calmed his wife sufficiently for her to be led back upstairs so that they could inspect her wounds. 'He said that it was his intention to mop up the worst of the blood and then call for the police.' Lucan went into the bathroom for a face flannel. While the taps were running he was momentarily deafened, and when he went back into the bedroom he found it deserted. Lady Lucan had got up from the bed and left. He went on to the landing and called after her. Then he heard the front door slamming down below and realized that Lady Lucan was raising the alarm. He heard her in the street screaming, 'Murder! Murder!' and it dawned on him that she would implicate him in the crime.

'I think he then panicked,' said Mrs Maxwell-Scott. 'He didn't *say* that he panicked but I think he did. There he was with the body and the blood. I think he thought to himself: "There's blood on me, blood all over the place. I'm not staying here." So he left.'

Having completed the story, Lucan asked if he could use the telephone to ring his mother and check that she had collected the children and that they were unharmed. Mrs Maxwell-Scott heard his side of the conversation in the subsequent call.

The Dowager Countess of Lucan had returned to her flat just before midnight. She had put the children to bed and was spending the night sleeping upright in an armchair by the telephone. PC Beddick was sitting across from her when Lucan rang.

According to Mrs Maxwell-Scott, Lucan asked, 'Have you got the children?'

The Dowager replied, 'Yes, they're here in bed, and to the best of my knowledge and belief they're asleep.'

Lucan said, 'That's all right, then. Has Veronica turned up?'

'Yes, she's been taken to hospital,' came the reply. 'She's going to be all right but I'm afraid that the nanny is dead.'

Silence. The Dowager said, 'Look, the police are here. They're in the flat. Do you want a word with them?'

Lucan seemed to hesitate. The Dowager tried to press the point. Much later she would say that it was a cause of 'lasting regret' to her that she didn't force him to speak to the officer sitting across from her. But Lucan said simply, 'No. I won't speak to them now. Tell them that I'll ring them in the morning. And I'll ring you in the morning, too.'

The Dowager then asked him what he was going to do next. 'But I got nowhere,' she said. Repeating the claim that he would speak to her tomorrow, Lucan hung up. The Dowager replaced the receiver and turned to PC Beddick.

'That was my son,' she said. 'He won't speak to you now. He'll phone you in the morning.'

Back in Uckfield, Lucan now tried to reach his sister-in-law and her husband, the Shand Kydds. He was told that they were out. So while Mrs Maxwell-Scott made some coffee, Lucan sat at her mahogany writing desk and wrote William Shand Kydd two letters, further protesting his innocence. 'The circumstantial evidence against me is strong,' he said, 'in that V[eronica] will say it was all my doing. I will therefore lie doggo for a while. I am only concerned about the children. If you can manage it, I'd like them to live with you. When they are old enough to understand, explain to them the dream of paranoia, and look after them.'

A second letter apparently took the form of a last will. It detailed Lucan's appalling finances and reminded Shand Kydd of a forthcoming sale of family heirlooms at Christie's. 'These,' he said, 'should satisfy the bank overdrafts.' He ended by saying, 'The other creditors can get lost for the time being.' He sealed both letters and asked Mrs Maxwell-Scott to post them for him in the morning. For a while, the two of them sat in the drawing room, sipping coffee. Then Lucan said that he had to be getting back. He exact words were: 'I must get back to sort things out.'

'I tried to persuade him to stay the night,' Mrs Maxwell-Scott said. 'I told him that he could have a wash and tidy up and then we'd go to the police in the morning. He almost wavered. I'm sure if Ian had been here he would have persuaded John to stay. But he repeated that he had to get back to find out what Veronica had been saying about him.'

Mrs Maxwell-Scott led him to the front door. He paused and said that he would be in touch again, as soon as he had spoken to the police. 'Goodbye, Susie,' he said, kissing her on the cheek, 'and thank you.'

She stood on the steps in her dressing gown. She watched him climb into his car and negotiate his way down the long gravel drive, and when she could no longer see the tail-lights winking at her in the darkness she went back inside the house and closed the door.

No one ever saw him again.

PART ONE

THE MURDER

I live at 46, Lower Belgrave Street with my Mummy, my brother George, my sister Camilla, and whoever is looking after us. Mummy and Daddy don't live together, but I usually see Daddy every other weekend. The last time I saw Daddy was on Thursday, November 7th, 1974. On that day I didn't go to school because the bus didn't come for me, so Mummy said I need not go. Camilla and George went to school as usual. I stayed home with Mummy and Sandra, our nanny. As far as I know nothing unusual happened that day and no one came to see us.

On Thursday evening Mummy, Camilla, George and Sandra and I all had our tea together. I think that was some time around 5 p.m. or 5.30 p.m. After tea I played with some of my games in the Nursery. Sandra brought George and Camilla upstairs and put them to bed. I stayed in the Nursery and then went downstairs to Mummy's bedroom. That would have been about 8.40 p.m.

I asked Mummy where Sandra was and Mummy said she was downstairs making some tea. After a while,

Mummy said she wondered why Sandra was taking so long. I don't know what time this was but it was before the news came on the television at 9 p.m. I said I would go downstairs and see what was keeping Sandra but Mummy said no, she would go . . .

Just after she left the room I heard a scream. It sounded as though it came from a long way away. I went to the door and called 'Mummy?' But there was no reply, so I left it. At about 9.05 p.m., when the news was on television, Daddy and Mummy both walked into the room together. Mummy had blood over her face and she was crying. She told me to go upstairs. Daddy didn't say anything to me and I didn't say anything to either of them. I don't know how much blood was on Mummy's face, I only caught a glimpse of her . . . I wondered what had happened, but I didn't ask. I went upstairs and got into bed and read my book. I didn't hear anything from downstairs.

I was very surprised to see Daddy at home on that Thursday night, but I didn't ask why he was there.

From the statement of Lady Frances Bingham

Chapter One

JOHN LUCAN

The Lucan family is a line of little antiquity but considerable prominence. They had originated in Sutton Bingham, near Yeovil, when Robert Bingham had become Bishop of Salisbury in 1229 (there is still a mural on the wall of the little parish church which depicts him in the role). Later, they had become sea-faring mercenaries for Elizabeth I. But the Earldom was relatively new, dating back to the end of the 18th century. Nonetheless, they were a family of immense grandeur. They had a vast estate in Ireland of 60,000 acres and a fine town house in Castlebar, County Mayo. They also had a seat in Staines, Middlesex, and a town house in London.

The Lucans were notorious in Ireland for their ferocity and their dissipation. The Third Earl of Lucan, who had ordered the Charge of the Light Brigade at the battle of Balaclava, was known in County Mayo as the Great Exterminator, because his ruthless policy of eviction during the potato famines cost thousands of lives. A contemporary account reports how the streets of the town became choked with the bodies of those who starved to death. Lucan's only reaction, when asked to give assistance, was, 'I do not intend to breed paupers to pay priests.'

Some in the line lived a permanent feast of pleasure. The Fourth Earl squandered enough of the inheritance to force his father to place considerable restrictions around the estate, lest it be lost to his son's creditors. Contemporary reports show him to be a model of 19th-century romanticism, who sacrificed a promising academic career to gambling and extravagance.

But the Lucans were also famed for producing throwbacks. They had the warrior qualities of cruelty and savagery. They confronted all obstacles with irritation and took whatever steps were necessary to ensure their own survival. When the Third Earl won command of the Cavalry Division at Balaclava it was, according to a contemporary report, because of the characteristics his line was most famous for: 'Ruthlessness, energy, and disregard for sentiment.'

Richard John Bingham had been born in December 1934, the second child of Patrick and Kaitilin Lucan. A girl, Lady Jane, had been born two years earlier, and another, Lady Sarah, would follow in 1936; a second boy, christened Hugh, was to appear just before the outbreak of the Second World War. The children were looked after by a number of domestic servants, including a nanny and several nursery maids. At that time, the Lucans lived in a tall house in Cheyne Walk, close to the river. Richard John, like many from his social class, had been born in the London Clinic, an exclusive maternity hospital in Chelsea. At home, he was the only one of the four children to be given his own personal maid, in addition to the family nanny, Flora Coles.

From the outset, the life of Richard John Bingham should have been an assured progression, from Eton or Harrow, to a stint in the Guards, and then Oxford or the Foreign Office. That was the way of his immediate predecessors and of his close relatives. His cousins had all gone to university. His father had gone into the army and then into politics. The way was open for Lucan to pursue either course, after suitable training, or perhaps to join the civil service or the Diplomatic Corps. Commerce, too, and high finance, had ceased in the last century to be considered unsuitable occupations for the nobility, and many of Lucan's friends would end up in the City.

But Lucan's life never quite made it on to that smooth, linear progression. This was partly because his own characteristics and temperament would not allow him to fit into the conventional work model. But there was also the question of his emotional background which, instead of equipping him with the mental discipline and security required for a conventional lifestyle, brought him a peculiar set of inner anxieties, and seemed to leave him largely unable to cope with the challenges of adulthood and independence.

The first trauma, one of many to scar his early years, was the war-time separation from his parents. Following the outbreak of conflict in Europe, it was widely considered to be prudent for the children of English aristocrats, who might be prominent on an execution list during an invasion, to be evacuated. Arrangements were therefore made for the four Bingham children to be sent to a retreat in North Wales, while Patrick and Kaitilin remained in the city, assisting the fire services. In due course, when the travel arrangements were complete, it was decided to evacuate the children abroad, to the United States.

Richard John did not cope well with this initial wrench. There were tantrums and violent headaches. He also suffered with nightmares. His parents were convinced that, in due course, he would settle down, and to an extent he did. It might be argued that he learned, in fact, to internalize the trauma, and we might speculate on the long-term effects of this later.

The children arrived in Washington, DC, in the late

summer of 1940, after sailing from Southampton to Canada
with Miss Coles, and then travelling across the Canadian
border. The Lucans had few connections in the United States
and their early days were nervously nomadic, but in September
a mutual friend put them in contact with Marcia Brady
Tucker, a banking heiress, who had agreed to accommodate
the four children on a permanent basis, at least for as long as
their parents felt England remained under threat.

'It was East Coast snobbery really,' said a family friend. 'It
was not the kind of commitment that was going to dent her
fortune and it gave her a certain status among the parvenus
of New York and the East Coast.'

Marcia Tucker was in a position to give the Binghams far
more than their own family could provide. She had come
from a family which had made its fortune at the end of the
19th century, chiefly in banking and industrial finance. The
Bradys were notorious, locally, for their rigid adherence to
the kind of sharp English gentilities that had become fashionable
social currency on the East Coast. Marcia would dictate
her orders each morning to a private secretary, who would
then deliver them to the staff by proxy. One family friend
wrote:

> The style was regimental and colonial. She was completely
> ruthless and the turnover of staff, whom she
> bullied relentlessly, was very fast. Her orders were
> always obeyed. She employed people, for instance, to
> walk around her estate – which was thousands and
> thousands of acres – just to frighten off the cats. She was
> a keen bird watcher and her orders were that no cats
> should be allowed into the grounds. This was a 24-hour
> surveillance.

Another friend, since dead, remembered how the head
butler, Herbert, had been forced to resign after being roped
and bound to Marcia by armed raiders. 'It was an indignity

too great for either of them to bear,' she said.

The Bingham children were given their own private house on Marcia's summer estate at Mount Kisco, Westchester. There were three tennis courts and two swimming pools, one in the sun, the other shaded. There were sixteen acres of woods, a farm and two large orchards. During the holidays Richard John was sent to the Adirondacks for summer camp. In winter, when the season began in New York, they transferred to Marcia's house on Park Avenue. There was also a beach property, Hobe Sound, in Florida, and an ocean yacht, *Migrant*, which was sufficiently powerful to be requisitioned by the US military after Pearl Harbor.

Relatives and friends were certain that the opulence left a residual mark. 'It stamped itself on us,' said Lady Jane Bingham, later. Her sister, Sarah, said, 'I suppose those years gave Richard John a taste for the rich life which he never lost.'

In February 1945 the children sailed back to England in the care of their American governess, Miss Harrison. 'It was perfectly apparent by then that there wasn't going to be an invasion,' said Kaitilin, 'and Pat and I thought they would feel bad if they hadn't seen anything of their own country.' The house in Cheyne Walk had suffered a direct hit and the Lucans had moved to a Georgian mansion in Eaton Square. Eaton Square had been listed before the war as one of the ten most exclusive addresses in London.

But the homecoming, like the departure, was a disturbing affair. In the war years Patrick and Kaitilin had decided publicly to declare their allegiance to Clement Attlee's Labour Party, with which they had been in quiet sympathy since the 1920s. Kaitilin had become an active member of the St Marylebone Constituency Association. Patrick had taken a junior position in the Commonwealth Office in the first majority Labour government. And their post-war lifestyles had now changed to reflect these positions. Although they occupied the house in Belgravia, family visitors recalled that 'it was virtually unfurnished'. Swords and scabbards and other family heirlooms lay around on the bare floorboards. A single rope, used for war exercises, dangled from the ceiling of the living room. Some of the windows had been blown out by the bombers and no one had bothered to replace the glass, so that rain occasionally seeped in and flooded the ground-floor rooms.

Richard John's uncle, J. Edward Bingham, recalled that Kaitilin would 'often come slopping in, wearing worn out sandals and awful baggy trousers'. She would rather have been 'plain Mrs Lucan, anyway'. Another relative recalled:

> They were not grand people at all. They were studiously eccentric English aristocrats. The house was never tidied; there were never any grand parties or anything like that. This was a time when it was quite fashionable for aristocrats to be Socialist, after the horrors of the depression and the war, but I don't think it was a fashion thing with them. They were quite sincere. They simply felt that politics was the serious business of life and all the upper-class things were trivia.

Jonathan Miller, a schoolboy contemporary of Lucan's, recalled: '[Kaitilin] was always wielding Labour Party pamphlets. She did look a sight in an impressive sort of way. Her hair looked as if someone had stabbed a sofa.' Another schoolfriend remembered being driven by Patrick Lucan in a car 'where the roof leaked on the whole journey'. But to his political friends, Lucan was seen as diligent and committed. 'He was a serious figure,' his agent said, 'not a lightweight.'

The effect of this domestic volte-face on the four children was unsettling. 'In America they had everything and thought nothing of luxuries,' said a relative, 'but back in London . . .' Richard John seemed to react particularly badly. 'John came back from the very rich life he'd had in America to this slum,' said his uncle. 'And he rebelled against it. What he wanted – and had when he was old enough – big cars, bright lights, the high life, were things his parents didn't approve of.'

'There were quite a lot of tantrums and sulks in the first few months after they came back,' said his aunt, Christine Bingham. 'John couldn't adjust to the rigours of self-denial after his experiences with the Tuckers.'

To the police and press in 1974, Lucan's addiction to pleasure, his obsession with extravagance and luxury, was one of the most striking features of the case. It was his impending bankruptcy, after all, which formed a central pivot to the supposed motive. Here, in his formative years, were the roots of that addiction. The unusual, almost neurotic emphasis that Lucan placed on hedonism was shown in a letter that he wrote to his uncle when he was barely out of his teens:

Too many people say that money isn't everything – it can't buy happiness, and all the usual patter. But this is either sour grapes or stupidity. Avarice is the spur of industry, whether it is avarice for oneself, or one's children, or for any other 'cause', it is avarice nonetheless . . .

I am perfectly happy now (that is to say that I am not *un*happy), but I know that with £2 million in the bank I should be happier still (who wouldn't?). It wouldn't be a case of 'buying happiness', but motor cars, yachts, expensive holidays and security for the future would give myself and a lot of other people a lot of pleasure. These are some of my carrots, and I'm certainly not ashamed of them.

In 1949, in spite of the Lucans' socialism, Richard John was dispatched to Eton. It was now possible to detect a hardening of his dissipation. He immediately began to pursue the two leading occupations of the leisured rich: gambling and sport. 'He was always gambling,' said his friend Charles Benson. 'There was a lot of it in our house, though it was strictly against the rules and was an expellable offence. He also played a lot of sport. He enjoyed games but he wasn't terribly good at them.' According to his mother he ran a secret book in order to supplement his pocket money, which took bets for the Thursday races at Ascot. 'He was always getting bawled at for going to the races,' she said. Another friend remembered him 'playing cards in the study of another boy, drinking gin and smoking. He would have been expelled if he had been discovered but he often seemed to be one step ahead.' Brian Masters, the writer, a friend of John Aspinall, relates a story that illustrates how deeply engrained in his psyche Eton had become, and how dependent he was upon it emotionally. After the upheavals and separations of his boyhood, Eton represented an anchor, some emotional stability, which he would not let go. According to Brian Masters, the Lucans had decided when Richard John was sixteen that Eton was incompatible with their socialism and elected to remove him to one of the new grammar schools. On hearing this, the boy sent a cable to his aunt, Christine, asking her to tea at the Ritz. When she arrived he told her that he was immensely happy at Eton but that his parents wished to remove him. They had jokingly told him that the only way he would remain there was by paying his own fees. So, he said, he intended to do just that. He knew that his aunt intended to leave him some money in her will, and he wanted the cash advanced to him now, in full, so that he could pay his entire fees, up to his eighteenth birthday. His aunt, not a socialist, wrote him out a cheque in the lobby of the Ritz, and he was able to remain at Eton for the remaining two years, eventually ending up as Captain of Roe's House.

'I think he really found himself at Eton,' said a contemporary. 'He had had a very insecure childhood after all, in

America, and then with his parents moving and becoming socialist.'

But the college failed to provide any tangible sense of direction, and when Lucan left in 1953 to do his National Service he had 'absolutely no idea' how he was going to make a living. 'He had thought of going to university to read English Literature,' said a friend, 'but his parents had told him that they would only allow him the money to go through university as an ordinary student, and of course that didn't appeal at all.'

For a 'born gambler', as Lucan described himself, the stock market seemed an obvious place. After completing his National Service, at Krefeld, in Germany, and passing out as a Second Lieutenant in the Coldstream Guards, he took a series of banking exams and joined William Brandts, the merchant bankers.

'I have come into the City in an attempt to make my pile,' he wrote:

> I don't know whether I shall succeed, because, in my opinion, it's not just a question of staring at ledgers. In my opinion the formula for success is as follows:
>
> a) 60% Luck
> b) 20% Industry
> c) 20% Gambling ability
>
> Mr Niarchos [presumably the tycoon] does not agree with me: he believes his success is only 40% luck and 60% hard work. Obviously, there are other require-ments, such as an ability to get on well with people, honesty, trustworthiness and all the usual virtues. But taking these for granted, all I now ask is ten times my ration of good luck! It's impossible to qualify for this unless full use is made of (c) on the 'nothing venture, nothing win' theory. Nothing has been ventured in this

family since our great-grandfather ran up a grocer's bill of £4,000.

He signed the letter John, the name he had adopted in preference to Richard, and added: 'PS If you ever "have a go" nowadays, a speculative interest in K.G. (Holdings) 1/ – sh. @ 6/9 is strongly recommended!'

Years later, when I was going through his personal files and documents, I was struck by how closely tied Lucan had remained to the City and the stockbroker world, in spite of eventually changing his profession. His papers were full of details about shares he owned in minor trading companies – from a sportswear manufacturer in the north of England, to a motor insurance agency he ran with several friends. There were numerous letters inviting him to shareholder meetings and his name appeared on the boards of directors of several company letterheads.

And yet the City was not adventurous enough. In the words of one friend, 'He lacked the application or powers of concentration to be a successful businessman.' Already, barely a year into his banking career, he had begun to look around for something more alluring.

What happened next was somewhat inevitable. Lucan was spending more and more of his time playing bridge with colleagues from the bank or with old friends from the Guards. He had formed Brandts' first bridge team the previous year, and this met every other Thursday at a house in Kensington. His evenings were devoted to prowling around Mayfair, looking for one of the big backgammon tournaments, and on Saturdays he would usually end up at Newmarket or Epsom races.

It was not surprising that, in time, he became a familiar figure within the Chelsea set, a select group of young aristocrats who, unshackled from the constraints of *noblesse oblige*, embodied a new upper-class spirit of extravagance and liberation. There were many parties, expensive cars, fights, pretty girls and, of course, gambling. Though Lucan resisted the label of playboy, he found himself increasingly sucked into this group.

The doyen of the gaming set was John Aspinall, a flamboyant and compelling personality, who had started gambling at Oxford. Aspinall was a noted raconteur and wit, and he attracted to his tables the richest young aristocrats of London. Inevitably, he and Lucan met, and Lucan began to form up with Aspinall's clique for regular poker games.

The attraction between the two men, roughly the same age, both from privileged backgrounds, was based on a sense of shared values. 'He was born out of his own time,' said Aspinall. 'He would have been better exposed in the nineteenth century. I saw in him a figure like myself – a warrior, a nobleman. He was a leader of men. In fact he wasn't, but in more rigorous times he would have found a better role in life.' One of the group thought Lucan 'had enormous presence and beauty'. Another remembered being struck by the fact that Lucan signed his name on cheques in a perfectly straight line.

But it was not just his enigmatic personality, or his title, which attracted the Mayfair set. It was his sense of style, which seemed a model of decadence and romantic inspiration.

'When we were in the army together,' said an officer stationed in Krefeld:

he stuck out as a particularly sophisticated and suave individual. He was always getting dressed up for dinner and going out to the best hotels when really the rest of us were quite happy to stay in and eat the most filthy food. Quite often he'd hire a car – it was the sort of thing that only John would do – and insist that we all put on our DJs and motor down to the casino at Bad Neuenahr. On one occasion he actually hired a little plane and took three of us to the casinos at Trouville. There he was; sort

35

of devastating to look at and always immaculately turned out.

'He was an enormously swish and elegant figure,' said another friend. 'Physically, he had a tremendous bearing, with all that height, and that terribly upper-class face. And he could be charming when he was on form.' Mark Birley, the proprietor of Annabel's night club, where Lucan was a frequent visitor, told me, 'He was a difficult man to get to know. You got the impression he was rather shy, but he could be witty and lively and he had a lot of intelligent conversation.' Dominick Elwes, the painter, who was to become closely attached to him, said, 'He was one of my best friends. He was really superb company. He exuded style and a certain smoothness.' A mutual friend remembered that, when Dominick and Lucan were drinking together, shortly after their first meeting, Lucan remarked that his family were illegitimate descendants of Charles II, and that their Earldom had been created by George III. 'Yes,' said Dominick, who was a noted wit, 'and you've been royal bastards ever since.'

Quickly, Lucan became an habitué in this circle. He would go racing with Aspinall and Aspinall's friend Ian Maxwell-Scott. He would holiday in the Bahamas with the rich stockbroker Stephen Raphael. Twice that summer he gambled at the casino at Deauville with Aspinall and the party of the Aga Khan, often ending the day by playing poker on the hotel balcony, in the moonlight.

In due course his parents began to comment on the amount of time he seemed to be spending with his new friends. 'I thought and think that gambling is a most disreputable way of earning a living,' said Kaitilin, 'chiefly because it's wanting to get something for nothing, and that, in my book, isn't what anyone ought to do.' Other members of the family echoed this concern. His uncle, Edward Bingham, wrote him a strong letter after finding him sitting on a stool, over a game of roulette, at the casino in Deauville. And his grandmother, Violet, the Dowager widow of the Fifth Earl, George Charles, who lived a fossilized 19th-century life, cocooned against the spirit and paraphernalia of the times, summoned him to an angry meeting at her flat in Orchard Court.

As the months went by, Lucan began to lose touch with his older friends, from Eton and the Guards, and seemed to be spending less and less time at his desk. His parents warned him against the risks of distraction. But their warnings were too late. Lucan had the gambling bug, exhumed from his ancestors, and he was hooked.

In the autumn of 1960 there were a number of decisive events. First, the law was changed in England to allow gambling, for the first time, to take place on an habitual basis at the same address. Previously, it had been an itinerant business, involving the weekly transition of cards and players from one site to another (this was to deter a congregation of criminals, for gambling was still caught, in the legal mind, in the trough of criminality). The move was in keeping with the mood of liberation and social revolution which was sweeping England at the time. For those who had the resources to gamble the way was now open to do so professionally, on a permanent basis, and still remain within the law.

Secondly, John Aspinall decided to take advantage of the new situation and set up his tables in a permanent club. Aspinall had gained a reputation as an engaging host who, at his flat in Marylebone, ran the most popular games in London. His private parties, where he supplied the finest wines and food, were always sumptuous affairs, designed to attract the rich, and he now moved to consolidate his position. Aspinall chose a tall Regency house in Berkeley Square, in the heart of Mayfair, with easy access for the West End, at number 44. This was the last remaining town house in London to have been designed by the architect William

Kent, who had built it for Lady Isabella Finch, one of the mistresses of Charles II. The building was eminently suitable for Aspinall's purposes. There was a basement and extensive cellars, which he sealed off and leased to his friend Mark Birley, for use as a night club. There was considerable space on the ground floor for catering facilities and a restaurant. The building, though narrow, receded sufficiently to allow a bar and drawing rooms. Upstairs, a network of smaller bedrooms and dressing rooms could be knocked through to create several large gambling saloons. And on the top floors Aspinall laid out his offices and guest rooms.

It was an ambitious plan, and Aspinall faced considerable competition from the established clubs of London: the St James's, White's, the Portland. But he pressed on in the knowledge that he could count on the patronage of the highly influential people whom he had impressed in Marylebone. He resolved that, to survive, the Clermont would have to work in two ways. First, it would have to be as exclusive as its competitors – if not *more* exclusive. The membership list was restricted to six hundred, unusually low for a London club, and the criteria for membership were rigorous enough to encourage the cosy accumulation of faces that were already familiar to each other in the little villages of London finance and commerce.

Secondly, the ethos of the club needed to reflect the status and expectations of its members. It had to do this both aesthetically and psychologically. So Aspinall decorated the club using the most exotic designs: he hung crystal chandeliers from the ceiling, bought rare paintings and antiques and used the finest materials to make carpets and curtains. The tableware was Georgian and Regency in style, and the cutlery was all solid silver. The carpeting was Wilton, dotted at intervals with Indian rugs. The curtains were largely satin, relieved by velvet drapes and over-hangs. In the bar there were rococo mirrors and sparkling cut glasses. The effect was almost overpowering, an assault on the senses by vast opulence and glamour. It was no wonder that the richest people in London came to the Clermont to gamble. The web that Aspinall spun around them was gilded and gilt-edged.

In addition to this, Aspinall sought out equally attractive human furniture, and this was where Lucan became pivotal. Lucan was an attractive individual, and his title and good looks were useful in making the punters feel that they were playing with a man of some standing and respectability. He was, after all, the genuine article. He had a title, breeding, and, for many, a beguiling personality. So an informal arrangement was made between the two men. Lucan would come to the Clermont and gamble there as a house player. By doing so, he would upholster the sense of status enjoyed by its members. And in return Aspinall would give him free meals, free drinks and the protection implicit in being a 'house player'.

And so, in Lucan's early adult life, a running pattern now began to prevail: breakfast at ten; a walk in the park; a free lunch at the Clermont; a bit of light gambling in the afternoons; home to change; then back to the Clermont for dinner and the big games. In due course the routine became fixed, and Lucan found, to his satisfaction, that he was able to make far more money playing poker than toiling in the City. After a spectacular £20,000 win at chemin de fer, he finally decided to change his occupation and resign from the bank.

That September, he became a 'professional gambler'.

This move was decisive, and would come to be seen as the greatest mistake of his life. He was now locked into a lifestyle that he would find impossible to break free from: a two-dimensional existence, which was divorced from the outside world and from the diversity of experience that one needs in order to keep a grasp on reality. It was a noted feature of the Clermont Club that it had no clock. In London it was famous for this. This was not an oversight, of course, but a deliberate attempt to remove a sense of time and place. 'When I opened the Clermont,' Aspinall was quoted as saying, 'I wanted to create a place where English gentlemen could ruin themselves as stylishly and suicidally as their ancestors had done.' As time went by, and the 1960s ushered in a wave of social liberation, Lucan and his friends retreated further into their *oubliette*. Lucan had always been disenchanted with the diminishing reverence for the aristocracy that was prevailing in the wider culture. Of course, he did not expect to enjoy the extraordinary powers of his ancestors, but he did expect his status to shield him from nonentity, and he believed that his title gave him certain privileges that he fully intended to utilize. As the levelling movement of the 1960s began to advance, and Lucan found his social position under threat, so he began to complain, to react, to suspect.

The state of the country particularly bothered him. From the perspective of the poker saloons of the Clermont Club, England seemed to be standing on the threshold of national disaster. Lucan and his friends could sense the imminence of change and dissolution everywhere.

The 1960s and 1970s were difficult decades for an unstable country. Britain was reeling from the effects of Nixon's dollar devaluation; hyper-inflation was beginning to crystallize as a permanent feature of economic life; there had been an oil crisis, then a gold crisis, then another oil crisis. Unemployment was rising, living standards were static or falling, the multinationals and the oil producers were tightening their grip on the Western economies. At the same time, as a reflection of the contemporary uncertainties, Britain appeared to be suffering greater political and social destabilization than at any other time in its history. Edward Heath's Conservative government had been destroyed after a titanic struggle with the miners. There had been two general elections in less than a year, the first unresolved, the second leaving Labour with an unworkable majority. To end it all, the political language of the time was laced with an undercurrent of intrigue. The prime minister was said to be a spy. The leader of the Liberal Party was reported to be involved in a plot to murder a male model. People in the Cabinet were suspected of having clandestine links with foreign powers.

It was no wonder that Lucan and his reactionary friends feared a revolution. 'He thought the country was on the edge of an abyss,' said Michael Stoop, a retired company director and a backgammon player, 'and Liberal solutions were no good any more.'

'He was worried about the state of the country,' said Aspinall. 'It was people's complacency he minded about. They see the ship sinking and they're still worried about getting their share of the cornflakes. He was going to make a speech in the House of Lords about immigration. He felt very strongly about that. You see, Lucan came from a family who, in their roots, were the old clan leaders of the Anglo-Saxons. He therefore had a responsibility. He hated what he saw as the hybridization and miscegenation of the Island Race. Of course, a lot of people in a bus queue in Nuneaton might feel the same way, but then it's not their responsibility.' According to Charles Benson, Lucan was 'very right-wing and refused to compromise in front of people'. He would talk about 'hanging and flogging and foreigners and niggers'.

Lucan invested whatever money he made in jewellery. He said he knew how he was going to leave the country when the revolution came. Jewellery, he said, was portable. In the meantime, he and his friends talked of military coups, of private armies, of tanks rolling over Westminster Bridge. 'He wanted to save England,' said a friend, 'for grouse moors and stately homes.' His friend, Michael Stoop, had joined Colonel Stirling's private army, which was dedicated to keeping the country moving in the face of a general strike. Greville Howard, another friend, had become the private secretary of the right-wing Conservative MP Enoch Powell, who had been admonished for making speeches that were racially divisive. Howard was the son of a former director-general of the BBC. He was a Clermont Club veteran. Prior to joining Mr Powell's staff his only claim to attention had been some years earlier, when he had featured in a newspaper, riding around Sloane Square on a bicycle, wearing gold pyjamas, pursued by a number of débutantes in a white Rolls-Royce.

Lucan's privileges extended to real action within the existing framework of the Constitution. He had his seat in the Lords. He could speak out, through the statutory channels, whenever he liked. But he never did address the Lords. He visited the place seventeen times in ten years. This was hardly a chronicle of passionate protest. Perhaps he recognised that his views were so reactionary that they placed him beyond the political pale, outside the mainstream of what was an acceptable view for someone of his position to hold. Perhaps he thought conventional protest was useless. At any rate, whenever the relevant debates came up at Westminster, on hanging or flogging, or any of the other subjects that caused him to foam at the mouth, he avoided speaking his mind and consoled himself with a round of golf, a game of poker, or an hour or two of backgammon at the St James's.

In 1960 Lucan moved out of his parents' house in Eaton Square and took the tenancy of a smart Regency flat at Park Crescent. This was tucked behind the grand columns and stucco frontages of a Nash terrace which overlooked Regent's Park. He bought himself an Aston Martin sports car and assumed the lifestyle of an old-fashioned man-about-town. He had his hair cut at Thomas's, in Curzon Street, and bought his suits in Savile Row and Bond Street. His hand-made brogues came from Oxford. His grocery accounts were with Harrods and Claridge's. When he was ill he took himself off to a specialist in Harley Street, and when he was well he interrupted his London routine with long touring holidays abroad: the United States, Canada, the Bahamas, Africa. It was a life of overwhelming pleasure and sensuality. 'Looking back,' said a friend, recently, 'he must have been having the greatest time ever. The greatest time of anyone in that group, certainly.' The luxury seemed to justify the risk of becoming a professional gambler. Certainly, Lucan felt more assured and self-confident than he had done at any time since leaving Eton.

Now, there was only one thing missing.

Chapter Two

VERONICA DUNCAN

Veronica Mary Duncan had certainly had a different education and upbringing to John Lucan, although in some ways their backgrounds were psychologically and emotionally similar. Her reticence in later years suggested a defensiveness about her roots, especially in the company of Lucan's friends, after what she called her 'elevation'. To me she was ostensibly quite candid, although there seemed no prospect of information being volunteered unless she was directly questioned. She had come, she told me, from 'the middle classes'. There was nothing sensational to report. It had been 'grinding poverty'.

She had been born in May 1937, in Bournemouth, Dorset. Her father, an army major, had been killed in a car crash, two months before the outbreak of war. Veronica's mother had taken the girls to Uckfield, in Sussex, and then, later, to South Africa. Veronica was two when her father died. Her sister, Christina, had just been born. In South Africa their mother met and married an RAF officer named James Margrie.

Veronica was popularly said to have loathed South Africa – the boarding schools, the climate, the constant upheavals. And it was well known that she disliked Margrie himself. She resented his intrusion into what she regarded as a close-knit family unit. She certainly recalled being unhappy at boarding school. In Grahamstown she and Christina were so sharply singled out, because of their accents and their late arrival into established groupings, that they were eventually removed from the school and sent to another. It was quite common, Veronica recalled, for them to return from lessons to find their beds stripped or their cupboards and drawers emptied. Veronica grew up into a pensive, highly strung teenager. The schoolgirl ragging, perhaps coupled with the loss of her father and the arrival of Margrie, made her highly competitive and over-anxious to be accepted. At one stage, she was even treated by a psychiatrist. Her ostracism from the Clermont, years later, would seem all the more cruel in this light.

In 1947, Margrie secured the tenancy of a little pub in North Waltham, Hampshire, called the Wheatsheaf, and the family returned to England. The girls were sent to the local private school, St Swithun's, which Veronica abandoned as soon as her exams were over. She returned to her native Bournemouth, to an art school, where she studied graphic design. After qualifying in 1954 she moved to London, a suitcase in each hand, her ambition to become a model.

For a while she was successful. She moved into a small bedsit in Gloucester Place and got a job modelling teenage clothes at a fashion house in Cavendish Square. But she was repeatedly rejected from other jobs because of her height. She was five feet, two inches tall, and she had been told that this was a sign of inferior breeding. Breeding then became something of an obsession with her. She talked about marrying someone of breeding, so that she could see her name in the Stud Book. Years later, when she was asked how her skull had been able to survive the terrible beating she had received at Lower Belgrave Street, she replied, 'Good breeding, that's how.'

In due course, Christina came to London and the two girls shared a flat together in Melbury Road. Another flatmate, Rachael Blacklock, had earlier met a bobsleighing German named Hans Heyman, whom she eventually married. Heyman had a friend, Bill Shand Kydd, whom he thought would be suited to Christina (Christina, unlike Veronica, was confident and pragmatic), and after two dates in London Bill and Christina became engaged. When they married, in January 1963, Veronica was chief bridesmaid. Later, when Bill and Christina began holding regular weekend parties at Horton Hall, their estate in Bedfordshire, Veronica became 'the spare girl who came for weekends'. She was then, having abandoned modelling, running her own business, Resumes Ltd, which printed stage scripts for the West End. She was 26 and, by her own admission, ready to marry. It was at one such party that she met a bobsleighing friend of William's. He was 28, and a highly successful sportsman and gambler. His name was John Lucan.

'I was looking for a god,' Veronica recalled, 'and he was a dream figure.'

Years later, neither of them could recall their meeting with any great clarity. The room had been crowded with golfers, fleeing indoors from the rain, and they had exchanged only brief, formal pleasantries. 'I think we just said "How do you do?" and sipped sherry and that was it,' Veronica told me. It was not until much later, as the summer progressed, that things became more concrete.

In August, Lucan took his powerboat, *White Migrant*, which he had built with the proceeds of a large gambling win, down to the South of France. By coincidence, while gambling in Deauville, he ran into Bill Shand Kydd, who invited him to another weekend golf match at Horton Hall on their return to England. When Lucan accepted, Shand Kydd asked him, 'What bird do you want?' and Lucan replied,

'The one I met in April; the blonde with lots of hair.' Veronica accepted the invitation. But she had no illusions about why Lucan had specifically asked for her. 'He knew I was Bill Shand Kydd's sister-in-law,' she told me, 'and he was always on the look-out for rich connections. He was always looking for people who might underwrite his precarious financial position.' Nonetheless, after the party, when Lucan offered to drive her back to London, Veronica quickly accepted.

'He dropped me off at my flat,' she said, 'and asked me out to the theatre the following night. I accepted and we began a courtship. We went out to parties, to the theatre, for dinner, and, yes, even gambling. At the weekends he took me down to the coast and we would go boating. I think we found that we felt the same way about things. I was running my own business. I was finding it harder and harder to make ends meet. His view was that the country was in a terminal decline and it was becoming impossible to make anything of your life or to live well. He used to say that anyone who lived well was either evading tax or spending all their capital. I had the same opinion. Life was an uphill struggle.'

Looking back, one is struck by the speed of the courtship. They had met in August, started seeing each other regularly through September and October, and then married in November. The engagement took place on October 14th, when an announcement appeared in the *Daily Telegraph* and *The Times*. But had the time-frame been sufficient for a proper exploration of their compatibility? And what were the linchpins of their mutual attraction?

Certainly, those who knew Lucan, particularly his family, greeted the news of his engagement with astonishment. It was not just that he was marrying someone out of his own background; more that he was marrying before the age of forty, which was curious for a professional gambler. 'Lucan always gave the impression of being entirely self-sufficient emotionally,' said a friend. 'He was a man's man, after all, and was very independent. I remembered thinking that he just didn't seem to *need* anyone.'

It was true that men were largely allergic to women in the circles that Lucan had frequented: Eton, the Guards, merchant banking, and now 'the boys' clubs' of Mayfair, many of which excluded women altogether. 'I think he saw women as an inferior race,' said Dominick Elwes. Stephen Raphael reckoned he was merely 'very shy'. 'He was so typically a man's man,' he said. 'When we were in Nassau he would water-ski, play some backgammon on the beach with myself and my wife. He had one or two girlfriends, but they were sort of secondary.'

There was a view prevalent after the murder that Lucan's two-dimensional personality put many women off; that they found his gambling obsession impossible to cope with. He might have style, and would whisk a girl off to dinner in some fabulous hotel overlooking the French Riviera. But when it came to whispering sweet nothings there would be very little on his mind except the winner of the Epsom 3.30.

However, many of Lucan's friends whom I spoke to disputed this: there had been no shortage of girls, they said. So why had Lucan chosen Veronica?

Undoubtedly, there *was* a problem with his gambling. In spite of his title, breeding and good looks, it was impossible to believe that some women – perhaps a majority – didn't value security, particularly financial security, above these attractions, and that, however tempted they may have been by his social position, they knew at the end of the day that they had to be pragmatic. Christina Shand Kydd remembered thinking that Lucan was attracted by the 'twin-set type' – tweed jacket and string of pearls – but that he knew that 'that type of girl would never live a gambler's life'.

In addition to this there seems to have been a genuine attraction on his part. Veronica was five foot two inches. Lucan towered over her. Her height seemed to emphasize her innate courage, to underline her resilience and her sheer gut determination. That would have appealed to him in a paternalistic sense. He, too, saw himself as courageous in the face of uncertainty, enterprising, prepared to risk everything because a conventional existence was beyond the pale. When he saw these characteristics in Veronica, curiously accentuated by her diminutive stature, something in him responded to them. He felt the urge to protect a fellow traveller, to shield her from the same difficulties that affected his own life. The attraction was therefore largely brotherly, or patriarchal, and she, having missed an element of paternalistic security since her childhood, immediately reacted to the protectiveness.

It was on this basis, surely, that their relationship progressed.

On November 28th, 1963, they married at Brompton Holy Trinity, near Harrods. Years later, Veronica showed me her wedding albums and described her feelings on the day. Her wedding gown was of white silk, cut with an apricot-tinted skirt. She carried a bouquet of gardenias, lilies of the valley and freesias, and she wore a large diamond tiara. The tiara, she said, had been hauled from the vaults of Lloyds and belonged to her mother-in-law. 'It was,' she remembered, 'extremely heavy.' Behind her, her bridesmaids wore long white dresses trimmed in emerald green, and emerald green satin coronets, an allusion to the Irish peerage. At the reception afterwards, at the Carlton Tower Hotel, she and Lucan greeted four hundred guests, mostly his family and friends, including Earl Alexander of Tunis and Princess Alice, Countess of Athlone. They honeymooned on the Orient Express, travelling from Paris to Istanbul, and on their return to London they spent their first Christmas together at the flat in Park Crescent.

The New Year brought both joy and sadness. Veronica discovered that she was pregnant, and they began to look around London for a suitable family home, concentrating on Belgravia and the West End. Then, in January, on the 21st, Lucan's father collapsed and died at the family home, Hanover House, in St John's Wood. Since the Lucans had been mostly blessed with longevity, particularly the males, this shocked and appalled those who knew him (he was 64, and had the previous week been passed as 'perfectly fit' during a test for life insurance). It did mean, however, that Lucan was now the new Earl, the head of the clan.

The title brought considerable pecuniary rewards. Although the Lucans had long since abandoned Ireland as a seat of residence, and their old ancestral home had fallen into disrepair, they still owned considerable acreage around the town of Castlebar, where six hundred tenants had to pay a weekly rent. There was also a golf course in Staines, which the Fourth Earl had bought, and a little property in London, including a mews house in Eaton Row. In addition, the family had a vault at Lloyds, where they kept jewellery and heirlooms, and there was a cash inheritance of about £250,000. Money had also been deposited in bank accounts abroad, including Switzerland, Africa and the Bahamas, but because of exchange controls this money could only be spent if one was actually living, or staying, in the relevant country.

To pre-empt the arrival of children, the couple decided to use some of their inheritance to buy a family home. They chose number 46, Lower Belgrave Street, in the heart of Belgravia. The house was exceptionally swish. It had five floors, including a basement kitchen area (and, under that, an old-fashioned cellar for food or coal). On the ground floor there was a large drawing room, facing the street, and a dining room that looked out into the long garden. Veronica decorated the dining room in heavy red wallpaper and hung a portrait of the Third Earl of Lucan on the wall, opposite his military rival the Earl of Cardigan. It was a notorious fact, historically, that, in spite of being

51

brothers-in-law, the two men couldn't stand the sight of each other.

On the floor above, there was a main bedroom with French windows that opened out on to a wrought-iron balcony. The balcony looked out towards the private residents' park below, and across, west, towards the Mall and Buckingham Palace. Veronica decorated the bedroom in blues and lemon yellows. There was also a nursery on this floor, and, on the floor above, three children's bedrooms. On the next floor Lucan had his study, which he lined with his family's leather-bound volumes, and his own collection of detective novels. He also kept his ermine robes here, and the engagement present that Veronica had bought him: an ivory backgammon board, from Asprey's, in Bond Street.

Like any residence in Belgravia it was expensive and insular. It encouraged its occupants to be reclusive, and it provided a timeless cocoon where, in a world increasingly liberated from social restraints, appearances were kept up and standards maintained.

Indeed, the house was just one facet of Veronica's exotic new existence. Six months earlier she had been plain Veronica Duncan, aged twenty-six, from Hampshire. Then she had become Lady Bingham. Now she was the Countess of Lucan.

As the months went by she began to make the most of her 'elevation'. She shopped at Hermès and Gucci and Belleville Sassoon. She had her hair done at Clarita's, in Sloane Street, and often dined à deux at La Popete in Chelsea. She and Lucan attended the Cresta Ball in January, and stayed with the Aga Khan that summer. Lucan bought her a couple of race horses, Travelling Light and Bombproof, to match his own, Le Merveilleux II, and they would fly to the races each weekend, or ride out to hounds with the Whaddon Chase.

'It was,' Veronica recalled, 'a golden life.'

But it would be unrealistic to imagine that things could continue in this vein. Lucan, after all, was a professional gambler, the most precarious profession in the world, and his wife was not celebrated for her sense of inner security. Beyond the glamour of their immediate circumstances lay all the terrible forebodings of defeat and despair.

Chapter Three

THE DRUMMING OF FINGERS

The problems in the Lucan marriage became apparent early on. They also had a number of disparate sources.

In the summer of 1964, Veronica made a conscious decision to start accompanying her husband to his clubs each evening. She was a late riser, rarely up before lunchtime, and her afternoons were usually spent at home with the children. But at night, evidently bored, she decided she wanted to go with Lucan to the Clermont. They would have dinner together at 9 p.m. and then Lucan would go off and join in one of the big backgammon tournaments. Veronica would then spend the evening sitting by herself, sipping champagne.

There were several reasons for her decision. First, though she would not openly admit it, she was worried about him having an affair. He was good-looking and young. His sexual charisma evidently appealed to every conceivable kind of woman. Though most upper-class debutantes would never consider marrying a gambler, there were many who would

certainly contemplate an affair. In addition, Veronica felt
that the Clermont males had an overriding preoccupation
with sex, and that they were 'quite capable' of planting a
prostitute on Lucan, so that they could 'find out what
Lucky's like in bed'.

The second reason was more pragmatic. Veronica was
newly married. She was already pregnant with her first child.
Her husband was out all day and almost all night, and she
was lonely. Like any newly married woman, she wanted to
spend as much time with him as she could, even if it had to be
in the formal and censorious environment of his gambling
club.

This was the first real problem that one can detect in their
marriage. Lucan's routine had been fixed before meeting
Veronica, and he did not intend to vary it after marriage. He
would rise at 9 a.m., read the *Telegraph*, breakfast, and then
take his dog, Otto, a Dobermann, out for a walk. At
lunchtime, with Veronica still asleep, he would go to the club
for a boozy lunch – lamb cutlets and smoked salmon in
winter; lamb cutlets and smoked salmon *en gêlée* in the
summer. In the afternoon he would watch a race on TV or
play a round of chemin de fer. Then he would take a cab
home for about 6 p.m., have a bath and put on his dinner
jacket, returning to the club for dinner and the big tournaments. He would finally come home at about 3 a.m. It was a
static, manically specific routine, and it would be repeated
day after day, without interval or variation.

When Veronica complained that the routine allowed her
no time to see him, Lucan responded by saying that she
should 'make her own life': go to the theatre, meet friends,
join societies or charities. Veronica dismissed that. She
hadn't married to lead her own life, she said, she had married
to be with her husband. Charities and coffee mornings were
occupational therapy for bored housewives. So, if Lucan
would not make time for her, she would join him; she would
go with him to the club, or to the races, or to his big poker

games at the St James's or the Portland.

This decision in turn led to its own problems. Lucan reacted against what he saw as an invasion of his privacy, of his secret world. He resented the implication that he might have an affair, and he may have resented the way Veronica seemed reluctant to be more independent. At any rate, her presence in the club, her ritual haunting of the place, appeared to put both of them under some strain.

But the central problems arose when Veronica actually crossed the threshold of the Clermont. A number of things then became apparent to her that severely corroded her own position. First, the club was an exclusively male terrain. Women were allowed in, it was true, but 'they had no business being there', in the words of the proprietor. 'Most of the men saw it as a refuge from women,' said one member. 'They were either unmarried or unhappily married.' The language, the style, the whole resonance of the place was laced with the flavour of a public school, and those women who did attend were expected 'not to interfere'. Veronica reacted against the prevailing ethos with a sharpness that irritated most of those who came into contact with her. In reality this was something of a defence mechanism, provoked by the censorious environment, but others saw it as snobbery or plain rudeness. 'She was clever, astute and subtle,' said Michael Stoop, 'but also aggressive and unbalanced. It made her an extremely dangerous type of woman.' 'She used to come night after night,' recalled Aspinall, 'and sit alone on the banquette, and she had a rotten life in that sense . . . But then,' he added, 'she had no business being there.'

After they had dined, at nine, Lucan would abandon his wife to 'the widows' bench', an ornate gold and velvet couch under the grand staircase, where the women spent their evenings chatting together, toying with their pearls, generally waiting for their husbands to finish gambling upstairs. Veronica hated the widows' bench. Small talk bored her.

Invariably, she would sit and participate for a couple of hours, maybe even play a little blackjack, but then she would be overcome by boredom and irritability and go upstairs and tell Lucan that she was leaving. He, relieved, would make no effort to stop her, and she would take a taxi home, alone.

Secondly, Veronica saw for the first time just how insecure their financial position really was. 'There were huge swings,' she recalled. It was not uncommon for a gambler to lose ten or twenty thousand in a single game. Indeed, just after the honeymoon Lucan himself had lost eight and a half thousand at the club, playing poker. Veronica now saw that his gambling was not just a mild diversion, a pleasant hobby for a bored young aristocrat; it was an obsession. And he did not possess the resources to gamble on a par with those at the Clermont. In addition to this, he now had a family to support. Veronica had given birth to a girl in October 1964, called Frances, and she was already expecting another child. There was the upkeep of number 46; provisions for the children's future; their long-term security as a family. Lucan had never had these responsibilities before; he had never had anyone to consider but himself.

In due course, Veronica began to harangue him. 'I told him that we needed some security for the future, that he ought to put money aside for the children and the house.' Lucan's response was simple. He had made adequate provision for the children. He had nothing particularly to leave a son anyway. The vast estate was in trust and didn't yield much return. The family seat had gone. He, Lucan, might actually make enough at the tables to restore some of the family fortune, as well as enjoy a good life from the proceeds himself. In addition he reminded Veronica that she had known he was a gambler when she had married him. He had made his position clear. He had taken her out to dinner and told her that he had no intention of changing his lifestyle after marriage. If gambling was something she couldn't accept, he had said, then she must refuse his proposal. 'She knew it totally,' said her sister, Christina, 'and she accepted it quite happily. She knew what she was going into.' Lucan had even bought her a library of gambling manuals prior to the marriage, so that she could understand the world he occupied. Now, in his view, she was reneging on that commitment, and making 'unreasonable demands'.

As the months progressed the situation worsened. Veronica was bored with the routine at the Clermont, with being abandoned to the widows' bench, and the hostile atmosphere was making her brittle and anxious. One evening she had thrown a glass of wine over a woman who was blocking her view of the TV. She had taken to chain-smoking; a doctor had prescribed mild sedatives for her depression. She was finding it harder and harder to control herself when it came to Lucan's friends. There were scenes in the poker rooms, shocking outbursts in public. Lucan felt she was an embarrassment, and when she took to attacking *him*, to reducing him in the eyes of his friends, he decided that something would have to be done.

There is some suggestion that Lucan was beginning to lose quite rapidly at the Clermont during this time, and that he probably attributed this to the general instability in his home life. Gamblers, he maintained, needed absolute tranquillity on their domestic ground if they were to operate successfully; it was a question of confidence, of smoothness. If a gambler lost his nerve it was only a matter of time before the pack scented blood. He refused to concede that his own inflexible routine, placing Veronica under severe strain, was at the core of most of their problems.

In September 1967, in the first of a series of bad mistakes, Lucan drove his wife to a private nursing home in Roehampton, called The Priory. Lucan had warned the doctors to expect her, but he had not told Veronica. There was a scene. The staff waited in the lobby while the Lucans argued at some length in their motor car. Eventually, as a compromise,

Veronica agreed to start seeing a psychiatrist regularly in London. Then they drove home. 'I only did it,' she said, 'to show him that I would co-operate. He told me that it was the sign of a mentally ill person when they refused to have treatment.'

She now began a regular series of counselling sessions. She was also prescribed a range of drugs, including Lithium and Moditen, for anxiety and depression. But things did not improve. She would spend most of her time at home, alone, in her bedroom. 'She practically *lived* in her bedroom,' said a nanny, resident at the house, 'in a sort of twilight world, with the blinds drawn all day.' She rarely went out shopping or to meet friends. She found it impossible to face the Clermont. If they went on holiday she would often fly back early, stricken with anxiety. And her anger towards Lucan's entrenched lifestyle did not seem to diminish with treatment.

In 1970 Veronica gave birth to a third child, Camilla. She had suffered with post-natal depression before and began to show all the cardinal symptoms again. Lucan's reaction was once again to broach the subject of in-patient treatment. She had her weekly counselling sessions, but she found them unproductive. She complained that the psychiatrist was biased against her from the start, that he would listen to Lucan's description of her behaviour and form a judgment based almost entirely upon that. She moved from psychiatrist to psychiatrist, but her notes, which forewarned of her conditions and treatments, trailed her wherever she went.

In the autumn of 1971, twelve months after Camilla had been born, Lucan drove her to another nursing home: Greenways, in Hampstead. This time she had agreed to be admitted, but when she actually arrived at the place she had a loss of nerve. 'I saw all this ghastly ECT equipment hanging up in one of the rooms when they showed me round,' she said, 'and I knew that I couldn't face it.' Lucan was furious. They rowed in the lobby. Veronica fled from the hospital and ran out into the streets around Hampstead. She made her way home, by bus and by taxi. When she got there she found the atmosphere sullen and pensive. Even the nanny, Lilian Jenkins, seemed disappointed to see her back.

The incident at Greenways apparently marked a new low in relations between the couple. At any rate, Lucan spent more and more nights away from the house, usually at the St James's or in the mews behind number 46. He tried to step up the amount of medication and treatment that Veronica received. But it was to no avail.

In January of 1973 they finally parted. Lucan had been away for the New Year, on a gambling excursion abroad. When he returned, he found that Veronica, 'in a state of hypo-mania', had sacked Lilian Jenkins, who had been with the family since the birth of Frances, nine years earlier. Veronica, if the truth be known, had never liked the idea of a nanny. She thought that they were 'an unnatural wedge' between a mother and her children. 'It might seem very grand to have someone who is always there to look after your children,' she said, 'to wash the nappies and change the beds and generally take them off your hands. But then you ask yourself: What is there for me to do? They're *my* children, after all.' She had tolerated the presence of Miss Jenkins for the sake of her husband, who 'had old-fashioned ideas about these things'. But now something inside her revolted against it. Frances was nine; George was six; perhaps she felt that they had grown up and she had not been able to participate in their development as fully as she would have liked. Perhaps the birth of Camilla brought home to her how much she might have missed, because of the presence of the nanny, in the rearing of the eldest two. Perhaps it was a conscious cry of anger, a determination to take charge, in spite of what her husband demanded.

At any rate, Veronica dismissed Miss Jenkins. She sent her belongings to the Helena Club, in Sloane Square, where the nanny had a room, and returned her references to the Beauchamp Agency in Knightsbridge. Lucan later claimed that Miss Jenkins had been 'dismissed at ten minutes' notice and against my wishes'. She remained fiercely loyal to Lucan, and he to her, and after the murder she was one of the fiercest advocates of his innocence.

But Lucan could not reinstate her. When he arrived home to find that she had been dismissed he was furious. He and Veronica argued ferociously, and after an hour he summoned his GP, Dr Christopher Powell-Brett, to talk, he said, about his wife's mental state. The clear implication was that he wanted some kind of sanctioning of another attempt to commit Veronica to a nursing home. They had had a terrible Christmas at his sister's house in Northamptonshire, he said, and had had to leave early because of a series of disputes in the family. Now she had sacked a loyal employee for no apparent reason.

Veronica remembered, 'There was no attempt to work the problem through, to really sit down and sort things out. He just said to the GP: "Is she fit?" and the GP said: "Yes, she is fit," and with that he just turned on his heel and went upstairs and began to pack. He filled up one of his sailing bags with clothes and then went round the corner to Eaton Row. This had happened many times in the past. Usually he would come back the next morning and we would sit in silence for a couple of hours and then we would start to talk. Usually, by the afternoon we would be laughing about it and things would be back to normal. I thought this occasion would be no different. Whatever had happened between us I was still his wife and I loved him and he was still the father of my children.'

But this time the pattern had changed. Lucan didn't 'reappear as usual'. And, as the days drifted into weeks, Veronica had to confront the prospect that this time he was apparently *not* coming home.

Chapter Four

A GRIM BUSINESS

One of the most striking features of the case remains the controversy that still exists over the break-up of the Lucan marriage. In the years after the murder, as I found when I began to rake through the documents and trace those involved, it was almost impossible to find any source whose views were not coloured by their loyalty to one side or another. The nature of the story, with all its sociological and emotional dimensions, invited one to adopt a position, defend a line, assume sympathy with one or other of the protagonists. There were rumours and counter-rumours.

Some people felt that Lady Lucan had put too much pressure on her husband to quit his chosen occupation. But how realistic was it of Lucan to expect a wife and mother to tolerate all the insecurities and long hours away that professional gambling entailed? Was it a coincidence that almost all Lucan's gambling friends were separated from their wives? Certainly, Lucan's intransigence must have been a central feature: years later, looking in from the outside, Chief Superintendent Roy Ranson said, 'Would you go night after night to the Clermont and have dinner with your husband and then he'd say, "Oh well, I'm going to play roulette or backgammon" or something and leave you sitting there like a lemon [for] three or four hours? You'd do it once or twice or three times, but come three *years* you'd say, "I've had enough of this," wouldn't you?'

In the months to come it became clear that, whatever problems they had had in their marriage, neither of the Lucans handled separation well. It is ironic perhaps that, in the final analysis, it was Lucan who finally came apart at the seams. Anyone looking at their backgrounds and psychology and taking a bet at the time would surely have concluded that it was Lucan, with his fuller lifestyle, his ebullience and social confidence, who would have come through unscathed: shrug off the emotional threads binding him to his wife; get a girlfriend after a suitable interval; install her at his flat; continue as usual. At the same time, Veronica – isolated, friendless – was the one with the terrible fear of loneliness, the one who craved the security of a companion. Whereas Lucan had apparently *not* depended on the camaraderie of marriage, and had been content in his clubs, she, never socially at ease, had clung to him, building her life around him, wholly committed to his emotional needs and the rearing of his children. Who could have doubted under these circumstances that it was Lucan, not Veronica, who would survive the ordeal in the fittest shape? And yet it was not to be. By the end, Lucan seemed half mad with the bleakness of his hollowed-out existence.

Shortly after leaving Lower Belgrave Street, Lucan embarked on a plan to win custody of his children. His devotion to his children was one of the few universally acknowledged features of the case. Some people thought that the children represented his hopes for the future – after the disaster of Balaclava, socialist parents and his own misfortunes. Some thought he saw them as his one lasting achievement. At any rate, he took a special interest in their welfare, paying for private tutors and indulging them during birthdays and holidays. 'He was fabulous with the children,' said one friend. 'There was no question of going off to dinner or going out in the evening until he had seen them to bed and kissed them goodnight. And at weekends he used to take them to the country, to [Lord] Suffolk's place [Charlton Park] or Horton [Hall, home of the Shand Kydds].'

And so, a fortnight after leaving his wife, Lucan took the tenancy of a five-bedroomed flat in Elizabeth Street, just off Eaton Square, and only a couple of hundred yards from Lower Belgrave Street. In taking a five-bedroomed apartment, Lucan was clearly signalling his intention to win care of the children [a live-in nanny would make five persons]. Two weeks later, he applied for an order from the High Court to take control of them, pending a full inquiry that summer.

On March 23rd, he sprang into action. He hired a team of private detectives and co-ordinated a meticulous plan to kidnap the children when they were out of their mother's sight. He waited until George and Camilla left number 46 that afternoon, with their nanny, for a walk in Green Park. This was an established routine. Then he approached the nanny, showed her the order, and took both children to his car. Next, he drove round to the school which Frances attended and waved the papers under the nose of the headmistress. She, too, had no choice but to hand Frances over. By the end of the day, all three children were installed at his flat.

Veronica was devastated by the news. The order was *ex-parte*, which meant that Lucan was not obliged to inform her of his actions. She learned of what had happened when a confused nanny and a confused headmistress rang her that afternoon. 'By then,' she said, 'it was too late.' In fact, the news so shook her that she spent a week in the Priory, under observation.

The stage was now set for a titanic struggle of wills. In retrospect, it is difficult to underestimate how important the children were to both parents. They had become central to

Veronica's existence. She did not go out or have any real form of social life. She saw no friends. She was even estranged now from her sister. She painted a little and she read. But she had no consistent diversions, no real preoccupations and she threw herself into looking after the children. She cooked them meals, washed their clothes, spent as much time with them as she could.

But Lucan's devotion was beyond question, too. Even his detractors accepted that. He believed that he was better equipped than his wife to raise the children. It is also possible that, in his autocratic, Crimean mind, he believed there was little a mother could bring to the rearing of children that could not be supplied by an efficient nanny. Maybe that does him an injustice. But he himself had been raised without a strong maternal presence in his formative years, living in America, surrounded by nannies and nursemaids, separated from his real mother.

And so, with both partners investing so much psychologically in the outcome, the approaching custody hearing was set to be violently traumatic, even by the cruel standards of those proceedings.

Lucan began by hiring a team of private detectives. He needed evidence to persuade the court that Veronica was an unsuitable mother. The private detectives sat outside Lower Belgrave Street day after day, week after week, photographing the house, recording the visitors, watching Veronica's sleeping habits. At the same time, Lucan himself also watched the house, presumably on those occasions when the private detective was not present. He would walk past it at night. Sometimes he would appear on the other side of the road, in his Mercedes, his face blurred by cigarette smoke. Occasionally, he would wear dark glasses. When the police found the abandoned Corsair they came across a hat in the boot. Presumably, therefore, he must have worn that, also. The idea was obviously to remain in disguise, perhaps even to be threatening, but to the outside observer there is more than a hint of comedy in this vaudeville performance.

In addition to this, Lucan also bought a pocket tape-recorder and took to secretly recording his conversations with Veronica. He would conceal the machine in his breast pocket and then switch it on when he arrived at number 46. While the tape ran, he would provoke Veronica into a ferocious argument, using every bait he could think of to make her sound unbalanced and hysterical. Then he would go home. He would take the tape out of the machine and edit out his own incitements. He was left, he hoped, with hard evidence of his wife's poor psychological condition.

Just before the hearing began, evidently confident of victory, Lucan wrote a letter to his American godmother, Marcia Brady Tucker, in which he outlined his position and his hopes:

> We do have against us the natural inclination of most judges to award custody to the mother, but I have the best QC in the country working for me, and what is more important he is not a man with a reputation for being too brilliant on behalf of his client, right or wrong. The judges all respect him. The fact that the children have now been with me for the best part of three months – that they are all happy and contented – will also weigh very much with us. Also on my side I have the very strong evidence of my own family, George and Camilla's headmistresses and, of course, Veronica's psychiatric record going back to 1962 (before I met her).
>
> The best result for me would be to be given permanent care and control, with four weeks' access for her.
>
> The worst result would be the return of the children to her with virtually no access for me.
>
> Both these extremes are unlikely, however.

In snatching the children before the case started, and in

conducting a ruthless smear campaign, Lucan was employing much more than mere military tactics. He had delivered a strike that had all the ferocity for which the Lucans were noted. He had also revealed his own autocratic edge. Others thought he saw the case was against him, with his profession and his position as an absentee father, and simply overstepped himself in the ferocity of his campaign. He believed that the end justified the means. And he expected the court to see it that way. Not only did the law *not* operate in such a way, however, but the central plank of Lucan's whole claim, which he believed negated his odious methods, was not endorsed by the court itself. His wife was run-down. She was highly strung. She had been emotionally wrecked by what had happened. And she was probably, at that point, physically and psychologically unable to cope with bringing up her children without some help from a nanny or other source. But she was *not* the unfit mother that Lucan pretended.

The case opened on July 11th and lasted just nine days. Lucan called a panoply of witnesses, including the former nanny Lilian Jenkins, and members of his own family. He had psychiatric records and affidavits. He played his tapes. He outlined the kind of care that he envisaged for the children. He talked of private schools and extra tuition. But to his amazement he lost. The judge apparently disliked him. He considered his methods sordid and suspicious. The non-medical witnesses were seen as too partial and the psychiatric evidence was countered by Veronica's current psychiatrist, who said that, with medical treatment, she was quite capable of looking after her children. It has been widely reported that Christina Shand Kydd gave evidence against her sister but this was not so. She, in spite of being estranged from Veronica, told the court that she thought Veronica could look after her children, if she had the appropriate help.

It must be added that Veronica, too, was a highly convincing witness. (She was to demonstrate the same skill at Sandra Rivett's inquest.) Her demeanour was controlled and articulate. She gave not the slightest hint of the conditions that Lucan had accused her of.

And so, on the morning of July 20th, Lucan's barrister, James Comyn, conceded the case. 'The consensus of opinion was that if it had gone on,' said Bill Shand Kydd, 'John would have lost.' The case had already cost him an estimated £40,000 in legal fees, since he was also paying his wife's costs, and he doubted that he could continue without going into bankruptcy.

The judge then formally handed the children back to Lady Lucan. His only acknowledgment of the claim that she was unable to look after them was a stipulation that she must employ a suitable nanny to help her. The nanny had to be approved by the official solicitor. That was it. Lucan, humiliatingly, could have access every other weekend and every other Christmas. But there was to be no other contact.

For him, 'the worst that could happen' *had* happened. And when Veronica walked from the courtroom, holding Camilla's hand, she saw him sitting on a bench in the lobby, his head in his hands.

'It was horrible,' she said.

There can be no doubt that this was the worst trauma of Lucan's life. He had pinned everything on the custody hearing and he had lost. At first, people remembered, it didn't seem to show; the façade held steady, despite the bomb-blast. He went about his normal routine as usual, meeting friends, dining and lunching around London, visiting the Clermont. But then, little by little, the cracks and faultlines began to appear.

'His expression changed completely,' said Lilian Jenkins, the ex-nanny. 'He didn't smile and he looked older. His faith in the law was quite shaken.'

'The court case was desperate for him,' said Caroline Hill, who gave Frances piano lessons. 'He couldn't believe – none of us could believe – that it would go against him.'

'He complained endlessly about the case,' said another friend. 'If it hadn't broken his spirit then it had certainly ruptured something very deep. Aspinall called it internal bleeding. He tended to internalize these things because he was a very controlled man. But those who knew him saw that there had been extensive haemorrhaging.'

Lucan was now alone at the big flat in Elizabeth Street. And how desolate it must have seemed. For three months he had had the children for company, each in their own room, surrounded by their toys and games and belongings. A nanny had been employed. Lucan had immersed himself in the minutiae of his case, confident that he was going to win, probably not even daring, for a moment, to contemplate losing. And now he was alone, again, having lost everything.

Each of his friends had a different recollection of the manifestations of his deterioration.

Dominick Elwes remembered how he would sit in the Clermont and harangue anyone who would listen, often for hours at a time, about the injustice of the court decision, about his wife's mental health, and – above all – about the children. 'He talked of nothing else,' said Elwes. 'It was an obsession.' Dominick remembered saying to him, 'Look, you're not the first person to be divorced [sic], nor to have a wife who is strange and erratic. You've got to brace up and be a man, and when they're grown up, you'll have the children around. You can't go on bending everyone's ear with this problem.' Elwes added, 'I thought I'd got through to him. But, of course, I hadn't.'

And now there was an additional problem: the legal bills had to be paid; so did the private detectives. There were the expenses of running two establishments and also the accumulating gambling debts, which stood at approximately £20,000.

Lucan may originally have believed that his gambling

would improve when he removed himself from Lower Belgrave Street – that, after all, would unshackle him from the immediate symptoms of a marriage in crisis. He would be able to return to the green baize, liberated from anxiety. But a central feature of that delusion must have been the need to win the children. He would probably have found that he could no more concentrate on recouping his fortune while they remained at Lower Belgrave Street than he could when *he* had remained there. That may have been an additional factor in the cruelty and ferocity of his campaign. And when he failed, it would have signalled a death knell for his confidence. He was already exhibiting some of the features of paranoia, according to Dominick Elwes. He may have felt the loss as a fatal breach of his position.

Whatever the case, his financial pressures mounted. He owed money to banks and to professional moneylenders; he also owed shops, businesses and private individuals. When I went through his belongings, I came across his cheque books, returned cheques, stubs and bank statements. I also found letters to bank managers in which he asked for extensions to his existing overdrafts and offered the surety of a sale at Christie's which would return the accounts to credit. In one letter he promised that the overdraft was not intended to be used for gambling purposes.

His overdraft at Lloyds stood at £4,379; at the National Westminster it was £1,290; at the Midland in Newgate Street it was £5,667; and at Coutts, the trustees of the Lucan estate, it was £2,841. The rent on his flat was £70 a week; he was required to pay £40 a week to Veronica, plus £25 for the nanny at number 46. He owed his mother £4,000 and had a legal bill that was estimated to be in excess of £40,000. He had weekly repayments on his new Mercedes of £85 and all the usual gas, electricity and telephone bills (for two establishments).

And so it was that Lucan began to come apart at the edges. His usually polite and personable behaviour started yielding

71

to a more hostile manner. He was rude and belligerent.
Dominick Elwes said, 'It wasn't the Lucan I knew. It was
perhaps the dark side of the moon.' Charles Benson remembered how Lucan would frequently appear to sweat profusely, even at the backgammon board. When he appeared
at the club at lunchtime he would often be drunk, and on one
occasion he arrived to watch Benson playing a backgammon
tournament and nearly ruined it by passing comments. 'It
would have led to anyone else but John being asked to
leave,' Benson said.

At the same time, his encounters with Veronica would
almost always degenerate into brawls:

> I told my wife on Friday that I was not prepared to pay
> £35 a week for the new nanny. She said it was impossible
> to get anyone for less. She accused me of trying to
> 'sabotage' her. In ordinary circumstances, £15–20 a
> week is the going rate. I recognize that the circum-
> stances are not normal, and that I must pay more. But
> there are limits. Am I obliged to bribe someone to live
> at 46 Lower Belgrave Street so that my wife may comply
> with the court order?

Again, towards the end of the year:

> Today was Camilla's Nativity Play and Frances's Carol
> Service. Veronica informed me of neither, but other
> parents had told me. I arrived at 11.10 for the play and,
> not seeing Veronica, I sat through it. At the end of the
> performance Camilla came down from the stage to see
> me. If I hadn't been present she would have been one
> out of just two or three children who didn't have a
> parent present.
> Camilla's new nanny came up to me after a short time
> and took her home. In the afternoon I went to Frances's
> Carol Service. Veronica arrived at 2.15 p.m., stood next

to me and started to tell me that I was in breach of the court order. I told her to be quiet. At the end of the service I left without saying Hullo to Frances.

In his own grieving, Lucan seems to have imagined Veronica to be exulting in her victory. She defeated him at every turn, even in court. He had landed the bitterest blow upon her that he could muster and still she had swum back up to the surface. His arguments with her appear to have been symptomatic of a wider sense of persecution. He was broke. He owed money wherever he looked. A sensible option would have been to go bankrupt. But for Lucan that was the ultimate humiliation. He could not stand the thought of the children seeing their father in court. Yet there seemed to be no option. Debts of £70,000. An income of £12,000. Something would have to be done.

And so, according to several of his friends, Lucan now began to feel the allure of violence.

In the dim drawing room of his empty flat, bleak, soulless, where the ghosts of his three children haunted his imagination, he toyed with the final solution. The situation was desperate. But perhaps there was still time for a last gamble. Perhaps he could still dictate events rather than accommodate them. He was a man of action, like his savage and wily ancestors, and he had the fearless blood of the Lucans rushing through his veins. The Lucans did not hesitate. They intervened in order to survive.

'I did everything I possibly could in court,' he wrote. And by and large, he was right. But there was still one conceivable way out.

Chapter Five

THE FINAL GAMBLE

There have been a number of published versions of Lucan's plans to murder his wife. Some have been more elaborate than others (and we may not have heard them all). But the central thread linking each account remains the same, and can be described as follows.

By the summer of 1974 Lord Lucan was on the edge of catastrophe. He was broke and he was an emotional wreck. He decided that the only way he could recoup his fortune was to kill his wife. Then he could sell the house where she lived and clear his debts. The red ink on his desk only hardened this resolve as the months went by. The murder of his wife would also bring a permanent end to the running sore of dispute about his beloved children. It would allow him to heal the wounds he felt had been inflicted upon him.

And so, during that summer and autumn, he began to make his plans. Lady Lucan never left the house. She was a recluse, barricaded behind the door of number 46. So, even though the children were with her, it would have to be done there. In order to eliminate the chances of the children or their nanny witnessing something, he decided to carry out the crime well into the night, long after the former had gone to bed, and to pick a night when the latter was off duty. Lady Lucan habitually came down to the kitchen to make herself tea at 9 p.m., and this presented itself as the perfect moment.

But what method to use? Guns were noisy and inclined to leave too many clues: the science of ballistics is a highly advanced one. Knives were messy and would involve a physical struggle. The victim rarely died instantly, unless the attack was frenzied, and usually had plenty of time to cry out and fight back. Strangulation would involve a physical struggle, and although Lucan was much stronger than his wife, he probably baulked at the idea of actually having to throttle her. Poison would be impossible to administer.

So he decided upon the bludgeon. One or two clean blows to the head and it would all be over. No noise. No clues. He would position himself behind the stairs, wait until she was crossing the room, and then surprise her from behind, sending her down on the first blow, with no chance to scream or to struggle. It would be finished in a matter of seconds.

The next problem was how to dispose of the body. This was his biggest concern. If his wife were left for dead on the floor of the basement, to be discovered by the nanny returning home from her night off, then he, Lucan, would be the chief suspect. Similarly, if Veronica were found to have disappeared in peculiar circumstances then it would be Lucan that the police hauled in for questioning. But every year, in England, thousands of people vanish, apparently of their own volition, and are never traced. It is very rare for these cases to come to the attention of the courts or for the police to open up a murder inquiry as a result of a missing persons report. Usually, they are teenagers, drop-outs, the mentally ill. Veronica was no drop-out. She was the Countess of Lucan. But she was highly strung and depressed and she had been treated by a psychiatrist. In addition, she was an isolated figure, cut off in a hostile environment, and she was rarely seen by her family or friends. If she vanished, with no clear evidence that she had been harmed, there would be very few people who would make inquiries about her; fewer still who would look beyond an explanation, by an august and plausible English Earl, that she had vanished of her own accord.

And so Lucan hatched a plot for his wife's 'disappearance'. He was an expert sailor. He had been a keen powerboat enthusiast when he and Veronica had first met. He had competed the following year in the Cowes race. He had a boat that he kept moored on the Hamble in Hampshire. He knew, as only someone who loves and respects the sea can know, what the tidal patterns were, the location of deserted beaches, where the deepest parts could be found; he knew, for instance, that if one dropped a weighted sack into the shipping lane around Southampton, then it would disappear into the waters and be impossible to retrieve. That, then, was where Veronica must go. Down into the depths of the Solent, a heavy object lashed to her body, down to the bed of Seven-Mile-Bottom.

And slowly, slowly, his soul began to blacken.

But what of the authorities, and an explanation for her absence? Lucan knew that the moment at which suspicion would fall heaviest was the moment when Veronica actually vanished: the night itself, the hours between the nanny's leaving the house at, say, 7 p.m., and her return at, say, midnight. It was here that Lucan must cover himself. The disposing of the body could then be done at his leisure.

So, his plan was this: he would establish an alibi for himself at the door of the Clermont Club at a quarter to nine. He would commit the murder at nine. He would drive from the murder (having hidden his wife's body) to establish another alibi for himself at another address for five past nine. In retrospect, the police would conclude that there was no way he could have stopped off between point A and point B to

77

kill his wife and dispose of her body. He would thus be in the clear. What they would fail to deduce (he hoped) was that he had only accomplished *one* part of the scheme in the interval between the two alibis; and the second part of the scheme would be concluded later.

And what of the disposal of the body? How would he hide it until he was ready to get rid of it? That was simple. Once his wife had been murdered he would place the body in a canvas sack and place the canvas sack in the safe. The safe, conveniently, was in the basement. This meant that everything could be confined to one room. It was a large safe and it was quite capable of holding a human body. He would clear up any signs of the deed that existed and then go and establish his second alibi.

At midnight the nanny would get home. She might go straight to bed, in which case Veronica's disappearance would not even come to light until the morning, or she might look in on the Countess and, not finding her, alert Lucan that his wife had vanished. Either way, he would be called at some point in the next twenty-four hours to take charge of his children. He would move them, and their nanny, to his flat, leaving number 46 empty. He would now have an easy run of things.

The next night, the Friday, he would dress up in his dinner jacket and bow tie and set off as usual for Mayfair. But he would not *arrive* in Mayfair. Instead, he would arrive at his wife's house. He would let himself in with a latch-key. He would go down to the basement, take the body out of the safe, go up the stairs, open the front door, and convey the sack down the three short steps to the boot of the car. This would probably be the most hair-raising part of the operation: the quick jaunt from door to pavement, normally done in the batting of an eyelid, would seem like an eternity. But there was simply no other way out of the house with the deadly cargo.

Now Lucan would motor down to the sea. He would have

his boat ready at a discreet location, a lonely cove some-where which he had discovered on his forays and sorties around the South Coast. He would load up the cargo, sail out into the Channel, locate the appropriate spot, and send his wife down to the sea-bed.

At once, he would set off back for London. He would probably have changed clothes at some point, or perhaps put a boiler suit on over his smart evening wear. Now, back on dry land, speeding back to the city, he would change again, returning to the dinner jacket. He would probably drive straight home to his flat, arriving for about 3 a.m., and would make a point of disturbing the nanny, in full Mayfair uniform, to confirm that he had just returned from a gambling club or a dinner.

The next day, a Saturday, Lady Lucan would have been missing for over twenty-four hours. He would go to the police station. He would explain to the duty sergeant that his wife had apparently disappeared some time on Thurs-day night, taking with her an overcoat and suitcase, and that he was concerned because she had a history of depression. He would add that she had disappeared like this before, though never for more than a day, and that she had attempted suicide the previous year. As a matter of routine, the police would test Lucan's alibis for the Thursday night and, finding them water-tight, would prob-ably drop their inquiries. So long as Lady Lucan was not thought to have met her death at the hands of her husband it is unlikely that the police would have pressed on. 'Most murders are the result of a dispute between husband and wife,' said Roy Ranson, later. 'Ninety per cent of murders, I'd say.' The official conclusion on Lady Lucan's missing person's file would be simple: a history of depression; the terrific strain of the custody case; the running uncertainty that she could cope; the previous attempt at suicide. The police would decide that she had simply wandered away and killed herself, that her body would turn up sooner or later, in a lake or hanging from a tree. The file would be closed.

And Lucan's problems would be gone.

This, then, was the broad summary of the police case, some of which was to be presented at the inquest, some of which dripped out unofficially years later. But what was the evidence for it? There are a number of sources, spanning the implied to the detailed and explicit.

First, there are Lucan's conversations with John Aspinall and his mother. Some weeks before the crime, according to Brian Masters' biography, *The Passion of John Aspinall*, Lucan told both Aspinall and his mother, Lady Osbourne, that he would like to kill his wife. Curiously, Lady Osbourne was, according to one source, 'the closest confidante of Lord Lucan'. They certainly seemed to enjoy an intimate relationship. Lucan was said to have regarded her as his 'substitute mother'. And, according to one journalist, '[Lady Osbourne] is said to have gone to her grave knowing all the secrets of this story.'

Masters continues:

> Aspinall was certainly not surprised that Lucan might have killed his wife [*sic*]. The missing earl had confessed to him some weeks earlier that he would like to, and had even gone so far as to tell Aspinall's mother that he intended to.
>
> She had replied to the effect that he must do whatever he thought was right.

The second source was the gambler, writer and Greek shipping tycoon Taki Theodoracopoulos. Taki was a friend of Lucan's and gambled with him at clubs in Mayfair. He revealed in the late 1970s that Lucan had done a number of things in the summer before the murder which with hindsight clearly indicated his intention to kill Veronica. Taki did not reveal his source but he was emphatic with his claims. First, Lucan had bought a twenty-foot speedboat, he said, which he kept moored 'on the South Coast'. Second, he had made two dummy runs in the car, with a sack in the boot weighing eight stone. Third, Taki recalled coming across Lucan jogging one day in Hyde Park, and this had struck him as odd because Lucan had never before shown any real interest in his physical health. The clear implication was that he was preparing himself for the rigours of the task ahead.

The third source – and the most persuasive – was Greville Howard, a fellow gambler at the Clermont, and one of the inner circle. Just after the murder, Howard went to Gerald Road police station and made a statement in which he said that Lucan had told him he wanted to kill his wife. Greville Howard's statement, in fact, was to form a linchpin of the police case. Howard said that he and Lucan had been drinking at Lucan's flat in the weeks before the murder and Lucan had mentioned his money worries. He had told Howard that he was finding it difficult to maintain the payments to his wife and to keep up with the expenses at Lower Belgrave Street. Howard's advice was to go bankrupt. Lucan replied that he could not do that because it would mean public humiliation and his children seeing him in court. Howard said that that was a stupid attitude to have. They talked some more and then Lucan said that there was another way out of his problems: to kill Lady Lucan. He told Howard that it was possible to bury a body for ever by dropping it into the Solent. Howard told Lucan that he was being absurd and added that the children would be far more hurt at seeing their father in court for the murder of their mother than for mere bankruptcy. Lucan responded by saying that he would not get caught.

In addition to these accounts, there were a number of incidents that ran together through late October and early November which seemed to indicate that the plot was coming to a head. On October 23rd Lucan had dinner with Michael Stoop at the Portland Club. During the conversation he asked if he could borrow Stoop's second car, a battered Corsair. He gave no explanation for wanting the car and, according to Stoop, he 'seemed sort of pent up when he asked'. Stoop, knowing that Lucan was accustomed to grander things, offered him the use of his Mercedes. But Lucan declined. 'I assumed through natural good manners that he didn't want to deprive me of my better car,' Stoop said. It was somewhat inconvenient for Lucan to have the car when he wanted, which was that evening, but Lucan was insistent. 'He did want it very much *that* night,' Stoop remembered. So Stoop told Lucan to get it insured and said he would leave the car keys in the car, outside his garage, so that Lucan could collect it when he wished. Lucan thanked him. Then he told Stoop to keep the matter a secret.

It was the contention of the police that Lucan wanted the car to transport his wife's body. There was nothing wrong with his own Mercedes: he drove around in it after borrowing the Corsair. But the Corsair was not associated with him; it had a capacious boot; and it was a nondescript vehicle, less likely than the Mercedes to be remembered by witnesses or to be stopped casually by traffic police.

At the end of the following week, on the weekend of November 2nd, Lucan drove his three children up to his sister's home in Northamptonshire. He used the Mercedes. On the drive there he taped the conversation (he did this as a matter of course when he was with the children, in case they revealed something that he could use against their mother). During a discussion about life at number 46 he asked Camilla if Sandra Rivett had any boyfriends. Camilla replied that she did. He asked when she went out with them. Camilla replied that she went out with them on a Thursday night. The next Thursday was November 7th.

On Wednesday the 6th, Lucan dined with Selim Zilkha and a

small gambling party at Selim's house in Portland Place. Afterwards, he went to Annabel's and sat drinking with a casual friend, Andrina Colquhoun, the stepdaughter of the timber millionaire Peter Montague-Mayer. They finished their drinks and left the place at about 2.30 a.m. The next morning, Lucan rose at 10.30 and rang Andrina to talk about their dinner arrangements. His plans were 'rather muddled', she said, 'so I told him I'd see him at the Clermont at lunchtime'. But Lucan didn't show up for lunch. Instead, apparently preoccupied, he went to Heywood's, the bookshop in Curzon Street, where he bought a book on Greek shipping millionaires and their hideaways. Then he went to the chemist at the bottom of Lower Belgrave Street, by the Plumbers Arms, and asked the pharmacist to identify a small pink pill that he, Lucan, had taken from his wife. Having been told that it was a tranquilliser, he then left.

Thirty yards up the street someone else had 'rather muddled' evening arrangements. She was Sandra Rivett, the nanny to Lord Lucan's children. In the vast plotting of the Lucan case, Sandra has been reduced to an almost Brueghel-like insignificance. Yet she was a kindly, attractive girl, with an even temper. She came from Basingstoke, close to where Veronica's family had run the Wheatsheaf. She had married Roger Rivett. He was a security guard at Gatwick Airport, and they had one son. After the marriage collapsed the son was looked after by Sandra's parents, Albert and Eunice Hensby, while Sandra stayed in London to work for an elderly couple in Paddington. The photograph of her which was widely used by Fleet Street and the British television companies after her murder does not do her justice. It was taken at a wedding four years before her death. In fact, from that bright and fresh-faced girl, rather too plump, she had flowered into an extremely attractive young woman. The hair was shoulder-length, the face had grown leaner and more sensual. In repose there was a quiet shadow of melancholy across her eyes which men found irresistible. At the time of her murder she was seeing the relief manager of the Plumbers Arms, John Hankins. There was talk of marriage, of returning to Hankins' native Australia.

That week, Hankins had phoned to say that his night off was going to be Wednesday. So Sandra, with Lady Lucan's permission, changed her night off. At four o'clock, she had taken the children out to post some letters. Now, at 6 p.m., she was back at the house, helping Lady Lucan with the children's dinner.

Round at Elizabeth Street, Lucan was having a drink with a friend called Michael Hicks Beach, a literary agent, who was advising him about an article that he had been asked to write on gambling. They had a couple of vodkas and arranged to meet over the weekend for lunch. Then Lucan drove Hicks Beach back to his flat in Fulham. 'I assumed that after he'd dropped me he was going to go back home,' said Hicks Beach, 'change clothes, have a bath and then go and meet his friends for dinner.' Earlier that evening, Greville Howard had phoned to say that he had some tickets for a Cole Porter show in Blackfriars. Lucan had declined the invitation but had invited Greville and his party to dinner at the Clermont. They had accepted. At half past eight Lucan had telephoned the club to book the table. 'We'll be along at about eleven,' he told the restaurant manager, Andrew Demetrio. 'I hope that's not too late.'

Lucan's next move was curious. Having just phoned the club, he then got into his Mercedes and drove round there. He did not get out of the car but pulled up at the door and called over the linkman, Billy Egson.

'Anyone in the club?' he asked Egson. Egson came to the window of the car.

'No, my Lord, none of the usual crowd.'

Lucan said, 'Okay. I'll be back later.' Then he drove off. Egson didn't notice which way he drove off.

It was approaching 9 p.m.

Chapter Six

THE BODY IN THE BASEMENT

At Lower Belgrave Street, the house was quiet and in darkness. Frances was playing in the nursery on the second floor. George and Camilla had been put to bed. Veronica was in her bedroom, watching TV. Sandra had rung her parents in Basingstoke to tell them how much she was looking forward to coming home for Christmas, and had then gone to her room to finish some ironing.

Sometime after eight thirty, she switched the iron off and walked down the two flights of stairs to Veronica's second-floor bedroom. She put her head round the door and asked if Veronica wanted a cup of tea. 'It was not usual for her to ask me that,' Veronica told me, 'but I accepted.'

Later, after an interval of about twenty minutes, Veronica began to wonder where the tea had got to. By now Frances had returned to the bedroom and was watching the TV with her mother. She takes up the story:

I asked Mummy where Sandra was and Mummy said she

was downstairs making some tea. After a while, Mummy said she wondered why Sandra was taking so long. I don't know what time this was, but it was before the news came on the television at 9 p.m. I said I would go downstairs to see what was keeping Sandra but Mummy said no, she would go. I said I would go with her but she said no, it was okay, she would go.

Then:

She left the bedroom door open but there is no light in the hall because the bulb is worn out and it doesn't work.

Then:

Just after she left the room I heard a scream.

Veronica had walked through the darkness of the house, down to the ground floor. That, too, was in darkness. She had walked along the hall towards the basement stairs. The basement door was open. It was dark down there as well. 'I knew then that she couldn't possibly be making the tea down there, so I called out her name.'

She now heard a noise behind her, coming from the downstairs cloakroom, a sort of shuffling sound. She turned to face it and:

He came at me out of the darkness [she told me]. There were four or five blows. I screamed as loudly as I could, not just because of the pain but because of the terror of being attacked in the dark. By screaming, I was also trying to alert Frances, upstairs. As soon as I screamed he slapped his hand over my mouth and said, 'Shut up!' He was obviously frightened of the children coming down. As soon as he spoke I recognized the voice as that

Sandra Rivett, the Lucans' nanny, who was brutally bludgeoned to death. Her battered body was discovered in a canvas sack in the basement of 46 Lower Belgrave Street (*Topham*)

The wedding of Veronica
Mary Duncan and
Richard John Bingham at
Brompton Holy Trinity,
November 28th, 1963
(*The Hulton-Deutsch
Collection*)

Lady Lucan plays with
two of her three children,
seven-year-old Lord
George Bingham and ten-
year-old Lady Frances
(*Syndication
International*)

The Seventh Earl of Lucan – a man of 'enormous presence and beauty' who exhibited all the characteristics for which his line was most famous: 'ruthlessness, energy, and disregard for sentiment' (*Topham*)

The Plumbers Arms, where a blood-soaked Veronica Lucan ran to safety from her attacker on the night of November 7th, 1974 (*Topham*)

46 Lower Belgrave Street, Lady Lucan's home, where the murder took place (*Syndication International*)

5 Eton Row, where Lord Lucan lived briefly after he and his wife separated; Veronica Lucan moved there after the murder (*Syndication International*)

of my husband. He pushed his fingers into my mouth and we started to fight. He started to throttle me and tried to gouge out my eye with his thumb. I moved about as much as I could in his grip. We fell into the basement doorway and he tried to push me down the basement stairs. I hooked a leg round the banisters to stop myself going down. He was throttling me and I remember thinking to myself that I was going to die. I remember thinking, You're going to die, you're going to die. You're thirty-seven and it's a bit young to die. I managed to grab his testicles and I squeezed as hard as I could. That made him let go and he sprang back. He was exhausted. We were both exhausted.

For a long moment, she recalled, they sat together on the basement stairs, panting. Then Veronica asked where Sandra was. Lucan replied that she had gone out.

'But she wouldn't go out without telling me.'

Silence. Then, 'She's dead. She's down in the basement. But don't look, it's a ghastly mess.'

There was some more dialogue and then Veronica persuaded her husband to take her upstairs. She resisted the suggestion that he had 'helped' her upstairs. He had 'frogmarched' her, she said. They had gone into the bedroom.

Again, Frances remembered:

At about 9.05 p.m., when the news was on television, Daddy and Mummy both walked into the room together. Mummy had blood over her face and she was crying . . . Daddy didn't say anything to me and I didn't say anything to either of them. I don't know how much blood was on Mummy's face, I only caught a glimpse of her. I didn't hear any conversation between them. I couldn't see if Daddy's clothes had any blood on them. I wondered what had happened, but I didn't ask.

87

Frances was sent to bed. The television was turned off. Lord and Lady Lucan went into the bathroom to inspect her wounds. Then, feeling dizzy, Lady Lucan returned to the bedroom to lie down. Lucan brought in a towel and draped it over the pillow. He didn't want her staining the sheets. Then he went back into the bathroom for a face flannel.

Now Lady Lucan had her chance. She told me:

> As I lay on the bed, I suddenly realized that the sound of the taps running would momentarily deafen him. I had about four seconds to decide what to do. I got up off the bed and went to the door. I left the room and ran down the stairs and out into the street. It was deserted. There wasn't anyone around. I felt sick and faint. I ran like hell down to the Plumbers Arms. I knew the Plumbers Arms because I occasionally used to go there for cigarettes.

Meanwhile, Lucan, oblivious, came back into the bedroom, the wet towel in his hands. The light was burning. The sheets of the bed were ruffled. The towel on the pillow was stained in blood. And the door was open. His stomach must have turned at the thought of what had happened. 'There he was,' Susan Maxwell-Scott said, 'with the body and blood and a wife gone away who would almost certainly try to implicate him.'

Frances, who was upstairs, reading in bed, recalled:

> After a little while, I heard Daddy calling for Mummy. He was calling: 'Veronica, where are you?' I got up and went to the banisters and looked down and I saw Daddy coming out of the nursery on the floor below. He came straight out and then went downstairs. That was the last I saw of him. He never came to the top floor of the house, either to look for Mummy or to say good night to me.

Precisely what Lucan's movements in the house were in those last seconds we do not know. But he evidently did not remain there for very long. When he got to the ground floor he may well have found the front door standing open, unless Veronica had pulled it shut behind her, to delay his pursuit. If he went to the door he might even have been in time to see his wife disappear through the doors of the Plumbers Arms, in which case he would have realized that the night, for him, was finally over.

She had won again.

At any rate, he decided not to be in the house when the police arrived. He closed the door behind him, conscious of the children, and got into the Corsair. Then he drove off, apparently avoiding his flat, out into the night.

PART TWO

THE INQUEST

The lives of the very rich are not for me.
They are interesting to observe at close
quarters for a brief spell. But they are also
strangely deadening to the heart.

Noël Coward
From *Remembered Laughter* by Cole Lesley

Chapter Seven

CLOSING RANKS

Detective Chief Inspector David Gerring had been a police officer for twenty years. He had served in Croydon and Catford and had earned the nickname 'Buster' for his 'gang-busting' successes in the 1960s. He had investigated the murder at Mr Smith's Club and had been on the CID team that had broken up the Richardson gang in 1968. In 1970 he had transferred to Gerald Road station, where he became the head of CID. His remit covered the whole of Belgravia and the area around Buckingham Palace, and in recent months he had been working on the shooting attempt on Princess Anne. He was an officer of considerable experience and aplomb and had earned several commendations.

On the night of November 7th he had finished duty at about eight o'clock and had gone straight home. At that time, he lived in Orpington, Kent. He and his wife had had dinner and watched the television news. A little after eleven o'clock he had gone upstairs to get ready to go to bed. It was then that the telephone rang. Gerring's wife answered and called him downstairs.

'It was my sergeant,' Gerring told me, 'ringing to say that he had a murder on his hands. His exact words were: "I've got a real one here, sir." He gave me a few details. He'd only just arrived at the house himself. I said I was on my way.'

A few miles away, in another part of Kent, Detective Chief Superintendent Roy Ranson was also getting ready for bed. Ranson, like Gerring, had handled a number of important cases in recent months. He had been involved in the same investigation into the shooting attempt on Princess Anne and placed regular reports of their progress to the Queen. He was also investigating Harold Wilson's claims that someone had stolen his tax papers.

The phone call came a little before midnight, Ranson recalled. 'It was Dave Gerring, calling to tell me that there had been a murder in Belgravia.' Gerring told Ranson that he was on his way to the scene and that he, Ranson, could leave it in his hands until the morning. But Ranson claimed to have some sixth sense about the case. 'Suddenly I was awake,' he said. 'I knew there was no way I could leave this to anyone else.' He told Gerring to pick him up on his way into London, and together the two men headed for Belgravia.

The sight that greeted them in Lower Belgrave Street was 'like a film set'. There were police cars and ambulances 'everywhere'. Television cameras had been set up at either end of the street and a group of reporters were gathering behind the cordon that Sergeant Baker had erected around the entrance to the house. Inside, the Dowager Countess was getting the three children dressed and ready to leave. In the basement, forensic experts and photographers were recording details of the scene. 'The house was pretty chaotic,' Gerring told me, later, 'with thirty or forty officers walking around.' 'I think what happens in these jobs,' Ranson said, 'is that there's such a flap everybody's there. We found we had to turf so many police officers out of that address. It was:

"Come and see the body!" and they all want to be first on the scene.'

The two men carried out their own inspection of the house, going from room to room. Already the implications of a Belgravian murder must have begun to penetrate: the rarefied world; the powerful network of friendships; the code of loyalty that united a group which was steeped in wealth and privilege. Certainly, both men had a sense of foreboding about the case.

Downstairs, in the hallway, they interviewed the Dowager Countess. She told them that she had received a call from her son a short while ago, asking her to go to the house and collect the children. She told them that he had been passing the house, had seen a struggle, and had intervened. The attacker had escaped. Gerring thought the Dowager was 'a very clever woman'. Ranson thought she was 'formidable'. In the weeks to come he would christen both her and her immediate family 'the Opposition'. As a result of the Dowager's story, a house-to-house search was started in the area and a team of officers began knocking on the doors of residents in Lower and Upper Belgrave Street. No one had seen anything unusual. No one had seen a man fleeing number 46, neither the Earl of Lucan nor anyone else. Although they had authorized the inquiries, both men were quickly to become sceptical of Lucan's story. Ranson thought it would be 'a miracle' if Lucan passed by at the precise moment of attack. 'Imagine,' he said, later, 'he just *happens* to be passing and he *happens* to see a man . . .' 'Basically,' he added, 'he's stuck with a story which he tells on the spur of the moment, and Lucan, if he's got an ounce of common sense, knows it can't stand up.'

Shortly after the Dowager had left with the children, Ranson and Gerring walked round the corner to the mews house in Eaton Row. Sergeant Forsyth had already smashed his way in through a top window and searched the place. Then they walked the hundred or so yards to Lucan's flat, in

Elizabeth Street, where the door had been forced and another search made. The flat had clearly been occupied until very recently, though there was no evidence that Lucan had returned there after leaving number 46. His Mercedes was outside with a flat battery. Ranson remembered feeling the bonnet and finding it cold.

At 1 a.m., the two officers decided that it was time to see Lady Lucan. Gerring told me, 'She'd been taken to St George's Hospital, in Hyde Park Corner. When we arrived she was in a terrible state. Really bloody awful. There were tufts of hair and skin all over the pillow. She was covered in dry blood and her scalp was open with the wounds. She'd been bashed about in a really shocking way. She was a tiny creature, sort of semi-conscious. She was only half with it, having been sedated, and she seemed very nervous. When I walked up to the end of the bed she sort of shied away. She cringed. I tried to tell her that I wasn't going to hurt her. I just wanted to know what had happened. The basement was a sight I'll never forget. Veronica Lucan was another sight I'll never forget.'

In due course, after receiving sixty stitches, Lady Lucan became more alert and lucid. She rested until the early morning and then gave the detectives her first coherent account of the murder. She told them how Sandra had gone to make tea, and how she had then gone to investigate, how she had been hit, and how she had escaped after the attack ended. She was emphatic that her assailant was her husband. Ranson and Gerring were both impressed. As a witness she was compelling and articulate. As a woman and a wife she demanded sympathy. 'She was absolutely convincing,' said Gerring. 'One hundred per cent convincing.' 'She never once wavered,' Ranson added. 'No matter how much we questioned her.'

The detectives left Sergeant Forsyth to prepare Lady Lucan's formal statement. By now, mid-morning on Friday, they were growing concerned at Lucan's continued silence. They had been assured by the Dowager Countess that he would contact them. He had said he would ring in the morning. They certainly had no reason to doubt that. He was, after all, the Earl of Lucan, resident in Belgravia, of considerable pedigree and conspicuous appearance. He was not the sort of man, typically, to run away. 'I fully expected him to walk into the police station that morning,' said Ranson, 'with a solicitor and a prepared statement. It would have been so true to character.' But it did not happen. At lunchtime the two men agreed to put out an all-force message requesting Lucan's immediate detention. An alert was also flashed to Interpol, as a precaution. Reluctantly, they had to conclude that Lucan was holed up somewhere, with a friend, trying to decide what to do, and that they must therefore weed him out.

Fortunately, they had found his address books at his flat. These, in Ranson's words, contained the sort of names 'that most of us only read about in the newspapers'. He and Gerring now began to divide the entries under the headings of the county police forces and rang round to ask fellow officers for assistance in checking addresses.

At this stage the paperwork for search warrants was still incomplete, so efforts were restricted to interviews and, in some cases, to clandestine watches on suspected addresses. Police constables were also deposited at the doors of London's finest restaurants and gambling clubs, including the Portland, the St James's, and the Clermont.

'A policeman came in at about lunchtime,' said an employee of the latter club, 'and told us that he was looking for Lord Lucan. He said he wished to wait at the foyer of the club in case he turned up. One of the managers said that this was not possible since it would disturb the members, but the officer refused to go. A chair was eventually brought and he waited all afternoon.'

By Friday evening, as the story broke on television and in the evening newspapers, Ranson and Gerring braced themselves for the first confrontations with Lucan's friends.

★ ★ ★

It was now that the two officers' early forebodings about the case began to be realized. News of the murder had spread quickly through the social milieu. A little after 11 p.m. a friend of Stephen Raphael's had seen two policemen smash their way into Lucan's mews house in Eaton Row. He had telephoned Raphael, to tell him that something serious was happening 'at Lucan's place' and Raphael, who assumed that Lucan had killed himself because of his debts, 'turned green and cried like a baby'. He then rang Charles Benson. Benson rang Gerald Road police station. He was told of the death of Mrs Rivett, and rang Raphael back. They then began to call other friends of Lucan.

As word of the catastrophe spread, a curious grouping process began to occur. People were dragged out of poker games and dinner parties, summoned from bars and clubs. Phones were taken off the hook; factotums were instructed to shoo the police away if they turned up asking questions. No one, in other words, was to say anything until a plan of action, a uniform response, had been agreed. The CID, who were, one senses, already uncertain of exactly how to proceed, became less and less sure of themselves in the face of sudden aristocratic hostility. One woman, interviewed in Chelsea, said, 'Murder is not the sort of thing which aristocrats *do*.' Another, waylaid at her estate in Surrey, said, 'Such a pity; nannies are so hard to find these days.' At the same time, the police received numerous calls – all of them hoaxes – saying that Lucan had just been seen in one casino or another across London. They had no choice but to follow up every lead, and wasted many man-hours in fruitless searching. Ranson called it 'the horse-play of the upper classes'. But another officer was less indulgent. 'You know how the Mafia work?' he said. 'They all stick together. And this lot stick together like shit to a blanket. They're used to being served and they look upon you as servants. You are not there to prosecute the aristocrat, if you're a policeman,

you're there to look after all the interests of the aristocrat.'
'We came up against the attitude of some of these people trying to put one over us,' said Ranson, 'to take us on and beat us.' He recalled how, when he rang people up to ask for an interview, they were likely to say, 'Terribly sorry, old boy, can't see you for three weeks, I'm off to Austria to do some skiing.'

On Friday morning, eight of Lucan's friends had met at John Aspinall's house in Lyall Street to discuss the murder. 'People were worried about what to do in case he turned up,' Aspinall said. 'I mean, he might have turned up at Howlett's [Aspinall's zoo] or he might have telephoned from Brazil. So every contingency was looked at.' 'Some of the suggestions were more melodramatic and ludicrous than others,' said Charles Benson. Dominick Elwes, always a romantic, had said that they must 'help Lucan flee'. They should, he said, smuggle Lucan out of the country on a cargo ship bound for South America. Shand Kydd told Dominick to 'piss off'. 'I said there was certainly no question of helping him flee. I said I certainly didn't think he'd done it and I wanted to get hold of him as soon as possible before he did something silly like killing himself or pissing off.' The lunch was concluded with the decision that, if Lucan contacted them, they would try to persuade him to give himself up. At the same time, it was decided that someone should see Veronica Lucan, to find out her version of events. Dominick Elwes, as the person she least despised, was dispatched with a bunch of flowers to St George's. He was accompanied by Christina Shand Kydd and by Lucan's younger brother, Hugh Bingham. When they arrived, Veronica, who was perched in bed with a bandaged head and huge black eye, looked at them and said, 'Well, now who's mad? Now who's the one with *paranoia*, eh?' Dominick, overcome by the injuries to Lady Lucan and the horror of what she told him, began to weep. 'His tears were not for me,' Lady Lucan said, 'they were for my husband.' Dominick, from then on, was convinced of Lucan's guilt.

The meeting at Aspinall's house was later to be dubbed 'the meeting of Eight Just Men', a strange term, lifted from an Edgar Wallace story, by a tabloid journalist. The lunch had in fact been entirely inconsequential and did not have the conspiratorial intent suggested later. 'They told me they were there to discuss ways of helping Lucan if he surfaced,' said Ranson, 'and I believe them.' But other acquaintances of Lucan, though again not part of any conspiracy, were continuing to make life difficult for the police. The team at Gerald Road had been nicknamed 'the Nob Squad' by the press, a phrase that was taken up and used with a more derisory tone in fashionable circles. The officers quickly resented what they saw as the condescending, patronizing attitude of the people they tried to question. The journalist, James Fox, wrote:

> What remains in the memory is the instant hostility that grew up between the various participants of the affair. Class lines were drawn up early on. The crime reporters and the CID, working as always in close proximity, soon found that the 'Lucan Set' were unapproachable and aloof, indeed defensively tight-lipped.
>
> It was as if, day after day, Ranson and Gerring were chasing the guests at some nightmare charity ball.

The matter soon began to arouse considerable national interest. It was reported in *Vanity Fair* that, when the police arrived to interview John Aspinall at his private zoo in Kent, they were shown into a dining room where Aspinall was seated at a table with two guests: his mother, Lady Osbourne, and a giant African gorilla. It was also reported that the police had come across a woman in Chester Square who had been disturbed on the Thursday night by the ringing of her front-door bell (which she had ignored) and a

100

telephone call moments later, which had been incoherent. She was sure that the caller had been Lucan, fleeing the murder house, but she had not contacted the police about it. 'It's their problem,' she explained to a *Sunday Times* reporter. 'They're obviously trained to discern these things.'

It was the same story in Uckfield, when the police finally traced Susan Maxwell-Scott. She also had not contacted them after Lucan's visit on Thursday night, and it was only when Shand Kydd turned up at Gerald Road with the two letters, bearing Uckfield postmarks, that Ranson and Gerring were able to establish the Maxwell-Scott connection. When they asked her why she had not called the police after Lucan's visit, she replied, simply, 'I had no reason to.'

As a result of their visit to East Sussex, the two detectives put out a special alert to Sussex and Hampshire police, asking them to keep watch for Lucan or for the car he was likely to be driving, the Ford Corsair. Subsequently, on the following day, Sunday, the car turned up.

Police Sergeant David De Lima, stationed at Lewes, in Sussex, was responsible for the Vehicle Investigation Bureau. He was on duty patrol in Newhaven, the Channel port, when he found the car, at 2.40 p.m.

Ranson and Gerring, who were both off-duty, their first break since Thursday night, hurried down to Sussex in Gerring's car. They were met by Chief Inspector Cyril Cornbil of Brighton CID, and together the officers decided to force the car open. Inside, there were blood-stains everywhere: across the steering wheel, the dashboard, the rear-view mirror, the windscreen and the glove compartment. And in the boot there was what Ranson called 'the clincher'. Lying between two bottles of vodka and a spare tyre there was a length of lead piping. It was sixteen inches long. It was bound in surgical tape.

And it was identical to the weapon that had been used to murder Sandra Rivett.

Chapter Eight

MANHUNT

'Obviously,' said Gerring, 'things were beginning to fall into place.' Once the car interiors had been photographed and fingerprinted, the Corsair was taken back to the forensic office at Scotland Yard for extensive microscopic tests. That afternoon, back at Gerald Road CID, Ranson and Gerring decided to flash a red alert to Interpol in Paris. The message read: 'Wanted for murder and attempted murder: Richard John Bingham, 7th Earl of Lucan. Please arrest. Extradition will follow.'

They now decided to switch their inquiries from central London to the English South Coast. Throughout Sunday night Gerring drove around Newhaven, checking local hotels and guesthouses. The forty officers who had been stationed at Gerald Road, conducting house-to-house inquiries in Belgravia, were redrafted to the Newhaven area, and officers from the local stations at Eastbourne and Brighton joined in the hunt. On Monday morning, having snatched a few hours' sleep in a local hotel, Gerring began to direct operations in the marina and ferry terminal. He questioned immigration staff to see whether a man resembling Lucan had tried to obtain a 48-hour passport on Friday morning. He organized a team to search the boats and fishing trawlers which were moored at the quayside. Another group checked the Sealink ferries which departed hourly for Cherbourg and St Malo.

At this stage, Ranson and Gerring must still have been fairly confident that they would make an arrest, since they asked for the inquest into Sandra Rivett's death to be postponed while they developed their lines of inquiry. They knew that an inquest jury's verdict, which might actually name Lord Lucan as Sandra Rivett's murderer, would have a prejudicial effect upon a future High Court trial. It was legally and morally incumbent upon them, therefore, to ensure that all possible steps had been taken to find Lucan, to give him the opportunity of a fair trial, before other legal proceedings were undertaken. The Coroner's Office duly replied that a postponement would be possible until the following month, although there was a degree of urgency because of the lucidity and fallibility of witnesses' memories.

The situation was not helped by the fact that, with the discovery of the car at Newhaven, Ranson and Gerring now became divided between themselves over whether Lucan was alive or dead. Ranson's reading of the aristocratic mentality implied a sense of honour that would have compelled suicide. 'I think he would rather die than let his children see him humiliated in court on a murder charge,' he said. There was also the question of whether Lucan had the tenacity to go on after the pressure of recent years. 'Don't forget,' the family GP had told the Dowager Countess, when the question of Lucan's silence was raised, 'he has been under the most fearful pressure for these last seven or eight years.' Ranson added, 'I think the strain of the murder on top of everything else has probably been too much for him. I think he may have parked the car and then got on board a ferry and thrown himself off halfway over the Channel.' Others agreed. Aspinall said that he would give 'even money' on whether Lucan was still alive. 'He was a warrior, a Roman,' he said, 'and he was quite capable of falling on his sword.' Kaitilin said publicly that she thought the strain had killed him. 'Everyone meets their Waterloo,' she told a journalist. Shand Kydd, when asked by the gossip columnist Nigel Dempster if he thought Lucan was still alive, snapped, 'Of course not.' And Jimmy Goldsmith said that he was 'convinced' that Lucan had committed suicide. The idea that he was still alive, he said, was 'absurd'.

Ranson marshalled a team of frogmen and deep-sea divers to plumb the River Ouse and the coast off Newhaven. It was, he pointed out, a notorious area for suicides. They extended their search along the coast towards Peacehaven and Eastbourne. He asked fishermen and powerboat enthusiasts to keep alert for the body. But nothing was found. Ranson also turned his gaze towards the Sussex Downs, which flanked Newhaven on all sides. Perhaps Lucan had parked the car and then wandered on to the Downs to die from exposure. Perhaps his body was lying in the undergrowth somewhere up on the hills, or perhaps he had crawled down into an animal trail, concealed by bracken and foliage, and swallowed an overdose of pills. At any rate, Ranson was convinced that the body was nearby. 'It was damn cold on the night he vanished,' he said. 'How far can a man get in the middle of the night, in the pouring rain and the wind, without an overcoat? If he *is* dead, then I'm convinced that he's dead within a five-mile radius of the car.'

While the sea search continued, a group of officers began to move across the Downs, trekking through the gorse, using tracker dogs, sticks and pitchforks. An army unit combed the forests and woodlands and a group of professional pot-holers went down to explore the caves that lined the cliffs jutting out to sea. 'Unfortunately,' said Ranson, when the searchers returned empty-handed, 'the whole area is extremely dense. It could take an army unit six months working full-time to cover the whole grounds. And even then they might not find everything. Also, the area is criss-crossed with animal trails, and if he crawled into one of those then we may not know about it for several years, until foxes or other animals bring out his bones.' 'But,' he added, 'we shall go on looking.'

A short time later Plessey offered the use of the new auto-gyro which they had been developing. The little machine had featured in the James Bond film *You Only Live Twice*, and had recently been adapted for use in the search for missing persons. Four cameras were mounted on the gyro's front and rear, two of them equipped with X-ray and infra-red facility, the remaining two using ultra-violet light. These cameras could photograph the whole area from the air and 'see' two or three feet beneath the foliage and soil. Any freshly decomposing matter would instantly show up on the photographs as red spots, and the police would then be able to dispatch a unit to check on the hidden remains. Astonishingly, as if to illustrate Ranson's earlier point, the first set of photographs revealed the body of a man hanging from a tree in a remote forest on the tip of the Downs. He had been there for three years. But the second set of photographs revealed only the remains of animals and rodents.

Ranson knew that time was running out. He sent the divers back down. More policemen were drafted in to search the cliff-tops and coves. The auto-gyro went back up, and the whole search was moved along the coast towards East-bourne.

Meanwhile, Detective Chief Inspector Gerring was convinced that Lucan was still alive.

'This man was a gambler,' he said. 'He was used to taking chances. I don't think he would have ended it all without a last throw of the dice, without some sort of a flourish.' Gerring told a press conference that, although they were looking for a body at Newhaven, and indeed he himself had been there for eleven days, supervising all the searches, they were also working on the theory that someone was shielding Lucan and that there were plans to smuggle him out of the country. Gerring had been to France to check on sightings up and down the French coast. He had interviewed hoteliers and restaurant owners in Cherbourg and St Malo. He had people watching air and sea ports. Addresses were being checked by Interpol in America, Africa and Australia. Friends of Lucan were being watched by their own police forces in cities as diverse as New York and Bombay. 'I am sure that he is still alive,' Gerring said, 'and I would like to remind everyone of what we said earlier: that anyone who harbours him or helps him will be prosecuted. It is as simple as that.'

Over the next few weeks, Gerring and his sergeant, Graham Forsyth, obtained search warrants for country estates from Kent to the Scottish Highlands. Holkham Hall, the seat of the Earl of Leicester, was searched, as was Warwick Castle, which belonged to Lucan's cousin. Claus Von Bülow wrote to Aspinall to tell him that the police had called on him to see if he was hiding Lucan, and *Vanity Fair* magazine reported that Jimmy Goldsmith's wife, Ginette Lery, had been visited by the *gendarmerie* in Paris.

By the time the police got to Aspinall's country zoo, Howletts, in Kent, they were weary and frustrated and in no mood for sarcasm. When Aspinall asked if they wanted 'to lift all the floorboards as well', Gerring rounded on him and asked if he was proud to be best friends with a man who had tried to bash his wife to death. Aspinall replied, 'Don't come that line with me, because if she'd been my wife I'd have bashed her to death five years earlier and so would you. Who knows into what red hell one's sightly soul will stray under the pressure of a long, dripping attrition from a woman who's always out to reduce you, from whom you've had children and to whom you're stuck.' 'Sometimes,' observed one journalist, 'Aspinall in full flow sounds like a violent version of Mr Micawber.'

The visit to Howletts had been prompted by a rumour

circulating through London that Lucan had shot himself and that Aspinall had disposed of his remains by feeding them to his tigers. Aspinall naturally denied this (it was astonishing to find the police taking it seriously, anyway). His tigers ate once a week and were said to be disinclined to consume any kind of food outside the boundary of their regular digestive patterns. Besides, if Lucan had come tapping on the windows of Aspinall's zoo on Friday morning it would, said Aspinall, have been for a different purpose. 'I would have taken him aside and had a long talk and looked at the problem,' he said. 'It may have involved giving himself up or getting him funds to go to Costa Rica. He could certainly have had a lot of money. I had many people calling me saying "If Lucan wants money, he can have it".'

Another man who denied knowing what had become of him was Michael Stoop, the owner of the abandoned Corsair.

Stoop received a letter at the St James's Club on the Monday morning after the murder. The letter, which was unstamped, was from Lucan. Stoop thought the paper and envelope were part of a selection that he kept in the glove compartment of the Corsair. Because the envelope was unstamped, the doorman had had to pay the postage due. The letter read:

My Dear Michael,
I have had a traumatic night of unbelievable coincidences. However, I won't bore you with anything or involve you, except to say that if you come across my children – which I hope you will – please tell them that you knew me and that all I cared about was them.

The fact that a crooked psychiatrist and a rotten solicitor destroyed me between them will be of no importance to the children.

I gave Bill Shand Kydd an account of what actually happened, but judging by my last efforts in court no one

– let alone a 67-year-old judge – would believe, and I no longer care except that my children should be protected.

Yours Ever,
John

Stoop rang the police from the foyer of the St James's Club. What happened next was to remain fiercely disputed. According to Stoop he was told by the duty officer to drop the letter in when he was next passing. There was some dispute of this from the officer at Gerald Road. But in view of the fuss they had made over the letters to Shand Kydd – sealing them in plastic envelopes and then sending them off to the Scotland Yard forensic department – it seemed odd that Stoop should be told casually to hand it in when he was passing.

At any rate, he finally appeared at 3 a.m. on Tuesday morning, more than thirteen hours later. He had the letter but no envelope. He told the duty officer that he had thrown the envelope away. It had not occurred to him to look at the postmark.

Where had he disposed of the envelope? At the club, in the bin in the foyer.

Two officers were dispatched to check on the bins, but by then they had been emptied. The envelope, in the words of the refuse collector, was 'probably floating down the Thames'.

The inquest into Sandra Rivett's death opened in December. She had been buried on the 18th, and four days later, on Monday morning, the Coroner agreed to suspend proceedings 'to await developments'. This meant that he was still waiting for the police to make an arrest so that High Court proceedings could begin.

But Ranson and Gerring were actually no nearer to finding Lucan than they had been on the night of the murder. Their search had not been made any easier by the time that was wasted in the pursuit of Lucan look-alikes, which had become a national sport. The log-book at Gerald Road was filled with moments of priceless absurdity. Police in Sussex had stopped a bus in Hove and formally cautioned a man who looked like Lucan but who turned out to be an Iranian student. In the House of Lords a spectator caused uproar when he leapt to his feet in the public gallery and pointed an accusing finger at Lord Raglan, who was speaking on a Housing Bill. Raglan's ancestors, like Lucan's, had commanded troops through the Crimean War. 'Right battle,' he said, 'wrong man.' There were two notable arrests in Australia. The first, in Sydney, was of a boiler-maker called Kenneth Knight, who was held for entering the country illegally after disappearing from his bijou residence in Kent. When she was shown a photograph of him by the police, Mrs Knight said, 'That's not the Lord of Lucan, that's my Ken that is.' Later, just before Christmas, a second arrest was made, in Melbourne, again of a tall, middle-aged Englishman who had entered the country illegally. This suspect turned out to be as significant a catch as Lucan, however, for it was John Stonehouse, the former MP and Postmaster General, who had faked his own death by leaving his clothes on a Miami beach in order to avoid embezzlement charges. On another occasion, when police in France stopped and arrested a man in a casino, Lady Lucan, when shown a photograph of him, said, 'This is pointless. The police obviously haven't got a clue.'

The British press seemed preoccupied with the idea that Lucan had absconded to either France or Spain. These were still the two most popular resorts for British holidaymakers. They were also resorts within the range of most tabloid expense accounts. Yet the idea that – without any money, dressed in blood-stained clothes, and with no opportunity to alter his appearance – Lucan would have simply climbed on board a boat in the Newhaven Marina that Thursday night and then sailed off to a foreign country was plainly ridiculous. It was as ridiculous as the idea that his flight was premeditated and that he had planned to leave the country after killing his wife.

Meanwhile, as the police continued their search, another group of investigators, driven by a rather different motive, were also busy at work. These were Lucan's creditors. And there were a lot of them. In due course, when it became apparent that Lucan had fled an impossible financial tangle, a certified accountant, Dennis Gilson, who worked in Islington, was commissioned to look into Lucan's affairs.

Years later, I met Mr Gilson for lunch in London, in the West End, and we discussed the complex web of technical procedures that had been carried out. He was a curious individual, with a shy and engaging personality. He had given up his offices in Islington, he said, and now operated out of Wigmore Street, in the hum and buzz of the theatre world. He had a clear memory, embellished with fine detail, about his dealings with the Lucan case and the trustees. 'I was a young man then,' he said, 'about twenty-five. Bill Shand Kydd and I shared a mutual friend; that was how I got involved.'

Gilson said that a decision had been taken by Lucan's trustees, in consultation with Bill Shand Kydd, to declare him bankrupt. Shand Kydd had been embroiled in the process because of the letter Lucan had written him on that Thursday night. Lucan had asked him to take a hand in organizing the sale of family silver which was taking place at Christie's on November 27th. The sale, Lucan said, 'should satisfy bank overdrafts'. But Lucan had sealed his own fate later on in the letter, Gilson told me, by adding that the other creditors 'can get lost for the time being'.

'That line, coupled with the fact that he had disappeared, enabled [the creditors] to move a petition for bankruptcy,' Gilson said, 'which was uncontested.' The petition, Gilson added, declared that Lucan had absconded abroad with the intent 'to defeat or delay his creditors on or around the 8th of November, 1974'. Shand Kydd and the trustees had then volunteered Gilson's name at a meeting of the creditors and passed a motion appointing him to oversee the sale of Lucan's assets and the full discharging of all his debts.

Gilson's first task was to find out where money was owed. His second was to find out what could be sold in order to meet the debts. The situation was complicated, he told me, by the fact that many of the assets belonged, not directly to Lucan, but to his family trust.

The list of claims reads like a props call for *Upstairs, Downstairs*. Lucan owed money to H.W. Motors Ltd for the purchase of his Mercedes. He owed Harrods £200 for 'cigars and fine wines'. Cartier's wanted £11.80 for a crocodile-skin watch strap, and a firm of gunsmiths in Knightsbridge called Boss & Co. were owed £163 for the repairs they had carried out to two shotguns. The military tailors in Mayfair, Cooling, Lawrence & Wells, presented a bill for £227 for the storage of Lucan's coronet and ermine robes, which he wore on visits to the House of Lords for the State Opening of Parliament. The coronet had eight pearls set into its lining, and the robes were threaded with gold lace. Cooling, Lawrence & Wells announced that they would withdraw their claim and keep the belongings instead. The belongings were worth about £2,000.

In addition to these claims, there were the usual bills for gas, rent and electricity, totalling £2,257. The Inland Revenue claimed £1,890 and Ladup Ltd wanted £11,800 for five dishonoured cheques given by Lord Lucan for the purchase of chips at a gambling casino.

'To satisfy all of these quite legitimate claims,' Gilson told me, 'I consulted Coutts [the trustees of the estate] and we drew up a list of assets that we could dispose of. The bulk of the estate could be preserved. I totalled all the debts together at £58,901. Lucan had assets way beyond that.'

Gilson now began to probe into Lucan's bank accounts.

He found that he had money in accounts in Bulawayo, the Bahamas and in Switzerland. He tried to establish how much was in the Swiss account, and whether any of it had been touched since November 7th, but the Swiss government refused to open it. He then asked the Foreign Office and the Bank of England to put pressure on the Swiss government to open the account, and eventually they did. It was only the second time in history that a Swiss account had been opened without the consent of its holder. 'There was money there,' Gilson said, 'but it hadn't been touched since his disappearance.'

Gilson also acquired permission from the trustees to sell Lucan's house in Lower Belgrave Street. He told Lady Lucan that she could have the pick of the furniture to keep, and he would sell only the items that she put aside for sale. Subsequently, the sale of silver went ahead at Christie's. Heirlooms belonging to the family, including the horse-whip used by the Third Earl during the Charge of the Light Brigade, were also sold. The belongings were auctioned under the heading: 'Property of a Nobleman', and many of them were purchased by Lucan's friends, leading to speculation that they were being preserved for Lucan's heir, George.

By the time Gilson had completed his work, the estate had been depleted by £118,000. This was double the original total of debt, but included all the fees, legal costs and interest. Every creditor, Gilson said, had been paid back in full.

Then he told me, 'The curious part about it is that it need never have happened. He would never have had to face bankruptcy if he had stayed, if the murder hadn't happened. His assets were more than enough to clear the debts he'd accumulated when he vanished. The bankruptcy only happened because he disappeared and there was no other option but to declare him bankrupt.'

The Lucan case, in later years, was to become celebrated for all its ironies. Veronica Lucan, desperate for security and 'a normal family life', had married the one man incapable of giving it to her. As a young girl in 'grinding poverty' she had craved the financial rewards of 'a good marriage', but as the Countess of Lucan she had ended up with nothing. Lucan wanted his children more than anything, but he succeeded in engineering things so that he could never see them again. As head of the clan, he acted to prevent the disgrace of bankruptcy, yet he managed to cover the Lucan name with the disgrace of murder. And, of course, there was the ultimate irony: that a blow aimed for the skull of Lady Lucan had crashed down upon the head of Sandra Rivett.

Now, here, too, was another: Gilson had said that Lucan need not have gone bankrupt. He had all the assets to avoid it. Presumably, besieged by creditors, he had been too money-blind to see this. And so the very circumstances that had driven him to act, the actual compulsion to dictate events, was revealed as an illusion. The pressure had sprung from the terrors of a situation that simply did not, and would not, exist.

Chapter Nine

THE INQUEST

And so it was decided, still with Lord Lucan missing, that the inquest could be delayed no longer.

On the morning of Monday, June 16th, 1975, more than seven months after the murder of Sandra Rivett, Dr Gavin Thurston arrived at Westminster Coroner's Court, in Horseferry Road, to begin the proceedings. Dr Thurston, a year from retirement, was Deputy Coroner to the royal family, and had gained some notability, at least in media circles, for presiding over several notorious deaths. He had conducted the inquest into the death of the actress Judy Garland, and into the suicide of Brian Epstein, the manager of the Beatles. He was noted as a cautious, reflective man, and had undoubtedly had a successful career. But he had also been criticized on one occasion for allowing evidence to go unheard. His inquiry into the apparent suicide of the boxer Freddy Mills was later to be challenged on the grounds that a considerable degree of evidence relating to Mills's Mafia connections had been ignored, and that the possibility of murder had been excluded too quickly from the proceedings.

The accusation of suppressing evidence was to be repeated again at the Rivett inquest, with startling results.

The opening moments of the inquest provided a striking and unforgettable spectacle. In the austere, wood-panelled courtroom, with the June sunshine pouring in through the huge glass dome in the ceiling, the central figures of the Lucan set squeezed in beside one another, wearing their morning suits and garden-party dresses. The public seats and the press benches were three rows deep as the world's media pushed into the court to record the battle ahead. A sense of drama, of history unfolding, was everywhere. Even in the street outside the police were having to restrain the crowds. Buses and cabs slowed down to allow their passengers to get a glimpse of the court. A lone woman from the battered wives society paced up and down, carrying a placard and shaking a can of money. The placard said: 'It affects us all, rich and poor.'

But it was the prospect of an Edwardian élite being stung at last by a British court that aroused the greatest sense of anticipation. In the weeks and months following the murder, the prurience and extravagance of the Lucan set had been minutely scrutinized by the press. So had their closing of ranks in the face of the police inquiries. Their callous ambivalence to the tragic and brutal end of a young woman, apparently slain 'by accident' in a bitter feud between two members of an upper-class family, had shocked everyone. And their hedonism, so devastatingly inappropriate at a time of national austerity and self-sacrifice, had assumed almost mythical status. Now it was all going to be accounted for; now the reckoning had come. Holidays in Portofino; chartered planes; private yachts; gambling casinos; wild and debauched parties; all the features of a champagne oligarchy were to be exposed against the background of a murder trial. If journalists and commentators were prone to descending into gratuitous contempt, or even sanctimony, there was nonetheless a feeling that such judgments had been invited, and that even the most impartial onlooker would find the details left a nasty residual taste in the mouth.

Peter Birkett, writing in the *Daily Mail*, thought that the style and demeanour of the Lucan set added 'an indecent splash of colour to a depressing chronicle of tragedy'. Clearly, he went on, they regarded the inquest as an occasion for a public display of solidarity:

> The leading personality of their set is wanted on a murder charge. Therefore, it is particularly important that they put on the right show; that they dress correctly; that they behave with proud confidence; that every move they make should reflect their loyalty to the missing man and the importance for them of Lord Lucan's sense of honour. So it comes down to a question of style. And if their style is not to the taste of the rest that is a matter of indifference. Proud, unbending and exclusive, they do not seem worried by what the world thinks of them.

Another central preoccupation of the media was the exaggerated ostracism of Lady Lucan. 'She is,' said a reporter, 'a woman deeply alone.' Each morning she would arrive in court in a police car with her personal bodyguard, Sergeant Forsyth. Forsyth had struck up a good relationship with her, based on a natural sympathy for her treatment by the gambling community and the way she had resisted their efforts to crush her. She would sit in court day after day, wearing the same black coat, sporting a small white turban to cover her head scars. One witness said, 'She sits staring ahead. She is emotionless, her eyes drawn through lack of sleep, sometimes yawning, sometimes looking around her defiantly, outstaring those prepared to play the dangerous game of trying to catch her eye.' Everyone had noticed the hostility between Lady Lucan and her husband's family, and the press made much of the fact that she was ignored 'by her relations, her in-laws, even her former friends'. The Dowager Countess and her daughter, Lady Sarah Gibbs, sat with Lady Sarah's husband, the Reverend William Gibbs, directly in front of Lady Lucan. Susan Maxwell-Scott, with whom Veronica had once holidayed, played tennis, swum, golfed and dined, remained at the back with her husband, Ian. On the front row, Christina Shand Kydd sat impassively with William. Throughout the proceedings, though they were only feet apart, neither of the two sisters exchanged a word or greeting.

But Lucan's family would also ignore all of Sandra Rivett's relatives, and for this they were severely criticized. The public expected the Lucans to observe certain courtesies, even under the trying circumstances of a legal inquiry. They were to be disappointed. Not a single member of the clan acknowledged the presence of the Rivetts. It was as if anyone who reminded them of why they were actually in court deserved to be treated as though they were invisible.

It was, of course, all part of the essential maintenance of morale and form. The inquest, with all its aim of inquiry and exposure, its propensity for revelation and punishment, was about to begin. And for the Lucan set, nothing would ever be the same again.

Dr Gavin Thurston opened with a long speech to the jury. He set out the reasons why the inquest was 'so unusual' and defined their duties and obligations. There had been immense pre-publicity, he said, and the scandal had become a burning topic of controversy right across the country. The jurors may already have formed opinions and prejudices about the characters involved from reading the newspapers or watching television reports. In this case, he said, they must put them to one side. Their job as the jury presiding over an inquest was to address only the facts. Whatever verdict they reached, it must be based solely on the evidence that they heard in the courtroom.

Dr Thurston then touched on a problem that had been preoccupying legal minds ever since Lucan's disappearance. He said that the responsibility of a jury in an inquest was different from that of a High Court jury in that they had to determine who had actually died, when they had died, and, if possible, how. But in certain rare cases they also had the right to name a person whom they considered responsible for murder – if murder was suspected. This was a privilege peculiar to English courts and had been recommended for abolition by the Broderick Committee in 1971. The problem was that a jury in an inquest might name someone as guilty of murder before his High Court trial, and obviously such a verdict would then prejudice that later proceeding. If, for instance, a jury at an inquest decided that Lord Lucan had murdered Sandra Rivett, and named him in their verdict, they would patently be affecting his chances of a fair trial in a High Court.

Dr Thurston said that he had therefore 'deliberately delayed this inquiry' in the hope that 'Lord Lucan would show up'. That would have rendered an inquest unnecessary. Under those circumstances, he said, Lucan would have been charged and tried; if he were found guilty, then the Coroner's Court could freely conclude that he had murdered Mrs Rivett; if he were acquitted, then the Coroner's Court would simply record that Sandra had been killed by 'A Person' and the police would have gone on looking for that 'Person'.

Ultimately, said the Coroner, it was for the jury to decide. Lord Lucan had been given every opportunity to come forward. He had not done so. He had therefore left others to make conclusions in his absence. The wheels of the law continued to turn, no matter what. If the jury decided on the evidence in front of them that they *could* name someone whom they thought responsible for the death of Sandra Rivett, then they had the right to do so. 'You have got to decide on the evidence whether you *can* name that person,' he concluded.

119

And there was a second problem. In law, no wife can give evidence against her husband. That is a privilege of marriage. She cannot give evidence against him *except* when he is charged with an assault against her. The Coroner had therefore 'agonized' over whether to allow Lady Lucan to take the stand. She had been assaulted, and she claimed to have been assaulted by her husband. But this was not a trial. This was an inquest, and Lucan was not officially in the dock. Therefore, by strict regulation, the Coroner should not have allowed Veronica to give evidence. But he did. He had decided that she could testify against her husband so long as she did not mention what she had already alleged him to have done to Mrs Rivett. (She couldn't, for instance, tell the jury, as she had told the police, about how Lucan had put his head on her shoulder after the fight on the stairs and confessed that the nanny was dead. She could, however, tell them how he had bashed her about the head with a length of lead piping.) Since the whole object of her testimony was to draw inference from evidence – inference that Lucan had killed Sandra Rivett because he had tried, in the manner that the nanny was killed, then to kill his wife – she shouldn't legally have been allowed to take the stand. But she was. She entered the witness box and gave evidence for nearly two hours.

The first witness was Roger Rivett, Sandra's estranged husband. He was a security guard at Gatwick Airport and had been separated from Sandra for about eight months. He had last seen Sandra alive in April. She had the use of their flat in Valley Road, Kenley, but he had no idea whether she had continued to live there. He had heard some time in October that his wife had got a job as a nanny to the children of an aristocrat. In answer to the Coroner he confirmed that his wife was 'rather a small lady'.

'How small exactly?'

'Five feet, two inches.'

The next witness was PC Patrick Sullivan, an officer who

had been on guard at number 46 after the murder. He explained the plan of the house to the jury and gave them evidential details which would become relevant later: it was not possible for someone who was in the bathroom which adjoined Lady Lucan's bedroom actually to see her bed from the sink; the door into the basement was hooked open; it was possible to see *part* of the basement from the street 'but only if there was a light on in the basement kitchen'.

'I understand the lightbulb was missing from the ceiling in the kitchen?'

'Yes,' replied PC Sullivan. 'It was found lying on a chair in the basement breakfast room.'

Then, at a quarter past eleven, Lady Lucan was called to the stand.

One reporter recalled later how 'painfully thin' she looked: 'almost emaciated'. There was such an air of frailty to her movements that the Coroner asked for a chair to be brought to the witness box. When Veronica then sat down to take the oath and give her evidence, she seemed to disappear into the box, so that only her head and shoulders were visible.

She started by telling the court about her relationship with her husband. They had met in 1963. He was a professional gambler. They had married eight months after first being introduced. Lady Lucan did not work. They had separated in 1973 after a row. There had been a court case over the custody of their three children, the youngest of whom was now four years old. Lady Lucan had won the case and this had devastated her husband, who was an anxious father. He had never really got over the case. Lady Lucan didn't see much of her husband after their separation. When he came for access weekends it was usually the resident nanny who dealt with him. She had last spoken to him on July 18th, 1974, when she had telephoned him to tell him that Camilla had chicken pox. She had seen him through the drawing-room window of number 46 on or around October 23rd. He

121

was sitting in his Mercedes, smoking, wearing dark glasses.

'Did your husband know Sandra Rivett?' asked Dr Thurston.

'He met her when he collected the children.'

'That was all?'

'As far as I am aware.'

'Did he have any connections with Newhaven, do you know?'

'None that I know of.'

'Do you know much about his financial situation?'

Veronica hesitated. 'I've read a bit about it. I read an article in the *Daily Express* which suggested that he had financial difficulties. But I don't know from my personal experience.'

'How many nannies have you had in the last six months?'

'Including temporaries?'

'Yes.'

'Seven.'

'And when did Sandra come?'

'Early in September.'

'Did you get on well with her?'

'Yes I did. She was very cheerful and she had an even temperament.'

'Did she have any men friends?'

'She talked of two.'

'You knew that she was separated from her husband?'

'Yes.'

'Had any man come to your house?'

'No.'

'Had she asked for any to come?'

'No.'

'What was her usual day off?'

'Thursday.'

The Coroner asked if Veronica knew anything about Sandra's 'stature'. She replied that she and Sandra were the same height, although Sandra 'was a little plumper'.

Turning to the night of the murder, Dr Thurston asked why Sandra had changed her day off.

'Her current boyfriend had his day off on Wednesday,' Veronica said. 'So she asked me if she could change hers to Wednesday as well so that she could go out with him.' Later, in cross-examination, she agreed that it was the first time that she had stayed in on a Thursday night. And she agreed that it would be unusual to find Sandra making tea in the basement on a Thursday night. 'But it would not be unusual for me to be there,' she added.

'What time did she look into the bedroom?'

'At about five to nine.'

'And what did she say?'

'She put her head round the door and said: "Would you like a cup of tea?" '

'Did she take some crockery down with her?'

'I don't know.'

'And then you went on watching the news?'

'Yes.'

'And what time did you start wondering about the tea?'

'At about a quarter past nine.'

'What did you do?'

'I decided to go downstairs and find out what had happened. I got as far as the ground floor. I looked round the stairs leading down to the basement and there was no light on. I saw that it was dark and that she couldn't possibly be down there.'

'Did you call out?'

'I called out her name.'

'And then what happened?'

'I heard a noise.'

'What sort of noise?'

'Just a noise. The noise of someone or something in the downstairs cloakroom.'

'What happened then?'

Veronica closed her eyes. 'I moved towards the sound.'

123

'And?'

'And someone rushed out and hit me.'

'Did this happen in the area at the top of the basement stairs?'

'Yes.'

'Was there more than one blow?'

'About four.'

'Did you hear anybody speak?'

'When I was hit on the head? No. Later I did. I screamed.'

'And then what happened?'

'The person said: "Shut up!"'

'Did you recognize the voice?'

'Yes.'

'Who was it?'

Veronica looked up at him. It was the first time she had done so when answering questions about the murder.

She said slowly, 'It was my husband.'

The Coroner: 'What did he do?'

'He thrust three gloved fingers down my throat and we started to fight.'

'And what happened during the fight?'

Again Veronica closed her eyes. 'It's difficult to remember,' she said. 'It *was* seven months ago.' Her hand went up to her forehead, to the parting in her hair, and she lightly fingered the scar. 'But during the course of it he attempted to strangle me from the front and to gouge out my eye. We fell into the basement doorway and on to the stairs.' Eventually, she said, Lord Lucan had had her on the ground, throttling her, when she got sideways between his legs and he desisted. He desisted, she said, because she had grabbed his testicles.

When the struggle had ended they had had a conversation on the stairs (which she was not allowed to repeat) and she agreed to go upstairs to inspect her wounds.

Exactly what had been said during that conversation was to remain a mystery. Whatever Veronica had said to persuade her husband to give her time, actually to help her upstairs and provide succour, rather than make another attempt on her life, was to be kept from the jury and the public.

What they did hear was that, once in the bedroom, Veronica told her husband that she 'didn't feel very well' and he went into the bathroom for a cloth 'to clean up my face'.

'Did he say anything about helping you further?'

'Very vaguely.'

'What did you do when he went into the bathroom?'

'I heard the taps running and I jumped to my feet and ran down the stairs.'

'Where did you go?'

'I ran out of the front door and about thirty yards down the street to the Plumbers Arms. From there I was taken to St George's Hospital.'

'Have you seen your husband since then?'

Veronica shook her head. 'No, I haven't.'

Dr Thurston looked down at her from his raised dais. To the rest of the court her head was barely visible over the lip of the witness box.

'You have no doubt that it was your husband?' he asked.

Again she shook her head. 'No doubt at all.'

Because the nature of an inquest is supposedly defined by its title, and because it is not generally regarded as a trial, there are no formal defence or prosecution counsels. Those involved may, of course, choose to be legally represented in the court by a qualified advocate, but there is no question of adversarial tactics. Because it is not a trial, no witness may be discredited or subjected to the sort of aggressive or provocative questioning in cross-examination that is the privilege of an advocate in the disputed proceedings of a High Court.

So, when Michael Eastham, appearing for Lord Lucan, whose services had been hired by the Dowager Countess, stood up to cross-examine Lady Lucan, the implication of his first question stalled the whole proceedings.

'Even before the separation,' he began, 'you entertained feelings of hatred towards your husband, didn't you?'

Immediately, the Coroner intervened and disallowed the question. 'Hatred', he said, 'is a very strong way of putting it.'

There were four lawyers in court during the Rivett inquest, each one representing a different camp. David Webster appeared for the Rivett family. His main concern was to ensure that the proceedings did not degenerate into a public brawl between the two opposing sides of the Lucan family. The police were represented by Brian Watling, who had been told that all efforts to trace Lord Lucan had failed, and that, in order to clarify the legal situation before the police closed their file, an official verdict which named him as Mrs Rivett's killer would be desirable. Lady Lucan was represented by Mr Brian Coles; and her husband by Mr Eastham. Mr Eastham said that he was there to 'prevent the jury from reaching a verdict which might bring a stigma to Lord Lucan's name'. But his task was a forlorn one, because witnesses may not be discredited during an inquest, and without discrediting Veronica he could not hope to convince the jury of Lord Lucan's innocence.

'The question is whether [Lady Lucan's testimony] is an honest recollection of what happened,' he said, 'or a fabrication.'

When the Coroner had intervened, Mr Eastham went on:

'You know that Lord Lucan has written certain letters and that in those letters he is saying quite clearly that he was *not* the attacker, and that Lady Lucan is deliberately making it *look* as if he was the attacker. Therefore, the relationship between them – whether or not Lady Lucan has feelings of hatred for her husband – must be relevant to the question of her testimony.'

He added, 'I don't enjoy my task but I would not be doing my duty in accordance with my instructions if I did not pursue this line.'

The Coroner appeared to hesitate. 'It's very difficult,' he said. He was naturally obliged to adhere to the rule which dictated that no witness be challenged or attacked. But since he had let Lady Lucan make her allegations he was also under a moral obligation to give Mr Eastham an opportunity to refute them. Dr Thurston dismissed the jury to develop the argument in private. For Lady Lucan, Mr Coles said that there were clearly laid down criteria under which witnesses could be cross-examined in an inquest. He did not need to remind Dr Thurston of the nature of those criteria. It would be a plain and intolerable infringement of Lady Lucan's rights if she were subjected to verbal attack or innuendo in the witness box. The police naturally agreed. So did the Rivett family. But Mr Eastham persisted.

The case was an exception, he claimed. The Coroner had said so himself. He had allowed Lady Lucan to testify. There had subsequently to be a right of reply by the Earl's family.

What of the scientific evidence, asked Dr Thurston. Couldn't the Lucans adequately harness that material for a defence?

Mr Eastham said that 'none of the scientific evidence will show this lady's feelings for her husband'. Lord Lucan could be vigorously defended only by establishing the nature of Lady Lucan's 'hatred' for him. There was the question of Lady Lucan's mental health. There was the issue of her plausibility as a witness. The phrase 'dream of paranoia' in Lord Lucan's letter, which might be seen as forming the crux of the whole saga, would be 'totally inexplicable to the jury' unless Mr Eastham could tackle Lady Lucan about it and call witnesses to embellish upon it.

Finally, after a further twenty minutes of discussion, the Coroner came down on the side of Lady Lucan. The rules of the inquest must be observed. Lord Lucan's family could challenge or attack Lady Lucan as aggressively as they wished in the appropriate setting of a High Court. But this

127

was not a High Court and her integrity as a witness had to be upheld. For a defence, said the Coroner, Mr Eastham would have to look to the field of forensic evidence.

When the jury filtered back in, half an hour later, the Coroner asked Mr Eastham if he wished to go on questioning Lady Lucan in the light of his ruling.

'In the light of your ruling,' said Mr Eastham, 'I don't think I can assist the jury at all and I have no further questions for the lady.'

Veronica was released from the witness box.

The first day of the hearing closed with a succession of minor witnesses. The statement which Frances Bingham had given to the police after the murder was read out in court. Sergeant Baker, the first policeman on the scene of the crime, described finding Sandra's body and the light-bulb on the cushioned chair near the window in the basement. Mr Whitehouse from the Plumbers Arms described Veronica's hysterical entry. And Dr Hugh Scott, the Chief Casualty Officer at St George's, told the court that he had given Lady Lucan about sixty stitches that night, mostly to her face and scalp. He had noticed evidence of an attempt at strangulation, and her neck had also been badly wrenched. Lacerations at the back of her throat could have been caused 'by fingers being thrust forcefully into the mouth'.

On the second day, the police and forensic witnesses dominated proceedings. First, Graham Forsyth told of arriving at Lower Belgrave Street and being confronted by the Dowager Countess. He said that the Dowager had told him that her son had been driving past the house when he had seen a fight going on in the basement. Mr Forsyth agreed that it would be impossible for anyone to see into the basement if they were driving past, especially if the blinds were drawn over the window.

He then read from Lucan's second letter to Shand Kydd, which was headed 'FINANCIAL MATTERS':

Dear Bill,
    There is a sale coming up at Christie's which should satisfy the bank overdrafts. Please agree reserve prices herein with Tom Craig (accountant).

There followed a list of the family heirlooms, ready for auction, and Lucan's estimate of how much each one would fetch.

Proceeds from the sale are to go to Lloyds, 6 Pall Mall; Coutts, The Strand; and Nat West, Bloomsbury Branch, who also hold an equity and law life policy.
    The other creditors can get lost for the time being.

Yours Ever,
LUCKY

After lunch Professor Keith Simpson, the pathologist, outlined the injuries to Mrs Rivett which he had found during his postmortem. Her body was doubled up inside the bag, he said, and although her clothing had not been disturbed and there was no sign of any sexual attack, the bag had been heavily soiled with blood. Death had taken place before she was placed in the bag. There were three major injuries to the face, mainly over the eyebrows; two on the neck and four on the scalp. There was heavy bruising from some 'near misses' on her shoulders, presumably where she had moved as she lay on the ground, trying to dodge the repeated strikes of the bludgeon. She had evidently raised her hand to try to grab the weapon as it came down, because there was some bruising on her hands, too.
    After she had been beaten to death the killer had grabbed hold of her arms and bent her double. There was bruising on

her arms where he had grabbed them. There were also some minor injuries to her face, which Professor Simpson thought to be consistent with a fist or hand slap.

Altogether, the injuries were sufficient to cause deep bruising to the brain, and had caused her to inhale a large quantity of blood through her nose. 'An unconscious person cannot clear the airways by coughing,' he said. When he was shown a photograph of the lead piping, which was twisted and bent, Professor Simpson agreed that it was highly likely to have caused the injuries to both Lady Lucan and Sandra Rivett.

The lead piping had also been examined by Dr Robert Davies, of the Metropolitan Police Laboratory. Dr Davies told the court that the piping weighed about two and a half pounds and was 'grossly distorted'. It had been tested at the atomic laboratory for fingerprints and several fingerprints had been found. However, they had been distorted by the stretching of the surgical tape around the piping and were, as a consequence, unrecognizable.

Dr Davies was asked about the second piece of piping, found in the boot of the Corsair. Were there any differences between the two? Yes, Dr Davies said, there were differences in the type of elastoplast used to bandage them; there were differences in the length (the piece in the car was just over sixteen inches long, almost double that of the other piece, and weighed about four pounds); and one piece was more corroded than the other. The corrosion itself suggested that they had both been water pipes at one time. But Dr Davies could not say whether they had ever been joined together as part of a single pipe. 'The highest I could say is that they *may* have been cut from the same length. But it is highly unlikely that the bit found at number 46 was ever joined on to the bit found in the car.'

Although Dr Davies had been unable to produce any useful prints from the piping, other fingerprints *had* been found at the scene of the crime. Mr Ian Lucas, a senior fingerprint officer at Scotland Yard, had produced sixty-two marks, of which forty-eight had been eliminated, four had been partly eliminated, and twelve were still outstanding. It was not unusual for prints to remain outstanding, Mr Lucas said. 'I've been in this work for over nineteen years. In my experience, even when persons are charged and convicted, there are still outstanding prints.' Although no positive prints for Lord Lucan were obtainable – Mr Lucas said he would need a control sample first – several prints found in the Corsair matched those taken from the flat in Elizabeth Street. Mr Lucas added that all the prints found in the basement at number 46 had come from police officers, children or from Mrs Rivett.

'So whoever attacked Mrs Rivett left no fingerprints?' asked the Coroner.

'No, sir. I didn't find any.'

On Wednesday, the third day, it was the turn of Mr Eastham. A succession of witnesses now came forward to give evidence on Lucan's behalf: to present the alternative view. In their anxiety to vindicate the missing Earl they occasionally crossed the line of the Coroner's ruling about what was admissible evidence. But the Coroner, sticking stringently to his earlier decision, refused even momentarily to indulge them in their mischief. Answers were struck from the record. Counsel were warned off lines of inquiry. It was classic partiality of the most heavy-handed kind.

The first witness was the Dowager Countess. Dry, bohemian, she had spent seventy-four years fashioning her eccentricity. In the witness box she displayed a combination of formidable intellect and homely, lady-of-the-manor charm.

She told the court that her son was a 'devoted' father, and took a great interest in the welfare of his children.

'Was it a disappointment to him that he did not have custody of them?' asked the Coroner.

'Yes,' she replied.

131

His feelings towards his children were 'strong and passionate', she said, 'almost like an obsession', and it was a source of great anxiety to him that they were not in his care. In reply to a question about her son's financial situation, the Dowager remarked that she did not know anything about his debts but that she had lent him £4,000 during the custody case. He was generally quite secretive about his financial affairs.

'When did you last see your son,' asked the Coroner, 'before this incident?'

'I am not prepared to say for certainty,' the Dowager replied. 'But I think probably the best I can say is that it was on the Sunday before the seventh of November.'

'And how did he seem?'

'He was in a state of great anxiety about the children as in the past, but not noticeably or more obsessionally so than was to be expected.'

'Were the children with him?'

'No. I almost invariably saw him in the evenings.' That Sunday night, she said, they had dined together and he had asked her to lend him a book she was reading called *The Intelligent Woman's Guide to Socialism*.

Turning to the night of November 7th, she told the court that she had spent the evening in a meeting at the local Labour Party, where she was an active member. When she got home the telephone was ringing. 'It surprised me by its lateness,' she said. 'It was between 10 p.m. and 10.30 p.m. I don't pretend to exactitude.'

'What did your son say in this phone call?' asked Dr Thurston.

'He said it was John speaking and he said: "There has been a terrible catastrophe at number 46. Veronica is hurt and I want you to collect the children. Ring Bill Shand Kydd and he will help." He also said: "The nanny is hurt." I asked: "Badly?" and he said: "Yes, I think so." That was about the whole conversation.'

The Dowager said that it was 'hardly a conversation I

would forget'. And yet already certain details had slipped her mind. Later, for instance, she would remember that Lucan had also said, 'Oh, Mother, there was something dreadful in the corner. I couldn't bring myself to look.'

Dr Thurston then asked, 'What did you do [after receiving the call]?'

'I first attempted to ring Mr Shand Kydd. I was told that he was not available. This was a mistake, although I didn't speak to him. I went to 46 Lower Belgrave Street. I returned to the flat and there was a second phone call. It was well after midnight. I had the impression that it came from a private house. There were no pips.'

The Dowager paused and then said, 'I must add that in the *first* telephone call he said: "I interrupted a fight in the basement".'

'He used those words?' asked the Coroner.

'Yes.'

'As regards the second phone call, what did he say?'

'He said: "Have you got the children?" I said, "Yes, they're here in bed, and to the best of my knowledge and belief they're asleep." He said: "That's all right, then." I said: "What do you intend to do?" I got nowhere. I also said: "The police are here. Do you want to speak to them?" He hesitated and then said: "No, I don't think I'll speak to them now. Tell them I'll phone them in the morning, and I'll phone you, too." Then he rang off.'

He had sounded 'more on all fours' in the second call, she said. In the first one he had sounded 'in a state of immense shock. As if he'd been knocked for six.'

The Coroner turned back to the question of how Lucan had come to see the fight in the basement. It was a central issue, he said. 'He told me he was passing,' the Dowager said. 'This didn't indicate whether he paused and peered in or whether it was so obvious on passing. I know he frequently *did* go past the house and look at it. It was very near his own flat.'

The Coroner seemed satisfied with that. But Mr Brian Watling, for the police, was not. When it was time for his cross-examination, he first of all asked the Dowager if she wanted to sit down, an ominous sign for any witness. She smiled and said she did not. 'I'm quite all right standing, thank you,' she replied. Then Mr Watling plunged straight in. Did the Dowager Countess of Lucan know that anyone who gave a false statement to the police was liable to be prosecuted? Kaitilin looked a little perplexed at that but said that she was aware of it. Mr Watling said that he wished to question her over the discrepancies between her original police statement and her statement to the court. There were some fundamental differences. In her police statement, for instance, she had placed the time of her son's first phone call at 10.45 p.m. Now she was saying it was between 10 p.m. and 10.30 p.m. The implication was that Lucan would have had less time to dream up a story about an attacker the earlier he rang his mother, giving, supposedly, an air of authenticity to his invention.

'I'm sure the statement must be correct,' the Dowager said, 'because that is what I said *at* the time. But I'm still under the impression that the hour mentioned was unduly late.'

She had earlier told the Coroner that the account which Sergeant Forsyth had given to the court of their initial conversation together at Lower Belgrave Street 'was substantially correct'. With regard to the call from her son, 'this was hardly a conversation I would forget'.

'Did you also say in your statement,' continued Mr Watling, 'that you "had the impression there was a third person present at number 46 during the attack" but that you "couldn't be exact about this"?'

'Yes, that's right . . .'

'Yet you've just told the court that your son "interrupted a fight between Veronica and another man".'

'Yes. And when I was asked by the police to repeat the

Lady Lucan leaves court after the inquest on Sandra Rivett, in June 1975 (*Syndication International*)

The policemen who led the hunt for Lord Lucan, Detective Chief Inspector David Gerring (*left*) and Chief Superintendent Roy Ranson at Canon Row Police Station (*Syndication International*)

Lord Lucan at the helm of his boat *White Migrant* at the start of the 1964 offshore powerboat race at Cowes (*Topham*)

Frogmen search the sea at Newhaven for the body of the missing earl (*Syndication International*)

Police with tracker dogs on the clifftop above Newhaven hunting Lord Lucan (*Syndication International*)

The auto-gyro which was used to search the Sussex Downs with infra-red cameras for signs of Lucan's body (*Press Association*)

Roger Rivett in sombre mood attends the inquest on his estranged wife, Sandra (*Press Association/Topham*)

Lord Lucan's mother, the Dowager Countess of Lucan, and his close friend Bill Shand Kydd after giving evidence at the inquest (*Syndication International*)

conversation in which he said he had interrupted a fight I quite unaccountably failed to mention this.'

Mr Watling continued: 'You see, you didn't say *anything* in your statement about your son interrupting a fight. You're just saying that *now*. At the *time* you merely said that you had "the impression that someone else was present".'

The Dowager was silent for a minute. 'Look,' she said, 'the words "I interrupted a fight" were *his* words and I imagine that when I made my statement the impression that there was a third person present was an obvious deduction from the statement that he had interrupted a fight.'

'Yes,' said Mr Watling (by now the Coroner was starting to look impatient), 'but why didn't you tell the police that he had interrupted a fight so that it could go in your statement – no deductions, just plain statement?'

'It *is* a plain statement,' said the Dowager, 'and *this* is a plain statement. The upshot of the two is the same.'

'*That* is a matter for the jury to decide,' said Mr Watling. 'The point is that you didn't use in your statement the words which you now tell the jury your son used.' He hesitated, as if checking that it all made sense. Then he waved his hand dismissively and sat down. 'I need go no further,' he said, 'the jury have seen this woman for themselves.'

At noon, as the June sunshine began pouring in thick columns through the glass dome in the roof, Susan Maxwell-Scott slipped off her black velvet jacket and produced a pink silk handkerchief to mop her forehead.

'He was always a close friend of my husband's,' she said. 'I first met him just before my marriage, about seventeen years ago. I got to know him well when we moved down to the country and he and Lady Lucan used to come down and stay with us.' Under cross-examination she said that she had 'always found him a very charming man. Kind and mild-mannered. He was devoted to his children, to a far greater extent than most men.'

135

Turning to the night of the murder, she went on, 'He called at about eleven thirty. I was in bed. My husband Ian was in London. He had previously told John that he was going to be in Uckfield on Thursday but, in the event, he had been unable to get home. I went to the window and looked down. Lord Lucan was standing below. I then let him into the house.'

'And how was he dressed?' asked the Coroner.

'Casually. He was wearing a light blue shirt, grey trousers and a brown pullover. The pullover was sleeveless.'

'Was there an overcoat?'

'No.'

'Were there any markings on his clothes?'

'I did notice a damp patch on the right thigh of his trousers.' Then she added, 'I forgot to mention that when he arrived he first of all asked for Ian. He said, "Hello Susie, is Ian around?" And I said no, Ian was in London. Then when we were sitting down he told me what had happened that night.'

Mrs Maxwell-Scott, who was a trained lawyer and the daughter of a QC, was determined not to get caught in the same trap as the last witness. 'I will do my best to repeat what he told me,' she said, 'but you have to remember that it was seven months ago.' That remark was for Mr Watling. 'Unlike police officers,' she said, going a stage further, 'I don't have notes and must rely on my memory.'

She then cleared her throat and looked directly across at the Coroner. She stood for nearly two hours in the witness box, her hands slightly in front of her, her fingertips resting on the lip of the stand. She spoke slowly and coolly and with an assured confidence. At one point she broke off her speech to search through the spectators for the face of her husband. Having found it, she said, 'That's right, isn't it, darling?' At which Ian gave an embarrassed nod and played with his straw hat.

'John said he had been through a most nightmarish

experience. He sat down and I gave him a good measure of scotch. He said that it was so incredible he didn't think anyone would believe him. He said he had been walking past Lady Lucan's house on his way home to change for dinner –'

'Now the word "walking" is very important,' interrupted the Coroner.

'Yes I know that. I am almost certain he used the word "walking" but he could have said "passing" and I assumed he was walking. I don't know what my police statement said but that is more likely to be correct.'

'The statement says "walking",' Dr Thurston said.

'Ah, well that would be correct then.' She went on: 'Through the venetian blinds he saw a man attacking his wife. He started by saying that this was "an unbelievable coincidence" and I told him I didn't think so because he was in the habit of going past the house to check on the children. He said: "Well, yes, I quite often go in to see if the children are all right." He said he let himself in through the front door – he had a key – and went down to the basement. As he entered the basement, as he got to the bottom of the stairs, he slipped in a pool of blood. He wasn't telling this like a story, you understand, it came out in bits and pieces, and this is my best attempt to tell it to you.

'The man he had seen attacking his wife ran off. Whether it was on seeing Lucan or on hearing him I'm not clear. But he ran off. And Lucan, perhaps unfortunately, rather than chasing the man, went straight to his wife.'

'Did he say which way the man ran off?'

'No, he just said the man "made off".'

'He went to his wife?'

'He went to his wife . . . who was covered in blood and hysterical. She cried out that someone had killed the nanny and then she accused him of having hired the man to kill her. This was something she frequently accused him of – a contract to kill – Lucan himself claimed she got the idea from an American TV movie. He said the scene in the basement was ghastly. He certainly saw the sack with Mrs Rivett's body in it. I think Lady Lucan indicated it to him. He described the basement as being horrific because of the blood. He assumed that the body was in the sack but he did not go over and examine it. I think he felt rather squeamish with all the blood and didn't want to look too closely.'

'Did he tell you what he did next?'

'Yes. He calmed his wife down – she was hysterical, as I said – and then took her upstairs to her room, where Lady Frances was watching television. Lady Frances was sent to bed. Lucan persuaded his wife to lie down. His intention was to get some wet towels to mop up the blood and see how severe her injuries were. Then he was going to telephone for a doctor and for the police. But while he was in the bathroom Lady Lucan left the house. He told me he heard the front door slam and Lady Lucan out in the street screaming: "Murder! Murder!"'

'Did he tell you what his state of mind was when he realized he was alone with a body and a lot of blood?'

'My words are that he obviously panicked. He put it another way. He said he felt there he was with all that blood, with the body, a murderer who had got away and with a wife who would almost certainly try to implicate him. He said he was sure she would try to implicate him. After all she had already accused him of hiring this man. He told me he reckoned no one would believe his story. I did my best to convince him that people *would* believe him. It was quite incredible that he should have had anything to do with it.'

Cross-examined by Mr Eastham, Mrs Maxwell-Scott agreed that she had raised the question of the killer's motives. 'We were discussing this probable killing and it seemed to me that it would be someone wanting to kill the nanny. But Lord Lucan said it wouldn't be anyone wanting to kill her. He said she was "a good kid" or a "good girl". He told me he'd spoken to the official solicitor and said the children had got a nice girl for a nanny, at last. He was very pleased with her.'

The Coroner asked about the phone calls Lucan had made from Uckfield.

'He looked at his watch and said something about the time. I think it was then about 12.15 a.m. He said: "Can I phone my mother?" He used the telephone in the drawing room. He spoke to her in my presence. I asked if he wanted me to leave the room but he said no. I heard him say something like, "Mother, it's John," and then he asked about the children. I gathered the answer must have been satisfactory because he said something like "Oh good," or "I'm glad." He then asked: "Has Veronica turned up?" I gathered that the reply was that she had been found and taken to hospital. He said: "I will phone you in the morning." Then he rang off. Next he dialled William Shand Kydd's number but there was no reply. After that he asked if he could borrow some note paper.'

Cross-examined by Mr Watling for the police, Mrs Maxwell-Scott returned to the identity of the alleged attacker. In an attempt to weaken the story, Mr Watling asked, 'Is it right that Lord Lucan at no time described to you this man he had "seen" attacking his wife?'

'Not entirely right,' she replied, with a smile. 'Lord Lucan did not see him *clearly* enough to describe him.'

'Did he describe him *at all*?'

'Yes, he said he was "large".'

Next Mr Watling asked whether or not Lord Lucan knew that the nanny was dead. If his story were true, of course, he would not know (unless he had inspected the sack). This was underlined by Mrs Maxwell-Scott's careful assertion that they had discussed a 'probable killing'. Soon the jury would hear Lucan's letters to Shand Kydd, in which he described the scene at number 46, and in which he stated that he had no intention of facing a charge of 'attempted murder'. The phrase 'attempted murder' as opposed to 'murder' was to perplex people no end. It skilfully underpinned Lucan's story of interrupting an attacker and of not knowing one way or the other whether Mrs Rivett was dead. 'Perhaps he did not know the nanny had been killed,' wrote one reporter. 'Perhaps he was not the killer.'

'Did he see the sack?' asked Mr Watling.

'Yes.'

'Did he examine it?'

'No.'

'But when Lord Lucan left that house he *knew* that the nanny had been killed?'

'Lady Lucan had *told* him that the nanny had been killed. She told him that the man had killed the nanny and attacked her. He saw the man attacking his wife, anyway.'

The use of the term 'attempted murder' was still left unexplained.

The Coroner asked if Lucan had said anything further before he left Uckfield.

'I asked if he'd like some coffee and I went and made us both some. He wrote his letters to Mr Shand Kydd. After he had written them he handed them to me and said: "Can you post these for me in the morning?" And I said yes and then put them on the drinks trolley.'

'After this there was general conversation, indifferent matters, the children and so on?'

'Yes.'

'Did you offer to let him stay the night?'

'I tried to persuade him to stay the night. I suggested it was a good idea to stay and then telephone the police in the morning. But after slightly agreeing he said no. He said he must – and he stressed the word "must" – get back and clear things up. When he said "get back" he did not mention London.'

'Did he ask you if you had any sleeping pills?'

'Yes he did. He said he was sure he would have difficulty in sleeping and he asked if I'd got any tablets. I said I hadn't. The best I could find was some Valium. There were only four pills left in the bottom. It wasn't a strong dose. But he took them with some water and then said he had to be getting back.'

'What time did he leave?'

'To the best of my recollection, about 1.15 a.m.'

'What happened then?'

'I went to bed.'

'And have you seen him since?'

'No.'

'Has your husband?'

'No.'

In the morning, she said, she had taken the letters off the drinks trolley and stamped them. She had failed to notice any traces of blood on the lips of the envelopes. She had given them to her daughter and asked her to post them on her way to school.

Mr William Shand Kydd told the Coroner that he had received the letters at his house in Cambridge Square on Saturday morning. He had originally driven to his country home in Leighton Buzzard on the Friday evening and Mr Maxwell-Scott had telephoned the next morning to inform him that Lucan had been to the house and written two letters. Mr Shand Kydd said that he had then rung his home in London and had been told by the butler that two letters with Uckfield postmarks had been delivered that morning. 'I drove straight down to London,' Mr Shand Kydd said, 'and having read the letters I took them round to the police station. There were blood-stains on them and I pointed these out to the police officers.'

The Court Usher then produced the first of the letters and the Coroner asked Mr Shand Kydd to read it out in court.

The letter read:

November 8th, 1974

Dear Bill,

The most ghastly circumstances arose this evening, which I have briefly described to my mother. When I interrupted the fight at Lower Belgrave Street and the man left Veronica accused me of having hired him. I took her upstairs and sent Frances to bed and tried to clean her up. She lay doggo for a bit, and while I was in the bathroom she left the house.

The circumstantial evidence against me is strong in that V will say it was all my doing, and I will also lie doggo for a while, but am only concerned about the children. If you can manage it, I'd like them to live with you.

Veronica has demonstrated her hatred for me in the past, and would do anything to see me accused.

For George and Frances to go through life knowing their father had stood in the dock accused of attempted murder would be too much. When they are old enough to understand, explain to them the dream of paranoia, and look after them.

Yours ever,
JOHN

After he had finished reading it to the court Mr Shand Kydd carefully folded the letter along its crease and handed it back to the Usher. The Coroner asked him when he had last seen Lord Lucan before receiving the letter. Mr Shand Kydd said that his memory was 'very unreliable' but 'it was probably about two weeks before the night of November the seventh.'

'And how did he seem?'

'He seemed very relaxed. He was looking forward to Christmas because it was his turn to have the children. He spent a lot of time with the children, both his and mine.'

The Coroner asked if Lord Lucan was 'unusually fond of children'. Mr Shand Kydd looked a bit perplexed at that.

'I don't think so,' he said. 'He was very fond of his *own* children.' Mr Shand Kydd agreed that he was 'very worried about his children. He considered that they were not being properly looked after.'

Mr Eastham then stood up to develop this line of inquiry in cross-examination.

He said that he would like to ask Mr Shand Kydd about some of the remarks that Lord Lucan had made in his letter, but 'bearing in mind the Coroner's ruling concerning what is admissible evidence, I must ask you to answer just yes or no. Do you understand?'

Mr Shand Kydd nodded.

Mr Eastham looked down at his notes. '*Veronica has demonstrated her hatred for me in the past* . . . Do you understand what he means by this?'

'Yes.'

'*And would do anything to see me accused* . . . Do you understand what he means by this?'

'Yes.'

'Could you give evidence about it?'

'Yes.'

'*When the children are old enough to understand, explain to them the dream of paranoia* . . . Did you understand that when you read it?'

'Yes.'

'Did you know what he was getting at?'

'Yes.'

'Could you, if asked, give evidence about the paranoia?'

'Yes.'

'Could you give evidence about all the sentences?'

'Yes.'

'Thank you, Mr Shand Kydd.'

After giving his evidence, Mr Shand Kydd asked the

Coroner if he could be excused from the remainder of the day's proceedings, in order to attend to 'important business'. The next day the *Daily Mirror* carried a front-page photograph of him in the Royal Enclosure at Ascot.

The last witness sympathetic to Lord Lucan was Michael Stoop, the owner of the abandoned Corsair car. Mr Stoop described himself as a 'retired company director'. Since he also added that he was 53 years of age, some of the older members of the jury looked a little confused by this. Stoop told the Coroner that he had known John Lucan for about fifteen years. 'We were both members of the Clermont Club,' he said. He told the Coroner that Lord Lucan had approached him one night over dinner at the Portland Club and asked if he could borrow Stoop's second car, the Ford Corsair. 'I had a Mercedes and I suggested that he might borrow that. I thought he'd prefer the Mercedes. My Ford is a pretty dirty old banger. But I imagined through natural good manners he didn't want to deprive me of my better car. He wanted the Ford specifically for that evening. I didn't ask any reason and he didn't offer any. I was going home to change for dinner. I left the keys to the Ford in the car and said that he could collect it when he wished. I hadn't seen the car between then and the incident.'

Stoop was shown some photographs of the interior of the car. 'The hat and newspapers were not there [when he lent the car]. The bag and battery charger are both mine.' He was then shown the Lion Brand pad found in the glove compartment of the car, on which Lord Lucan's last letter had apparently been written. 'I've seen so many of these before,' Stoop said. 'It's possible it *was* in my car. I can't really say whether it was or not. I haven't lent my car to other people.'

The Coroner asked Mr Stoop to read the letter out to the court. After he had done so he handed it back to the Usher and then faced a series of questions from Mr Eastham. Like the questions to Mr Shand Kydd, said Mr Eastham, he only wanted replies of 'yes' or 'no'.

Mr Eastham referred to the part of Lord Lucan's letter in which he said that, after his last efforts in court, *no one, let alone a sixty-seven-year-old judge, would believe* . . . Did Mr Stoop understand that?

'Yes.'

'Do you know what it meant?'

'Yes.'

'Did it refer to custody proceedings . . .?'

'Yes.'

'. . . involving Lord Lucan?'

'Yes.'

'. . . *and I no longer care except that my children are protected* . . . Did you understand that?'

Stoop hesitated. He glanced across at Veronica. He had once felt some sympathy for her. 'She didn't have it very easy,' he had said, 'with John forming up night after night and having dinner with bores like myself.' He looked back at Mr Eastham.

'I can't answer that with a simple yes or no.'

'I know you can't, but I'm in a difficulty. May I put it this way: if I asked you against what or against *whom* the children had to be protected, could you answer that?'

But before Stoop could reply, the Coroner intervened again. 'I warned you,' he told Michael Eastham, 'about this line of questioning. If you have any questions, please restrict them to the direct evidence.'

Mr Eastham said that he had no further questions in that case, and Mr Stoop was released from the stand.

At lunchtime the Lucan set left the courtroom and went across the road to the Barley Mow public house. The Barley Mow was evidently the place to be. One ate well there. By Wednesday the proprietor said that trade was so brisk he had completely run out of beer. The Dowager Countess ate there each day with her daughter and son-in-law, as did Michael

Stoop and the Maxwell-Scotts. And the Shand Kydds, when they were not attending to 'urgent business', lunched there as well.

Veronica Lucan, perhaps understandably, chose not to eat at the Barley Mow. When the Coroner adjourned proceedings she would slip out through a side door, climb into a police car and lunch at the local station, in the canteen, with Sergeant Forsyth.

After lunch on the third day, when the court had heard Lucan's side of the story, the police returned to the attack. Of the six police witnesses appearing that afternoon, two were to disclose fresh and vital evidence about the night of the murder.

Dr Margaret Pereira told the Coroner that she was the Senior Scientific Officer in the Biology Division at New Scotland Yard. She apparently had an international reputation in this field as a result of her pioneering work in the typing of different blood groups. Dr Pereira said that she had been called to Lower Belgrave Street at about midnight. 'There was an enormous amount of work to do,' she said. 'There were blood splashes on the ground floor and on the first floor and in the basement.' Samples had been taken from Lady Lucan and from the body of Sandra Rivett. It was established that Lady Lucan had blood Group A (found in about 42 per cent of the population) and Sandra had blood Group B (found in about 8 per cent). The next task was to find out whose blood was where. This would enable her to tell the police where Sandra Rivett had been attacked and where Lady Lucan had been attacked (whilst there was no dispute about where Sandra had been attacked, there was of course serious dispute about the location of the assault upon Veronica).

In the basement, Dr Pereira had taken samples of blood from the walls and the floor. This was 'the first obvious site of attack'. In the area at the bottom of the stairs there was a large pool of blood; another in the direction of the kitchen doorway. There was 'directional splashing' against the wall of the stairs and much of the blood had trickled down the wall to the skirting board. Dr Pereira told the court that in her opinion the attack had taken place at the bottom of the staircase, that the victim had collapsed near the piano (three or four feet to the right of the stairs), and that she had then been battered repeatedly in that position as she lay on the ground. The sprays of blood on the ceiling would have been made by the continuous raising of a soaking bludgeon.

On the ground floor, Dr Pereira had also taken blood samples from the staircase and the hall. This was the second obvious site of attack. The radiating patterns of blood on the hall walls had been caused 'by someone striking a wound which was already bleeding'. As the weapon came down on the victim's head it sent splatters of blood shooting off in a sideways direction. The attack had been so ferocious that a good deal of Veronica's hair had gone flying off and was to be found stuck to the blood which was trickling down the wall. As the weapon was raised upward for each successive blow it had, as in the basement, flicked a fine shower of blood, a necklace pattern, across the ceiling and across the wall behind. This evidence, the fact that the blood was showered on the far wall, opposite the front door, supported Veronica's story of having faced an attacker who was in the cloakroom. Further, Dr Pereira said that she had taken blood from a lampshade in the hall, between the stairs and the cloakroom, which had been trajected backwards. And this also supported Veronica's story of having approached the area leading towards the basement from the position of the ground-floor stairs.

The crucial point, however, was this: the blood which was found in the basement was almost exclusively that of Sandra Rivett, while the blood which had been found in the hall was exclusively that of Lady Lucan. This flatly contradicted Lord Lucan's story of having seen and rescued his wife from an attack in the basement. If, as he had claimed, she had been assaulted down there, spraying blood in the quantities proportional to the injuries she received, then obviously a good deal of the blood in the basement should have belonged to her Group A category. But it didn't. It was almost exclusively Group B. Veronica's blood was confined to the hall and the cloakroom, to the areas where *she* claimed Lucan had battered her.

Dr Pereira said that she had found a single droplet of Group A blood on the floor in the kitchen basement – 'not even the size of a pencil-end' – which could have been transferred there accidentally by the police officers swarming round the house after the murder. But there was no evidence to suggest that anyone with Group A blood had been attacked in the basement.

This, by any standards, was pretty conclusive. Ranson must have been delighted by Dr Pereira's evidence (he did later describe her as 'first-rate'). But Mr Eastham was determined to pursue some of the finer discrepancies in order to cast doubt in the minds of the jury. Could Dr Pereira tell the court about the groupings of blood found on Veronica's clothes? Dr Pereira said that she had found three groups: A, B, and AB, which could have been a third and separate group or, more likely, a mixture of the two. The Coroner intervened to ask whether the discovery of Sandra's blood on Veronica's clothes could have been the result of her struggling with an attacker who was saturated in Sandra's blood. Dr Pereira said that was very likely.

Mr Eastham tried again: Was it true that some of Sandra's blood had been found under the arch of one of Veronica's shoes?

Yes, Dr Pereira said, she had found a small stain of Group B under the left heel.

How could it be that Lady Lucan had some of Sandra's blood on her shoe? Could she have picked it up by walking through the basement?

Dr Pereira agreed with Mr Eastham that it was possible

that Lady Lucan had gone into the basement. 'That is a likely explanation for the Group B blood on her shoe,' she said. Once again the Coroner intervened. Could Veronica have picked up this blood by struggling with an attacker who was saturated in it; as she had probably done in the case of the Group B blood on her clothes?

Yes, Dr Pereira agreed with that. If Lord Lucan had been covered in Mrs Rivett's blood he might have passed some on to his wife's shoe during the course of their struggle.

But which was the more *likely* explanation, asked Mr Eastham.

Dr Pereira couldn't say. Mr Eastham pressed the point.

'It's a difficult question,' she replied. 'Perhaps if I could have the shoes . . .'

The shoes were produced.

Dr Pereira stood in the witness box and carefully examined them, turning them over, peering at the heel of the left shoe. Directly in front of her, Veronica strained forward, watching intently.

'No,' she said, finally. 'I can't tell.' She handed them back. 'The blood-staining could have come from either source.'

Mr Eastham asked next about the murder sack into which Sandra's body had been stuffed. This was a United States mailbag, made of canvas, about five feet long. Sandra's body had been bent double, so that her head was lolling between her feet. She had been stuffed inside head and feet first. Dr Pereira had taken samples of blood from six areas on the bag. Four of the areas gave a reaction to Group B. The remaining two areas gave a reaction for Group A, Veronica's group, with some minor Group B activity. This suggested a probable contamination of the two.

Again Mr Eastham was trying to find evidence to support Lucan's story of Veronica being in the basement. How could blood from her group have been found on the murder sack unless she had gone down there? This time Dr Pereira was without a satisfactory explanation. She could not explain the presence of the blood. It was possible, she said, that the sack had brushed against the wall as it was being carried out of the house by the police. Dr Pereira had decided not to examine the sack at number 46 but had waited until it was brought to her laboratory at Scotland Yard. She had had to wait until 10 a.m. on Friday morning.

Surely, by then, said Mr Eastham, the blood on the walls at number 46 would have been dry. Even if the sack had come into contact with it, it would not have smeared sufficiently to give a positive reaction. Dr Pereira said that yes, it would. In relation to another matter she would later say, 'Blood is still capable of making smears if it is clotted or not. It's difficult to say how long blood remains wet. It could take a few minutes or a few hours to dry.' Had the blood on the bag come from transference in the hall?

Later, a press photographer who was doorstepping the house as the police brought the body out would say that the bag had been wrapped in polythene sheeting. This, of course, would have prevented it from becoming contaminated with blood from the walls. But there was still a degree of uncertainty.

Accidental transference of blood by the police accounted for the Group A stain in the basement and for the small amounts of blood which were found on the leaves in the back garden. Further, the house had two resident cats. These were allowed to roam around for three days before they were finally caught. According to Ranson they would dart off every time an officer tried to pick them up. The cats could have picked up blood on their paws or tails and spread it around, giving a distorted picture to later investigators. It was a major failing on the part of the police that this had been allowed to happen.

And even if the murder sack *had* been wrapped in polythene sheeting and had *not* been contaminated by the policemen or by the animals, there was no certainty that the polythene sheeting had been applied *before* the sack was taken from the basement. It was equally likely that the sack had been picked up and carried into the hall, accidentally acquiring some of Veronica's blood as it was being man-handled through the narrow basement doorway, and *then* been wrapped in polythene sheeting before it was taken outside. Perhaps it had started raining in Lower Belgrave Street and, as the police got to the front door, they had decided to apply the sheeting before carrying the sack outside into the waiting van. But the question was never to be satisfactorily answered.

Aside from testing the blood at number 46, Dr Pereira had also examined the murder weapon. She had found several of Veronica Lucan's hairs sticking to it. The blood on the weapon gave reactions to Group AB (more precisely AB HP 2–1, which was a mixture of Veronica's A HP 2–1 and Sandra's B HP 2–2, but with a higher proportion of Veronica's blood). The weapon was bandaged in elastoplast to a margin of three or four millimetres from both ends. The elastoplast, appropriately enough, had a yellow streak running through it. Also on the piping were a number of 'greyish blue wool fibres'. These greyish blue wool fibres were microscopically indistinguishable from other greyish blue wool fibres that Dr Pereira had found in other parts of the house, *and* in the abandoned Corsair. She had taken four of them from the bath towel which lay on the bed upstairs; seven of them from the downstairs cloakroom; and a further thirty-two from the inside of the Corsair.

Lucan had been wearing dark grey trousers that night, probably wool.

The conclusive test would have been if fibres found at his flat matched those at number 46, but such a test was never carried out. Again, this was a serious error by the police.

Nonetheless, it seemed reasonable to suggest that Lucan had deposited the fibres found in the house because, of all the people in the house that night, he was the only one who also had access to the car. And if the fibres *did* come from him, the very fact that several of them had been found adhering to the murder weapon indicates that he must – at the very least – have *touched* it at some point in the evening.

Lucan's account of seeing his wife being attacked in the basement was further demolished by the evidence of Detective Chief Inspector Gerring, who followed Dr Pereira into the witness box.

Inspector Gerring told the court that it was not possible to see into the basement under the conditions described by Lord Lucan.

After he had received Lucan's letter at Gerald Road he had taken a colleague to number 46 and carried out certain corroborative experiments to prove or disprove the assertion that a struggle had been witnessed.

While Inspector Charles Hulls went down to the basement and weaved around at the foot of the stairs where Sandra Rivett had been attacked, Inspector Gerring walked past on the pavement and casually glanced down to the basement window.

He could see nothing.

Mr Hulls then switched on the basement light and went back to his position on the stairs, where he started moving again.

Again, Mr Gerring wandered past and glanced down, and again could see nothing.

But, he told the court, if he stopped outside the window and crouched down on all fours with his head two or three feet from the pavement – and if the light was on – he could just about distinguish Hulls's feet at the bottom of the stairs. He could clearly see Mr Hulls when Mr Hulls stood in the kitchen, by the kitchen window, and if a struggle had been taking place there 'it would have been obvious on passing'. But the fact that there was no evidence of a fight having taken place there, and that the light would have had to be on for Lord Lucan to have seen anything clearly, still left his stated motive for entering the house *without explanation*. It is not quite right to suggest, as one writer did, that to believe Lucan's story one had to accept that the light had been on when he walked past (miraculously at the very moment of attack), that he had crouched down on all fours for no reason at all, and that on his entry 'Veronica and her assailant had stopped fighting, removed the lightbulb, placed it carefully on the cushioned chair, and then started fighting again'. But the sentiment of ridicule was perfectly justified.

Mr Gerring also told the court that he had first arrived at Lower Belgrave Street at midnight on the night of November 7th.

'To the best of my knowledge nothing had been moved,' he said. 'Coming down the stairs to the basement I saw the pools of blood and the body in the sack. There was one saucer lying broken on the floor at the bottom of the stairs. Half the saucer was on the last step, the other half on the ground. There was no sign of a fight in the basement. I then went to St George's Hospital to interview Lady Lucan. I saw her at about 1.30 a.m. It was obvious she'd taken a sedative because of her injuries. She looked as if she'd taken drugs. She made a verbal statement to myself and Mr Ranson on the evening of Friday the eighth, at about six o'clock. Her understanding was extremely good. I left Sergeant Forsyth to take the written statement. The written statement was remarkably close to the verbal statement.'

Cross-examined by Mr Watling, Inspector Gerring agreed that he had been unable to trace anyone with a key to number 46 apart from Lord and Lady Lucan. He also said that there had been no signs of forced entry into the house.

'And have you been able to trace any third person who might have been in the house that night?' asked Mr Watling.

'None whatsoever, sir.'

'Have you made very extensive efforts to do so?'

'Very extensive, including inquiries in the area and forensic work across the whole of Belgravia.'

'How long have you been a police officer, Mr Gerring?'

'Over twenty years, sir.'

'Have you made extensive efforts to trace Lord Lucan?'

'Yes, sir. We have conducted a national and international search for him. We have made inquiries in nearly every country in the world. I myself have spent eleven days at Newhaven going over the evidence and the possibilities.'

'And?'

'And there is no trace of him.'

'None?'

'None at all.'

On the Thursday morning, Dr Thurston began his summing up. The courtroom was once again packed to capacity. The crowds outside included many people sporting top hat and tails, waiting for the verdict before going off to the races at Ascot. Even Mr Shand Kydd was back in his seat.

Dr Thurston's address lasted only seventy minutes. This was admirably brisk.

He started by examining the tense atmosphere in which the proceedings had been conducted.

'You know that Lord and Lady Lucan are separated,' he began, 'and that they have been on either side of custody proceedings. You also know that there are certain tensions in the family which, if aired, could only be painful to the people concerned.' People had particularly sensed the hostility between Lady Lucan and her sister and Lady Lucan and her mother-in-law.

The Coroner had decided to exclude certain evidence about Lady Lucan, 'because it would not benefit this inquiry'. 'If it could benefit this inquiry then I would have taken a different view. But simply to turn this into a forum for airing family tensions would be a wrong thing.' (Such a decision might have been justifiable if the court were concerning itself exclusively with the cause of Sandra Rivett's death; since it was also concerning itself with the identity of the person alleged to have caused the death, the question of whether 'tensions' should have been aired was irrelevant. If a suspect could not probe the credibility of his accuser, a basic right of English justice, then the law itself was clearly at fault.)

Turning to the two separate versions of the murder, Dr Thurston first examined Lady Lucan's story. He pointed out that Sandra and Veronica were the same height and that it was Veronica who should have been making the tea. Lady Lucan's evidence was the only account which fitted with the scientific discoveries. Blood in the hall belonged to the Countess. Blood in the basement belonged to Sandra Rivett. Was it likely, therefore, that Lord Lucan had seen a struggle in the basement between his wife and an attacker?

On this question of how Group B blood came to be found on the heel of Lady Lucan's shoe, indicating that she *might* have gone down to the basement, and Lord Lucan *might* then have been able to see her through the window, Dr Thurston reminded the jury that 'the blood-staining could have come about through contact with soggy clothing'. 'If it came about through walking in the basement that would not be compatible with what Lady Lucan has told us. But we must remember that the assailant would have Sandra's blood splashes on him and in the act of struggling with him some of this blood could have been transferred to Lady Lucan's shoe.'

As far as Lord Lucan's story was concerned, this did not fit with the established facts. It did not fit in regard to the areas of blood. And it did not fit in relation to whether or not it was possible to see into the basement through the kitchen window. Dr Thurston reminded the court that Inspector Gerring had said he could see part of the basement if he stopped outside and bent down, and if the light was on. 'But there was no light on,' he concluded.

'Then we have this question of an intruder. We have not been told which way this intruder went out. It is possible to get out through the back door but it would be extremely difficult to get out of the garden without leaving traces [the wall was seventeen feet high]. And no such traces have been found.'

Returning to his decision to disallow certain questions involving Lady Lucan, he pondered on the question of whether she was the type of woman who would, as her husband had suggested, 'do anything to see him accused'. 'Well,' Dr Thurston said, 'you have seen Lady Lucan for yourself. You have had her sitting there in the witness box for over two hours. You've heard her give evidence. You've had the advantage of seeing her for yourself and of observing her demeanour, of the way she answered questions. She answered very carefully and gave each question a great deal of consideration.'

Lord Lucan, on the other hand, 'was obsessed with his children'. He was 'absolutely devoted to them, and more so since the custody case'.

'As regards motive,' he went on, 'there is the question of Lord Lucan's financial situation.' (Dr Thurston's speech was beginning to sound like the transcript of a trial.) 'There is no doubt that he was having to keep two establishments going instead of just one. It could have eased his financial situation if he had the outgoings of just one.'

On the murder night, said the Coroner, Lord Lucan's behaviour was not exactly the behaviour one expected from a man who had just stumbled in on a murder. 'If – as Lord Lucan says – he was only trying to help his wife and give her succour – why did she then run out into the street screaming, "Murder! Murder!"?'

Why, on discovering the carnage, hadn't Lord Lucan telephoned at once for the police? 'What is an instinctive reaction for someone in that situation?' Dr Thurston asked. 'Would an instinctive reaction be to do what the barman of the Plumbers Arms did when he telephoned at once for an ambulance and the police?' (But the barman had not 'instinctively telephoned at once for an ambulance and the police'; he had instinctively done what Lord Lucan did – fetch a cloth, hold it to the wound, and *then* think about ringing for help. Nonetheless, the point was valid in the sense that Lord Lucan was at the scene of the crime for approximately fifty minutes and did not call for help during that time or at any time after.)

Finally, Dr Thurston asked the jury to retire and consider their verdict. 'The circumstances are quite clear. If you're satisfied on the evidence that you have heard that there was an attack by another person, then your verdict will have to be murder. And you've got to decide on the evidence whether you can name the person responsible.'

The jury began to shuffle out. Dr Thurston had told them that he could accept a majority verdict, 'provided there are not more than two dissenters'. He also said that he had 'agonized over this unusual and difficult case for almost seven months'.

Now, however, the anxieties were at an end. The responsibility was with the jury.

The courtroom emptied as the spectators and witnesses made for the benches in the hall. The crowd outside was now larger than ever. The streets of Westminster were lit by one of the hottest summer days on record. Across the road, the Barley Mow had opened its door half an hour earlier than usual and was serving iced tea and lemonade. The reporters who stood around chatting at the bar had already filed their copy. As far as they were concerned, the question was not what the decision of the inquest would be, but when it would be delivered.

A little before noon, the jury announced that they had reached their verdict and were ready to present it. They had been out for just thirty-one minutes.

Dr Thurston told the foreman to stand and then formally asked if they had come to a majority decision. 'Yes,' he said, quietly. 'It is Murder by Lord Lucan.'

157

Chapter Ten

THE SHADE OF LORD LUCAN

Dr Thurston thanked the foreman and then addressed the rest of the court. His final remarks took the effect of a formal committal at a Magistrate's Court. 'It is very unusual for someone to be named as the jury have done,' he said, 'but I will record that Sandra Eleanor Rivett was murdered on the seventh day of November, 1974, by Richard John Bingham, the Seventh Earl of Lucan. It is now my duty to commit that person for trial. In this case, of course, there *is* no one to commit for trial because we do not know where he is. But there is no doubt that he will be charged if he turns up.' Dr Thurston then thanked the jury and dismissed the court.

Outside, in the sweltering sunshine, the central characters hurried out to their cars, giving only brief reactions. Susan Maxwell-Scott continued to believe 'implicitly' in Lucan's story. Christina Shand Kydd felt 'saddened' and continued to believe in her brother-in-law's innocence. The Dowager Countess left the court on the arm of Mr Shand Kydd and said merely, 'No comment. No comment. It is a usual phrase and I shall be having a record made of it.'

Lady Lucan left the court by a side door, accompanied by a police detective. After she had been driven away, her solicitor came out and issued a statement on her behalf. The statement said that Lady Lucan was 'neither pleased nor displeased with the verdict'. 'I was only concerned with establishing the facts,' it went on. Her husband's interests had been represented in court and the jury had made up their minds. Now she hoped to 'resume a normal family life'.

It was left to Lucan's brother-in-law, the Reverend William Gibbs, to voice the Lucan family's anger at the verdict. 'This is not British justice,' he said. 'To me, it is frightening and amazing that a man can be named in court as a murderer without the jury hearing all the relevant evidence, and without being given a chance to defend himself. I know and the family know that Lord Lucan is innocent and we will do anything in our power to prove this.' Then, in an audacious moment, he added a flourish: 'This is not British justice and must therefore be ignored.' Perhaps that remark, more than any other, gave an indication of the aristocracy's attitude towards their own position. The verdict was not to be contested or fought or undermined by legal inquiry. It must simply be ignored.

It was certainly true that the verdict represented a breath-taking breach of contemporary legal etiquette. There had been a clear suppression of evidence. The Coroner had considered his motives for this suppression to be in the best interests of the chief witnesses, but those did not necessarily coincide with the best interests of the court or the inquiry – in fact the evidence was that those interests were diametrically opposed. In addition, Dr Thurston had permitted the jury to exercise its anachronistic right to name a suspect as a murderer in the absence of any formal defence. Undoubtedly, he would have countered the charge of inequity by saying that Lucan could have come and defended himself at any point in the proceedings. But there are many reasons why someone will not come forward to face a charge. Usually it is because they are guilty and do not wish to suffer the penalty they have incurred. But sometimes there are more complex reasons. Lucan's friends believed that he lay 'doggo' to avoid the recriminations of false accusation. 'I do not expect my brother-in-law to appear until the police have found the real murderer,' said the Reverend Gibbs.

Finally, there was the manner in which the proceedings had prejudiced a future trial. The Coroner obviously felt that his committal had merely the same effect as a committal at a Magistrate's Court; that it represented simply a 'case to answer', not a formal finding that would lead to a sentence. But this was rubbish. Unlike a Magistrate's Court the inquiry had led to a verdict. In popular terms, it had the same effect as a verdict in a High Court trial. It meant that Lucan was formally listed as having killed Mrs Rivett and was popularly recognized as having done so. It was therefore fair to say that it would be virtually impossible for Lucan to get a fair trial, or even that a jury could be composed of twelve men and women who did not bring popular preconceptions to their judgment as a result of the reporting of the inquest. That the police maintained a rule of *sub judice* over inquiring journalists *after* the inquest verdict was humbug of the most hypocritical kind.

In due course, the matter came up for review. Earlier, in 1971, as we have seen, the Broderick Committee had recommended the complete abolition of Coroners' Courts. The review of the Criminal Justice Act of 1977 did not go that far. But it did initiate a fundamental change in the structure of the court proceedings and it clearly suggested that the right to name people as guilty of a crime prior to a High Court trial should be abolished.

In that sense, then, the Rivett inquest was historic: the last one in Britain formally to accuse a suspect of murder prior to the change in the law. But for Lucan that was too late.

Absent and undefended, he had still, somehow, been convicted.

Ostensibly, the inquest into Sandra Rivett's death seemed to bring the Lucan case to an end. The verdict brought, as verdicts do, an attendant sense of finality. But in fact this was an illusion. The body of Lord Lucan might have been lying at the bottom of the Channel; he may even have been living it up in some casino in South America. But the ghost of Lord Lucan continued to prowl the streets of London, a powerful and evocative shade. Furthermore, it had the propensity to cause mayhem and ruin wherever it appeared. The central drama had passed; but the aftereffects would continue to shatter careers and ruin lives for a while to come.

The tone of the inquest, which had been hostile to Lucan from the start, had been principally set by a single newspaper article that had appeared the week before, in the *Sunday Times*. This was entitled 'The Luck of the Lucans' and was written by the journalist James Fox. Fox had previously worked with Cyril Connolly, on another *Sunday Times* article that had caused a storm, 'Christmas at Karen', about the shooting in Kenya of Lord Erroll. Fox was an Old Etonian and was thus able to enlist the aid of several of Lucan's friends in compiling his copy for the inquest. The final piece was essential reading for anyone interested in the story. It was widely regarded as a pioneering work. But on the whole it was sympathetic to Lady Lucan, not to her husband. Fox's politics were realistically to the left of those espoused in Mayfair, and many were outraged and stung when his article finally appeared. They had imagined a favourable presentation of *their* case, a chance to address the grievances they had about the way they had been treated by the press since the murder story had broken. But Fox would not toe the line. He talked about Lucan's narrow social life and about the right-wing causes – then so resoundingly out of fashion – which, Fox said, were institutionalized in the boys' clubs of west London.

In due course Fox was to win a special commendation in the British press awards for his article, which was immensely well received. But Lucan's friends felt exposed by it and began to blame each other for allowing Fox to penetrate the group in the first place. They thus cast their net about in the search for a scapegoat. Eventually, someone from within their own ranks was singled out and ostracized.

Dominick Elwes had helped Fox by painting a picture to accompany his article. The picture, for which he was paid £200, showed the 'inner circle' at lunch in the Clermont. It was done in caricature and was as unflattering to the set as the article itself. Dominick had also made several verbal contributions. He was known to believe that Lucan was guilty of the murder and told Fox that he had been suffering the 'classic symptoms' of paranoia beforehand. All of this had a fairly disastrous effect on Dominick's position when the article appeared.

Later that month, he received a letter from Robin Birley, the son of Lady Annabel, who was married to Mark Birley, proprietor of Annabel's, and mistress to the tycoon Sir James Goldsmith, accusing him of selling private photographs of his mother to the *Sunday Times*. Lucan had been on holiday in Acapulco with Elwes, Lady Annabel, Goldsmith and others in 1973, and several 'holiday snaps' had been reproduced in Fox's article. Elwes, who was unsuccessful as an artist and businessman, seemed the obvious source for the photographs, and though he wrote back to Robin Birley denying that he had sold them, the fact that he had painted the group portrait undermined his position, to the extent where he was not believed. Mark Birley banned him from Annabel's nightclub and sent out writs for two outstanding debts. Slowly, the curtain went down on Elwes; he was hounded, excommunicated, and blackballed.

He committed suicide.

The demise of Elwes, in fact, was a slow and gruesome affair. A kind man by nature, he had been shocked and appalled by the attacks on Sandra Rivett and Lady Lucan. He claimed the affair 'shattered' his life. He had suffered with depression for many years and took medication regularly. Lately, he had lost money in the property crash and several other investments had gone sour. When the *Sunday Times* article appeared, and his friends began to turn on him, he left England in a state of severe depression and went to stay in a villa in Portugal. There he fell down a mountainside and broke his wrist. In pain, moribund and anxious, he started drinking heavily. He wrote letters to anyone who would listen, pleading his innocence in the sale of the photographs, threatening to sue James Fox and the *Sunday Times*. (It later emerged that Dominick had been innocent of the sale, as Fox and the *Sunday Times* said at the time.) But all to no avail. His friends were implacable. When he returned to England he was in a state of clinical depression. Several journalists tried to intervene on his behalf, to restore him to favour with the old crowd. But nothing happened, and Elwes sank ever deeper into his decline.

On the weekend of September 6th, he was being driven back to his little studio in Chelsea by a girlfriend. He told her that he had not 'slept a wink for two nights' and said, 'I need my Tunial. I have a standing prescription at a pharmacy in Knightsbridge. I'll call them and tell them you're coming. Don't bother to ring the doorbell, just pop them through the letterbox.' The girlfriend did exactly that, and Elwes took the lot. The next day, another girlfriend let herself into the apartment and found him dead in the bed, the empty bottle on the bedside table.

Elwes had been a curious addition to the Lucan set. Although he came from a traditional upper-class background, having been to Eton and served in the Guards, and although he had embellished his credentials by joining Colonel Stirling's private army, he did not in fact possess the resources to keep on an even footing with the magic circle. Lucan had been broke, too, but Lucan had a title and the title opened all doors. Elwes's father, Simon, had been a portrait painter for the Queen, but in the end Elwes remained the outsider. His friends did not really accept him, it was said later, because he just didn't have enough money.

What he did have, however, was a remarkable gift as a wit and raconteur. Even Peter Ustinov had said that Dominick was the one person to whom he would defer in conversation. Thus, he was permitted entry into the Lucan set in return for the promise of laughter. He was always ready with an amusing story, a verbal parody. His friends agreed that he was the funniest person any of them knew. He became the Lucan set's court jester. But that, of course, was not enough to save him when the accusation of treachery began to gather momentum. He had betrayed his hosts, criticizing the very people who had granted him his position of social prestige and privilege. So far as they were concerned, he deserved no second chance.

At his memorial service, in Mayfair's Farm Street church, the great theatre critic Kenneth Tynan portrayed Elwes as a romantic monarchist, and lamented his pathetic adulation of a group that he, Tynan, considered worthless. Some people had elected him their court jester, he said, and Elwes had happily embraced the role. But in the final analysis he was simply too poor for them. It was a tragedy indeed that Elwes set such store by the opinions of his friends, many of whom were manifestly his inferiors.

In the second address, John Aspinall gave an astonishingly inappropriate eulogy. Aspinall suggested that Dominick's inability to find all the fame and fortune to which he thought he was entitled was due to a 'genetic flaw'. Some of the grieving family looked a little perplexed at that. Then he said, 'He resented the fact that many lesser men had found fame through the media and through the newspapers. He knew many people who had achieved much, but he never managed it. His business affairs had never been the success they might have been. He was happiest entertaining a dozen or more close friends with his amusing stories or his wit. But, unfortunately, modern society does not repay someone like him. It is the man who can entertain television audiences with his banalities who gets its rewards.' As he left the service, coming out onto the steps of the church, Aspinall was socked in the face by Elwes's cousin, Tremayne Rodd, a former rugby international player. 'That's what I think of your bloody speech, Aspinall,' he said. Aspinall, nursing his jaw ruefully, replied merely, 'I am used to this kind of thing in dealing with wild animals.' The next day the front page of the *Daily Mail* carried the headline: 'RIGHT HOOK ENDS MEMORIAL SERVICE TO MAN FROM LUCAN SET'.

In a sense, one can see the Elwes memorial service as almost a requiem mass for the set itself. Certainly, Elwes's ostracism betrayed the inner struggle and conflict that was wrenching apart a group which found itself exposed and wounded in a hostile world. If the Lucan murder had opened up a war – about privacy, about social values – between the Lucan set and the wider world, Dominick's death was surely its final, fatal blow.

PART THREE

THE QUESTIONS

Error of opinion may be tolerated only when reason is left free to combat it.

Thomas Jefferson

Chapter Eleven

LUCAN – NOT GUILTY?

In the mid-1980s I was working for a television company based in Regent Street, London, as a researcher. I had previously worked for provincial newspapers and in Fleet Street as a freelance journalist. The television company survived mostly on pop promotions and commercials, although every now and then it would find itself a 'serious' director, usually from Europe or the United States, and plunge into an expensive documentary, which it then sold around the world. It was an interesting organization to work for, although it cultivated a certain insularity. Media preoccupations consumed the staff. The goings-on in the outside world held very little interest for people who did their business almost exclusively in the restaurants around Covent Garden, spent their evenings, absorbed in each other's projects, drinking in bars, or watching surreal foreign films at alternative cinemas, and whom I hardly ever saw at our offices.

One afternoon in early October 1985, we were throwing ideas around for a drama documentary that could be based on one of the great social or political scandals of the last twenty years. Someone inevitably suggested the Profumo case; then the Windsors, the Earl of Erroll, Victor Grayson, and then, as the lights started going on in Regent Street and down towards Shaftesbury Avenue, the mystery of the missing Earl of Lucan. I confessed a resistance to the idea, principally because of the legal implications, and within a few moments, as other doubts surfaced, the subject was dropped. Now it was Anthony Blunt, the Jeremy Thorpe trial, Harry Oakes. Eventually, we concluded our meeting without any clear idea of which topic to pursue. Lucan, however, was way down the list.

My next immediate memory is of walking out of the building, turning right into Great Marlborough Street, and then pausing outside the entrance to the Oxford Circus tube station to buy a copy of the *Evening Standard*. The newspaper's lead story, by some bizarre coincidence, was the Lord Lucan case. I remember putting my briefcase down and standing at the corner of Argyll Street, under a lamppost, reading the front page. It seemed that another nanny to the Lucan children had been murdered, earlier in the year, and the case had come to the Old Bailey, where Nicholas Boyce was charged with the murder of Christabel Martin.

Christabel had left the Lucan house in the summer of 1974 to get married. Sandra Rivett had been her replacement. Boyce, Christabel's husband, had strangled her to death with the flex of the vacuum cleaner and then dismembered her body and dumped it in plastic bags around London. He received a four-year sentence for manslaughter.

The *Standard* gave an absorbing résumé of the Lucan case in a short by-line to the main piece, and for several minutes I was lost in the drama of that old story. Something in me responded at once to all the appeal of an unsolved puzzle and to the controversial social context in which the mystery had unfolded.

The following week we had our meeting again. This time I

was certain what the programme topic should be. The others, on the whole, were against the idea. We wouldn't get any cooperation from the people involved. We would end up being sued. Lady Lucan would threaten us with an injunction. And at the back of the mind there was always the possibility that Lucan himself might – just might – decide to turn up and wreck everything. On the whole, it was deemed too risky.

Nonetheless, we ended the meeting with an agreement that some preliminary research should be done, to establish whether it was worth pursuing, and we began to put out feelers into the networks for finance. In the meantime, I had taken myself off to Colindale, in north London, to the British Newspaper Library, to get a first-hand flavour of the contemporary reporting. This was quite an odd experience. For three days I sat at the big pine tables turning over the pages, watching the story slowly unravel. Some of the splinter articles were fascinating (there was a particularly good one, dated November 28th – Lucan's wedding anniversary – about the sale at Christie's). But the real interest was in watching the central story gather momentum, reading the predictions, reading the possibilities, and knowing how, in the final analysis, so much of the story would turn out. I had also read Norman Lucas's book on the case, called *The Lucan Mystery*, which was long out of print, and which had been compiled, as far as I could tell, from the press cuttings I was consulting. Lucas took the story from the arrival of the police at number 46 to the climax of the inquest. But there was virtually no speculation about Lucan's ultimate fate and very little about the various theories behind the murder. Lucas was quite content to drop the thread of the story at what seemed, ostensibly, to be the end.

But of course it was not enough to leave things there. Nothing had been resolved. The verdict of the inquest was in doubt. The question of Lucan's disappearance was unanswered. And the whole backdrop to the case had – apart from James Fox's article – barely been touched upon.

In the New Year I began to approach Lord Lucan's family and friends. I spoke to the Reverend William Gibbs. I spoke to Christina Shand Kydd. I wrote to Lucan's mother. The response never varied: they were cooperating with a journalist who was writing a book which would 'prove' that Lucan was innocent. They would not talk to anyone until this book came out. Then they would think about it.

In due course, after she had published a couple of frisky trailers, Sally Moore's book, *Lucan: Not Guilty*, finally appeared in 1987. It was well researched and an enjoyable read, and it had the advantage of being able to claim, truthfully, that many of Lucan's friends and most of his family were speaking about him for the first time. But what they had to say was, on the whole, of little interest. In fact, there was virtually nothing about the book that would have astonished the casual reader. Sally Moore portrayed Lucan as a sort of amicable, middle-class liberal; the kind of aristocrat who would only use his title to get the best seat in restaurants. She advanced the cause of his innocence in three separate ways, with varying degrees of success.

First, she set out to give some plausibility to Lucan's 'unbelievable coincidence'. She quoted several of his friends claiming that it was his habit to walk past the house at night, to check on his children, so that the likelihood of him accidentally witnessing a murder scene was considerably increased (this, as we have seen, had been raised at the inquest, when Susan Maxwell-Scott and the Dowager Countess both indicated that Lucan's anxieties drove him to 'regularly check on Lower Belgrave Street'):

> By now, neighbours and many of John's friends were well aware of the regular spying trips he made to the street where his children lived. Stephen Raphael and John Wilbraham were only two of those who walked to

or from his flat with him, specifically via Lower Belgrave Street, in order that John could try and check that Frances, George and Camilla were all right.

There was, of course, no way of knowing for sure whether Lucan did in fact walk around Lower Belgrave Street like a sort of Banquo's ghost, only that it was useful for his supporters to say that he did, but the picture does fit with the desperation and paranoia which are common features in descriptions of his last days. At the same time, Sally Moore had to show that a struggle could have been going on in the basement at the time Lucan walked past. Here there was the obvious difficulty of the evidence about Veronica's blood distribution. How could Lucan claim to have seen her being attacked in the basement if her blood was found by the forensic experts sprayed and splashed across the walls of the ground-floor hallway? Sally Moore made two points. First, she won a concession from the pathologist on the case, Professor Keith Simpson, that it was medically possible for Veronica to have been struck once in the basement area and then, on fleeing upstairs, to have bled extensively on the ground floor. Simpson's point was that a wound to the head will not begin to bleed for several seconds, until blood wells up into the damaged area, and splashing of blood will occur only if the victim is hit again on the same wound. Technically, then, it was possible that Veronica had been in the basement when she received a single blow to her head, which broke open her skin, and which Lucan, outside, saw through the window, and that she then fled from her attacker, up the basement stairs and into the ground-floor hall, where he, in pursuit, caught up with her, landed more blows to the wound, and so caused the splashing and spraying effect.

Sally Moore tried to bolster this scenario by utilizing two stray pieces of forensic evidence. A picture had been found awry on the wall of the basement, as one went up the stairs, and a smear of Veronica's blood was on the basement wall at the top of the basement stairs. Veronica claimed in her police statement that this was because she and her attacker, fighting on the ground floor, had fallen through the basement doorway, and that her attacker had tried to force her down into the basement. That assertion fitted with the nature of the smear and the disturbance of the picture. But, said Sally Moore, it *also* fitted with the idea that Veronica, struck by a blow in the basement and fleeing upstairs, had been hit again in a struggle at the top of the basement by an attacker chasing her from behind. Additionally, the police had revealed at the inquest that a small droplet of blood, 'the size of the end of a pencil', had been found in the basement kitchen, on the formica work surface near the window, which gave a reaction when it was tested by forensic experts to Lady Lucan's blood grouping, Group A. How could it be, asked Sally Moore, that a droplet of Veronica's blood had been found in the basement if she claimed never to have gone down there? At the inquest, too, Dr Margaret Pereira had spoken of finding blood Group B, Sandra's blood, under the heel of one of Lady Lucan's shoes. She conceded at the inquest that this meant that it was 'a likely possibility' that in fact Lady Lucan *had* gone into the basement.

How safe, then, was the police assertion that Lucan could not have witnessed a fight in the basement because the fight had not taken place there? When Ranson and Gerring were questioned about this they gave a simple answer: there had undoubtedly been some 'accidental transference' of blood *after* the arrival of the police. Sally Moore found that an implausible explanation. The police found any alternative view 'a red herring'.

Although it was possible to raise doubts about the police version of events, it was another matter entirely to provide a convincing alternative for what might have happened – particularly one that exonerated Lucan. Of course, in a court of law it would not have been incumbent upon the defence to provide such an alternative, but it was a measure of how deeply entrenched was the general certainty of Lucan's guilt that Sally Moore and the Lucan family felt obliged to offer another explanation. It might also have been seen as an indication of how great their failure was to really dent the police case; the need for an alternative explanation grows or recedes, one supposes, according to how successfully one has diminished the case advanced by one's opponents.

At any rate, those of us who had read Sally Moore's trailers had high hopes that a breakthrough was coming. I was particularly nervous in case it short-circuited all the preliminary research we had already done. We knew that the Lucan family had hired a team of private detectives, back in 1975, to find some evidence to support the presence of Lucan's second man. But we were to be disappointed. Sally Moore could only suggest that she thought the 'real murderer' was a policeman or a former policeman, and that Sandra Rivett had disturbed him burgling the house. The evidence for this came principally from Lilian Jenkins, the former nanny.

Shortly after the murder, she told Sally Moore, a man who claimed to be a police detective called to see Miss Jenkins at her home. He said that he had come for the letter which Lady Lucan had written to Miss Jenkins when Miss Jenkins worked at number 46. At first, Miss Jenkins had no recollection of any such letter. Then she remembered a sealed envelope that Veronica had given her many years previously. Veronica had said that Miss Jenkins was to give the envelope to the Commissioner of the Metropolitan Police if she, Veronica, were ever 'mugged or found dead'. This was because Veronica had been 'indiscreet' about security. She had arranged for a local policeman to come and advise her on the matter. During the course of their conversation she had taken him to the little mews cottage behind number 46, where the Lucans kept some of their jewellery. Then she had become convinced that the officer was corrupt and that she had exposed the family to the threat of robbery. She had duly written a letter to the Chief Commissioner, relating the incident and naming the man in question, which Miss Jenkins was to hand over in the event of Veronica being attacked. Miss Jenkins found the letter and gave it to the man claiming to be a CID officer. He then drove away, saying that he would return. He never did return.

And this was the sole evidence for the supposition that a 'bent policeman' had murdered Sandra Rivett. It was not exactly overwhelming. Sally Moore went on:

> Let's suppose, for the sake of argument, that a police-man or ex-policeman was involved in the murder of Sandra Rivett. Perhaps he knew there was valuable jewellery and silver at 46 Lower Belgrave Street. Per-haps he went there with the intention to rob. Would the facts fit?
>
> John said the killer was large. Veronica agreed that the man who rushed out and hit her over the head – a man she did not *see* in the darkness, was much taller than she was, which a policeman necessarily would be . . . If Sandra disturbed a policeman trying to burgle the house, perhaps a local cop she recognised, there was a clear reason why she had to be killed. And why Veronica, arriving downstairs, had to be silenced.

It did not help matters that Roy Ranson, in a remark to Sally Moore in 1975, had said that the real murderer 'could have been a policeman, the real murder weapon could have been a truncheon'. It was obviously this remark – quite a slip for a senior officer to have made – which gave Sally Moore her next line of thought. One assumes that Ranson was merely suggesting that in the Lucan case anything was possible. But he should have foreseen that such a comment, in the hands of a journalist, would provoke its own suspicions, in what was still a sensitive area.

In other areas, Sally Moore had less success. She was

unable to address the fact that Lucan had told Aspinall that he would like to kill his wife or that he had told Lady Osbourne that he intended to, because Brian Masters's book, which contained these revelations, was not published until after her own book had appeared.

But she overlooked the same story, from Taki Theodor-acopoulos, which had been published in 1978. Furthermore, when it came to Greville Howard's statement, in which Howard said that Lucan wanted to kill his wife and dump her body in the Solent, she was only able to say that 'this conversation took place one night when Lucan was very drunk, months before the murder'. In fact, according to Howard, the conversation occurred 'comparatively recently' (to the murder), and Lucan, though drinking, was *compos mentis* enough to discuss other subjects with Howard in a clear fashion.

Finally, there was the problem of the bludgeon. The only alternative to Lucan's having put a twin in the boot of the car was that someone else had 'planted' it. But this presupposed that someone had set out to frame Lucan. And that scenario did not fit with the earlier claim that he had accidentally disturbed an intruder, that there had been 'an unbelievable coincidence'. For him to have been framed would have required a premeditated luring of him to the house. And yet it was his advocates who said that he had arrived there through chance.

And so the Sally Moore book came and went, and after all the media attention the public's verdict remained the same: Lucan had murdered Sandra Rivett. Then he had attacked his wife. Then he had fled. He had taken his speedboat out in the Channel, tied himself to it, and, in the words of one journalist, 'gone down with his ship'.

But there *were* some real areas of doubt. For me, these did not appear whilst I was reading the books that had been published, nor while I was going through the cuttings at Colindale. They started when I read the transcripts of the inquest. During the inquest, when the story was still fresh to the ears of contemporary reporters, its sheer momentum would no doubt have carried those attending past the clogs and blots of evidence that didn't apparently tally. No one had made anything of the blood discrepancies at the time, for instance. But a retrospective analysis showed that much of the evidence was not impervious to criticism or doubt.

First, there was the testimony of Keith Simpson, the Home Office pathologist, who gave evidence on the second day of the hearing. His evidence broadly tallied with the version of events which the police advocated. But it did not *entirely* tally.

Simpson said that he had conducted a postmortem at 10 a.m. on the Friday morning. He found that Sandra had died from serious head injuries. After she became unconscious her lungs had filled with blood because an unconscious person 'cannot clear the airways by coughing'. This, he said, had precipitated death. Additionally, there was severe bruising on Sandra's hands, face, shoulders and arms. These had been made by a heavy blunt instrument, probably the lead piping. But some of the marks on her face were *not* consistent with an attack by someone using the lead piping. They were more consistent with a fist or hand slap. Sandra, in other words, had been *punched* by her attacker.

This was potentially devastating news for the police.

The police believed that Lucan had waited in the basement, positioned behind the stairs, ready to strike his victim on the back of the head when she reached the bottom step. The element of surprise was vital if the victim was to make no noise. And that scenario was supported by the discovery of the tea-tray at the foot of the stairs, by the broken crockery, and by the pattern of blood, which radiated up the wall behind the stairs.

But now Professor Simpson was giving a different view.

He was saying that Sandra had been hit in the face with a fist in addition to being hit with the piping, and possibly *prior* to being hit with the piping. He was saying, in effect, that the attack could have started with a face-to-face confrontation, and that she had not been taken by surprise as the police suggested; the blows to the back of her head, he went on, were 'parallels', which meant that Sandra was lying still when they rained down upon her, whereas those to her face were 'singles', which meant she was moving to dodge them as they were delivered. It was thus impossible to think that the fight had not started with a face-to-face assault, and that the blows to the back of the head only came later, when Sandra was lying unconscious.

In addition to this, the random nature of the marks on her face and her hands, together with the degree of bruising, suggested, according to Simpson, that Sandra had resisted her attacker and that they had grappled together. She had not silently succumbed to a single blow from behind.

This evidence was clearly troubling: a fight starting from the front, not from behind; shouts and cries from the victim as she fought back; punches and slaps to the face – the *face*, not the anonymous 'back of the head', as the killer and his victim struggled.

How likely, in this kind of scenario, was it that Sandra Rivett had therefore been killed 'in mistake' for another woman?

Secondly, there was the incongruity of Lucan's chosen method: his use of a bludgeon; his use of a canvas sack; the ferocity of his attack.

No one was going to suggest that, in a plot to do away with his wife, Lucan should have turned to the aid of a gun, however adept he may have been at using one (he still kept up his practice with the Grenadier Guards and owned several pistols and shotguns). A gun would have made a heck of a noise, and there are no obvious reasons why a man like Lucan should have legally possessed a silencer. A gun is also

179

likely to leave behind too many clues: a trace of powder; the markings and manufacture of the bullet. It was not a very discreet weapon for the act of murder, at least in England, where gun crimes are far less prevalent than in, say, the USA.

But then, neither is the bludgeon discreet. And in many ways it seemed just as improbable to suggest that Lucan would have used a bludgeon as it was to suggest that Lucan should have used a gun. A bludgeon is certainly effective in rendering your victim unconscious, and it does so more or less silently. But it also makes a very considerable mess, mess of a kind that is unequalled by any other type of lethal weapon. Even a blade does not produce the same quantities of blood. The blade is used to damage those parts of the body which contain a large amount of blood, like the chest and the stomach, so that a certain amount of bleeding is inevitable. The victim will haemorrhage from the open wound and bleed from the nose and mouth. If they are left untreated they will haemorrhage until they die, leaving large pools of blood all around them. But a bludgeon is not used to damage those parts of the body which contain a large amount of blood; it is used to damage that part of the body which contains the *most* blood: the head. When you strike the head, blood will not quietly seep out from the wound, or slowly haemorrhage away. As each blow is delivered, blood will splash and spray in different directions. It will squirt up walls, over furniture, across the torso of the attacker. It will flick off the end of the soaking weapon as it is raised over the attacker's head. It will leave a devastating physical record of its presence.

Consider, for instance, what happens in a nose-bleed, the way in which blood seems to get everywhere in the early seconds before a handkerchief is found. Then consider the effect of a dozen or so such wounds: one thing becomes obvious. Whoever wields the bludgeon must be prepared to withstand all the exposures of evidence that it will bring.

Lucan, as far as we know, had made no such preparations.

His schedule probably did not incorporate the time that would be necessary to clean up all the signs of the attack. We are told that he wished to keep the murder a secret – indeed, it was vital if he was to avoid suspicion. He had gone to great lengths to plan the disposal of the body and to plot the circumstances of his crime. And yet he was prepared to execute the murder in a manner that – more than any other – would betray him.

Of course, you could start by saying that Lucan's intention was merely to cosh his wife and then strangle her when she was helpless. This would have the advantage of keeping the evidence of her demise to a minimum. But whoever attacked Mrs Rivett did not do that. He punched her in the face six or seven times and then landed about a dozen blows to her skull. He obviously wasn't concerned about the mess he was making.

One might suggest that Lucan did not *know* that his attack would produce that effect. This can't be ruled out, but it is surely unlikely. He had gone to great lengths to plan everything else. It is improbable therefore that he would have slipped up in this most vital area. One might also suggest that Lucan, being the attacker, simply lost control of himself, and that he was seized by a sudden, overwhelming ferocity. There was certainly a tendency for over-action. But that is not consistent with his poker-face manner or with his meticulous and premeditated plan. To have lost control of himself would have been to ruin everything.

Anyone who cast a glance around the carnage at Lower Belgrave Street could see that, either the killer was unconcerned about making an unholy mess, or that he had gone berserk. And both explanations seem unlikely to apply to Lucan.

Thirdly, there was the strange and baffling use of the canvas bag. It was assumed that Lucan intended to use the bag to transport his wife's body away from Lower Belgrave Street. But consider the use of *canvas* material in this exercise.

A canvas bag will not hold liquid. If someone bleeding from severe head wounds is placed in a bag that leaks, they are going to stain every surface that they come into contact with. There would be blood in the safe, in the boot of the car, in the boat. Of course, a *plastic* bag produces an altogether different result: a plastic bag will hold an enormous amount of liquid unless it is pierced.

You would naturally expect all this to be rather obvious to someone who is actually weighing up the effects of using different kinds of material in this exercise. If an attacker is going to make someone bleed profusely, and lose three or four pints of blood, and if he is intending to store their body for a period of time in the boot of a car or in a family safe, then he would be far more likely to choose a plastic bag for this purpose than a canvas bag.

So, again, it seems that the murderer of Mrs Rivett, in choosing the least likely method of concealment, was not worried about any of the things which Lucan should have been worried about: the timing of the plot, the mess that would be made, or the investigations that would have to be thwarted.

Dr Margaret Pereira, Senior Scientific Officer in the Biology Division at New Scotland Yard and an expert in blood-grouping (*Press Association/Topham*)

Home Office pathologist Professor Keith Simpson, who, at the inquest, gave vital evidence regarding the nature of the attack on Sandra Rivett (*Press Association*)

Ian and Susan Maxwell-Scott leaving their home in Uckfield, the last place Lord Lucan was seen before his disappearance (*Topham*)

Sarah and John Aspinall. Aspinall was the flamboyant owner of the Clermont, where Lucan gambled as a house player (*Syndication International*)

Michael Stoop. Lucan had borrowed his Ford Corsair, which was later found abandoned in Newhaven. The car was covered in bloodstains and a piece of lead piping, identical to the murder weapon, was found in the boot (*Press Association*)

Christina Shand Kydd, Veronica Lucan's sister (*Syndication International*)

Lady Veronica Lucan in November 1977. Just three years after the murder, the strain of the tragedy had clearly taken its toll (*Syndication International*)

Chapter Twelve

BUSTER

In the summer of 1986, twelve months after I had started my research, I met David Gerring. Gerring had now retired from the Metropolitan Police and was running a pub in Kent. It took me ages to find him. At first he was against the idea of being interviewed. It was not a question of money. He didn't want money. It was a question of the invasion of his private life, which he cherished.

The village where he ran his pub was one of the quietest and sleepiest in England. It had recently won an award, according to a sign I saw as I turned off the motorway, for being the most beautiful village in England. It was not hard to see why. The fringes of the village were guarded by poplars and oaks. To the south were the lush pastures of flat, postcard Kent. To the north the rivers Swale and Cant made their way through high valleys towards the sea. Inside the village itself, the scene was vividly English: red phone boxes, a tiny post office and general store, small timber-framed cottages at the end of stone-paved paths. Some of the cottages were lavishly overhung, with ivy and lilac. Some had unusual varieties of trees – quince and mulberry were two favourites – or formal beds ablaze with colour. Everywhere, it seemed, the place betrayed months of tireless Sunday pruning.

Gerring's pub dominated the village. The brewery had wanted to call it 'The Vanished Earl', but Gerring had resisted the idea. I arrived early for lunch and sat at the back with a glass of beer. Most of the people were regulars and had come for lunch in large family groups, straight from Sunday service. Glancing around, I fully understood why Gerring disliked the intrusions of writers and journalists. The only indication that he had participated in one of the biggest manhunts in criminal history came from a picture hanging on the wall of the restaurant. The picture was a cartoon of Gerring's retirement party. It was done in caricature. Gerring, enormously round, was looking at his farewell card, signed by his fellow officers, and the caption underneath had him saying: 'This bit here – "Best Wishes David, Signed LL" – check it for fingerprints!' Behind him, to the left, a moustached waiter in dark glasses was grinning slyly.

Far away, on the other side of the pub, I could see Gerring carrying trays back and forth from the kitchen. Occasionally he would put a tray down, hitch up his trousers, and stand in surveillance. Then his wife would call him and he would disappear. Finally, after about an hour, the place cleared. Gerring dispatched the last of his customers, and I came down from my seat to introduce myself (we had only spoken over the phone). 'You should have introduced yourself earlier,' he said. 'I thought you were a bloody sales rep.'

The last of his staff went home. 'Can't seem to get staff nowadays,' he said. 'Advertise as far away as Sevenoaks, but you can't get 'em. What d'you want for lunch then, so as I can tell the Ayatollah?' Eventually Mrs Gerring brought us egg mayonnaise and gammon steak. 'Been bloody busy today, always is at lunchtime. People get a good meal here for a fraction of what they'd pay in a restaurant. They all come at lunchtime; weekdays I get the publishing people over from Sevenoaks. They like it here. Can't get the staff, though.' He opened a bottle of wine. 'So, how is the publishing world? I'm always getting calls from you chaps.'

'Cutthroat.'

'Eh?'

'The publishing world is cutthroat.'

'Yeah.'

Before we approached the subject of Lord Lucan, I asked about his career in the force. He had started as a bobby, in south London, on seven pounds a week. He had been commended three times and he had lectured on criminal law at Hendon Police College. He had been involved in some of the most notorious cases of the last thirty years: the murder at Mr Smith's Club in Catford, the Richardson gang, the Spaghetti House siege. He had earned the nickname 'Buster' after his gangland raids in Croydon and Catford. On their retirements, he and Roy Ranson had been presented by the Nob Squad with blue satin ties, which bore the initial L in gold over a green coronet. I had spoken to Ranson earlier in the research, but it was really Gerring that I wanted to interview. Ranson had been based at Cannon Row. Gerring had been the man on the spot. While Ranson had coordinated things, Gerring had been out and about, conducting interviews, doing the experiments at Lower Belgrave Street, organizing the searches at Newhaven and elsewhere.

I asked him if he had ever thought about writing his autobiography. 'What for?' he replied.

'Money,' I said.

'Doesn't interest me now. I'm comfortable. I can afford to go away on holiday when I like. I make enough to keep everyone happy. I don't have the worries that I did, anyway.' He started to trail off, then came back, 'You know, it really makes me sick when I see these fellas selling their stories to the newspapers.' That same week a senior Scotland Yard officer had retired and sold his story to the *Sun*. 'I felt sick when I saw that. What would he get? Ten, fifteen thousand . . .?' He shook his head. 'I don't begrudge them the money, I just don't think they should do it.'

'A story to tell, then?'

'Eh?' He came back.

'Write your autobiography because you've got a story to tell.'

'Wouldn't want the publicity. You know, tours and speeches and so on. It's like on the Lucan case, when I told my wife I'd be back in time for breakfast. She didn't see me for about four days. I've had enough of that. I like it here. Me and the Ayatollah are going to enjoy it.' He called Mrs Gerring over and put his arm round her waist. 'How long've we been married, love?'

'Thirty-five years this year.'

He winked at me. 'Thirty-five years.' Then he gave Mrs Gerring an enormous slap on the backside and watched her disappear with the dishes.

Gerring was convinced of Lucan's guilt. At one point he gave me a discreet smile, raised his eyebrows and said, 'He did it, James, I can assure you of that.' But at other times he seemed to talk like a man who still felt that he had a case to prove. Our first meeting, one of several, took place before it had become fashionable to retrace the evidence with a doubtful eye, or to suggest that the police had got it wrong. In spite of this, Gerring was still prepared to go over the ground with me and answer all my questions directly.

My own impressions of Gerring were to an extent coloured by the warmth he projected. A reporter I knew, not given to hyperbole, had said that he liked Gerring 'immensely' and that he would trust him 'with my life'. It seemed a curious remark to me, but the reporter was a generation ahead of mine and remembered Gerring from his days with the Spaghetti House siege and the East End gangs. To him, Gerring's name had a different, grittier connotation than to someone writing about the English aristocracy.

After speaking twice to Roy Ranson, who had also retired and was also living in Kent, then working for the BBC, I had written:

A highly cautious man. Not intuitive but engages with the facts. Long pauses between what I say and his responses. Listens to every word you say and doesn't attempt to speak or interject until you have finished. Then he reacts. Obviously intelligent. Is prepared to be fair about all of the evidence – not to jump to conclusions. He feels he was misrepresented [over his cooperation with a particular journalist] but it's hard to see how. Perhaps he has a different agenda and sense of priority. Perhaps he's sensitive to internal police politics.

After the lunch with Gerring I wrote:

Tremendous charisma. A huge man [he was probably five foot seven, but stocky]. He enjoys his retirement. When he leaned forward at the table and rested his chin on his hands, his forearms bulged out as thick as thighs. Probably lugs great barrels of beer around singlehandedly.

Was a lecturer at Hendon. A charming man who is probably very popular in the village. A man's man. Highly coloured language and great flair. Talked with affection and some bemusement about women. A wide variety of topics. He obviously enjoys an argument in good spirits and likes the cut and thrust of a discussion. He can widen it out or home in.

Just right for a lecturer or, in retirement, a publican.

As far as Lucan is concerned it might have happened yesterday. No embellishment, a perfect, linear narrative of the story. Has everything fixed indelibly in the mind and can snap the facts out.

I arrived for the interview with Gerring with a list of about fifteen questions, though of course I was happy for the field to widen out once we had begun our discussion. I particularly wanted to explore with him the forensic problems, to try to clear up the matter regarding the blood.

I started by commenting on the ferocity of the attack. That, I said, was inconsistent with Lucan's motives. I said that it was also inconsistent with Lucan's motives to use a bludgeon and a canvas sack.

Gerring's response was twofold. First, he said, it had been 'incredibly dark' in the basement. Light did come in – *some* light – from the glare of a streetlamp on the pavement outside, but if the kitchen door was shut then that light didn't penetrate the breakfast room. Although it was possible to discern vague shapes in the blackness – the movement of a figure, the outline of furniture – it wasn't possible for anyone wielding a bludgeon to see how much blood his attack was producing. An attacker would not have been able to see blood spurting around the basement and would not have realized the extent to which his victim was bleeding. By the same token, he went on, the killer wouldn't have known that a canvas sack would be insufficient to hold so much blood.

'I tested the basement myself,' Gerring said. 'My sergeant, Graham Forsyth, had tested it with light meters but I wanted to do it for myself. You have to. And there was no way that Lucan would have been able to see just how much mess he was making with [the bludgeon].'

His second point was that Lucan did not have a sufficient grasp of the effect that his attack would have on his victim. Gerring had been a technical adviser on several television programmes, he said, including a leading crime series for ITV. When the programme makers had asked him how much blood they should show after a bludgeoning, they had, he recalled, been horrified by his advice: 'We go out at 9 p.m. We can't have that.' The average man who goes through life without experiencing the effects of violence at first-hand would not know what effect his attack would have. People striking with a bludgeon, he said, were likely to 'underestimate their own strength'. They were also likely to underestimate the effect of their assault. 'You're tensed up. You're on edge. The person appears and you cosh them. You'll always cosh them harder than you think, it's a natural instinct. And Lucan was an extremely powerful man.'

Then Gerring made a striking point. 'You know,' he said, 'the first thing that struck me when I arrived was the floor in the basement. It was that kind of wooden tiling. Parquet. I mean, if you're going to kill someone with a piece of piping then you do it in a room which can be cleaned up pretty fast. That basement had no carpeting. You don't hit someone in a carpeted room, do you? The basement was a premeditated site of attack, that was what struck me.'

Next, I asked Gerring about the claim that the attack on Sandra had started with a face-to-face confrontation. He returned to his point about the darkness of the basement. He added that several people who saw Lucan before the murder had said that he had been drinking. Selim Zilkha's girlfriend, who saw Lucan the night before, on the Wednesday, said:

We had a big dinner the night before the murder – a men's dinner with bridge and backgammon, at Selim's apartment in London. I was the only woman there. Lucky arrived early that night. Guests were asked for eight, but he came at seven-fifteen. He had had a lot to drink. I remember he also stayed very late. There was a parcel that Selim wanted delivered, and Lucky said that he would do it on Friday or Saturday. You see, the murder was on Thursday. He made an arrangement to do something on the day after, or two days after.

We had a film that night, *Black Orpheus*, for anyone who didn't want to play, but everyone drifted away to the tables. He was his complete normal self. We loved him. He was a great friend. We saw him several times a week. He was very charming and very intelligent. He loved his kids and was panicked by his wife's behaviour. He had been drinking so much. Otherwise you wouldn't make such a mistake.

It was certainly not beyond the realms of possibility that Lucan had been drinking to steady his nerves. Those who knew him well always spoke of his squeamish nature, his inability to stand violence. When dogs fought, said Bill Shand Kydd, Lucan would leave the room. And Lilian Jenkins remembered Lucan asking her to cover a cut finger with a plaster because he couldn't stand the sight of the wound. If he had decided to bludgeon his wife, therefore, it is reasonable to suppose that he would have strengthened his resolve with several stiff drinks beforehand. But it must also be remembered that those who saw him prior to the murder did not think he was drunk, and that drinking heavily would have robbed him of the meticulous precision and fastidiousness for which he was famous and which was vital to the success of his plan.

The day before the interview, I had assembled a section of notes under the heading 'Blood'. These listed all the contradictions in the police case about the distribution of blood in the basement and hallway. Prior to seeing Gerring I had spoken to Lucan's brother-in-law, the Reverend William Gibbs, an emphatic believer in Lucan's innocence. Gibbs had seemed a remote and aloof individual and he was not prepared to go into any great detail about Lucan or the inquest. But, he said, for anyone concerned about the evidence, the question of the distribution of blood was vitally important. There were 'problem' stains and smears everywhere you looked; spots of blood in the 'wrong' place; even blood outside the house, in the garden. 'No one ever mentioned going in the garden, did they?' he said.

Dr Pereira's evidence about the location of the blood

appeared at first to give a simple and clear picture of what had happened to Veronica and Sandra at their points of attack.

In the basement there was clear evidence of Sandra Rivett having been bludgeoned at the bottom of the basement stairs. There were radiating patterns of blood on the walls and splashes on the furniture and ceiling. The foot of the stairs was the obvious site of attack. There was also Group B blood, Sandra's grouping, outside in the yard, on a couple of leaves. And Dr Pereira had found Sandra's blood on Veronica's clothes and shoes.

As far as the attack on Lady Lucan was concerned, the forensic evidence indicated beyond question that it had taken place on the landing at the top of the basement stairs. Lady Lucan herself recalled going to the door of the basement, peering down, calling out Sandra's name, and being assaulted by a man who lunged at her from the cloakroom. Dr Pereira found Group A blood, Veronica's grouping, on the wall and ceiling of the ground-floor hallway, by the cloakroom, and more of Veronica's blood on the top of the basement stairs. Later, Veronica recalled how her attacker tried to force her down the basement stairs, how she hooked her leg through the banisters to stop him, and how one of the balustrades came away in the struggle. There was all the key forensic evidence to support this.

But Dr Pereira had also found Veronica's blood on the murder sack and in the kitchen at the front of the basement. There were two or three tiny drops, no larger than the end of a pencil, which the police had at first thought were gravy stains. How had these smears and drops appeared in the basement if Veronica had not gone down there?

Broadly, although the blood indicated that the points of attack were at the foot of the basement stairs and on the ground-floor hall, there were a number of smaller discoveries that didn't entirely endorse that conclusion.

The explanation which the police gave was of 'accidental

transference'. This certainly accounted for some of the discrepancy. The smear of Veronica's blood on the murder sack, for instance, could have been made, as Dr Pereira said at the inquest, when the police took Sandra's body, which was still in the sack, out of the house and into the van waiting in the street. Even though Veronica's blood on the wall upstairs would probably have dried, Sandra's blood on the sack would not have done, and when the two surfaces came into contact with each other it is entirely plausible to assume that some of Veronica's blood was smudged on to the sack. A photographer who was doorstepping the house remembered the sack coming out in plastic sheeting, but no one could remember if this had been wrapped round the canvas sack before it left the basement or once it was in the hallway ready to leave the house. Logic would have suggested the former. But logic does not always prevail. Perhaps the police took the sack up the basement stairs, brushing it against Veronica's blood, and then, on reaching the hall, saw that it was raining outside and sent someone out for the sheeting. There were other ways the canvas could have been contaminated, too. Perhaps one of the police officers, passing the Group A blood in the hall, smudged some of it off the wall, on to his sleeve, and then, when looking at the sack, perhaps peering in, transferred the Group A blood from his sleeve to the bag. That was not beyond the realms of possibility. Everyone who went down to the basement to examine the sack had to pass the large amount of blood-staining and smearing that was on the ground floor. And a great number of people had probably examined the sack. Sergeant Baker, the first uniformed officer on the scene, had done so. So had Sergeant Forsyth, the police officer from CID. Then there was Ranson and Gerring. A police surgeon, Dr Michael Smith, had examined the sack in order to certify death. And in between, there would have been the 'forty or so' policemen who turned up at the house 'wanting to see the body'. How likely was it, therefore, that some of the blood from the hall wouldn't get transferred to the sack?

That was the first discrepancy that could be explained by 'accidental transference'. But what of the Group B blood – Sandra Rivett's group – that had been found on Veronica's clothes? Several stains had been found on her jumper and dress. A smear of blood had been found on her left shoe, too, under the heel. The blood on the clothes had probably been acquired when Veronica was wrestling with her attacker. He would have been saturated in Sandra Rivett's blood and would inevitably have transferred some of it on to Lady Lucan. Similarly, the shoes could have become stained during the fight. Veronica said that the attacker pushed her to the ground and tried to force her through the basement doorway. There was a struggle, with both of them lying on the floor at the top of the basement. Veronica hooked her feet around the banister. She was, in her own words to me, 'as slippery as an eel'. Later, she got between her husband's legs, still on the ground, and grabbed his testicles. If he was drenched in Sandra's blood, and the two of them were wrestling at the top of the stairs, it seemed probable that some of the blood would transfer to Lady Lucan's shoe.

Gerring was dismissive of the controversy that had been whipped up about the blood. Accidental transference was inevitable, he said, where there was so much blood and so many people around. 'Come on,' he said, 'you've got blood splashed and sprayed everywhere – on walls, furniture, carpets. It was a blood bath in the basement and upstairs. Then you've got forty or fifty policemen and photographers and forensic walking around. Of course you'll get blood transferred. It would be a miracle if you *didn't*.' The smear of Veronica's blood on the sack, he said, was the result of its being brushed against the bloody walls on the stairs. Sandra's blood on Veronica's clothes and shoe was simply the result of her struggling with Lucan. The blood on the leaves outside came from the blood-stained shoes of the police officers who'd walked about. Sergeant Baker had gone into the garden. So had almost every other officer on the scene. To get there they had all walked over the blood-soaked carpet upstairs and through the basement. And the drop of Veronica's blood in the kitchen, Gerring said, could have been caused by a police officer 'or by one of the two cats in the house'.

Gerring made an analogy with wet paint. 'After you've finished painting and someone comes in and you say: "Mind that, it's wet . . ." and then you imagine forty people all coming in, how safe is your paint then?' Then he said, 'The thing is, you have to look at the picture as a whole. You have to read the whole evidence. Clearly, the whole picture says that Sandra was killed in the basement and Veronica was attacked upstairs. If you're going to start saying that Veronica *wasn't* attacked upstairs, that she was attacked in the basement, you've got to ask why you didn't find large quantities of her blood down there. It's no good going on stray bits and pieces. As a policeman, you have to go on the whole thing . . .'

By now twilight was coming. Our shadows were stretching out across the bar. The meal was over. Soon it would be opening time. We discussed briefly the problems of being a father to a teenage daughter, and then Gerring yawned and said, 'I think I've earned fifteen minutes in the chair.'

We shook hands, vowing to meet again for lunch in the future. Then I drove off, confused, into the Kent countryside.

Chapter Thirteen

THE COUNTESS OF LUCAN

I don't want to build a castle and moat around myself.
But sometimes, because of the reaction you get, you just
have to run away and hide a bit . . .

Alan Bleasdale

By now it had become clear that I would have to try to
arrange an interview with the Countess of Lucan. This
seemed a rather remote prospect, since she had become a
recluse, estranged from her family and former friends. Her
shopping was done for her by her milkman, who delivered
bread, eggs and cheese. Her neighbours in Eaton Row,
where she had moved after the murder, saw her 'very
occasionally', when she came out at night, perhaps, to leave
the rubbish for the dustmen. And she certainly never gave
interviews. One of the researchers on the Granada programme had written to her to inform her of the proposed
production and to ask her for an interview. By that time she
had evidently adopted a formal rebuttal which she would use

for all journalists and writers seeking to speak to her on the twentieth anniversary. 'I do *not* give interviews,' she wrote back, briskly. Three books had been published on the Lucan case but Lady Lucan had refused point-blank to see any of the authors. Without her cooperation, I felt that any book on the case would lack the confident and lucid ring of authenticity. She was the most vital surviving witness. It surprised me that three detailed accounts of the drama could be published to significant fanfare without any first-hand contribution from her.

My own approach to her therefore presented itself as the classic writer's dilemma. I was aware that a letter or telephone call would not be a suitable approach. My obsession with the case would not translate to paper and you could sink everything in a split-second if you rang up at an inconvenient moment. It was far easier to dismiss an unwanted presence by simply putting down a receiver than by closing the door in his face. That is why the door is the favoured battleground of everyone from religious zealots to insurance salesmen. Yet this realization didn't help much. Just because the telephone was out of the question, it didn't make the doorstep seem any more inviting. Impressions are quickly made, and there would be no second chance, no going back and trying again.

Finally, one day when I was sitting in the offices in Regent Street, sipping coffee and listening to someone drone on about a forthcoming meeting, I got an overwhelming sensation that the moment was right and that I should go round there. It was four o'clock in the afternoon. I picked up my briefcase and headed for the door. When I told Richard, the head of the company, where I was going, he looked at me and said, 'Like that?' Then I was gone, out into the flurry of Regent Street and Oxford Circus, down into the tube and across to Victoria.

I walked past the Plumbers Arms, not yet open for business, past number 46, glancing down at the basement to see how much of the interior was visible (I could see the sink and the kitchen work surface, but the venetian blinds weren't drawn), and then round the corner into Eaton Row.

Number 5 looked deserted. It also looked terribly shabby. One of the trees from the back garden of number 46 was hanging over the flat roof, and the driveway of the mews was covered in leaves. A top window was boarded over. The others were covered by grey net. Some workmen were busy at the far end of the mews, so I could not stand out of sight of number 5, as I would have liked to do, and spend a minute gathering my thoughts. Instead, when they turned round and saw me pausing in the entrance, I had no choice but to walk quietly and quickly up to the front door of Lady Lucan's house and ring the bell. I glanced back at the workmen. They knew who lived there all right, and they knew that I was not a social caller. At any rate, they acquired a sudden lethargy. Cigarettes were produced. They stood around chatting, watching surreptitiously.

I rang the bell again. I was just starting to think that – thank God – she was away, on holiday somewhere, when I heard the quietest of movements behind the front door. There was the sound of a chain being released, bolts being drawn back, keys turned. And finally the door opened and she stood there, quizzically, blinking at me.

I had a momentary glimpse of long grey hair and cold grey eyes, the latter made up with dark mascara. I launched into a brief explanation of who I was, saying that I was aware she disliked the intrusions of reporters but that I had certain questions for her, which would have to be addressed if I were to try to do justice to the story. She blinked a little more. Then she said, 'Have you got any identification?' Unfortunately, I had neglected to bring my wallet, so the only means of identification lay in my briefcase, which had a combination lock that entailed clicking round the digits to line up the correct sequence. The next few moments were spent in a pantomime attempt to balance the briefcase on one arm while I tried to fathom out the lock with my free hand.

Behind me, the workmen were watching, spellbound by this charade. Eventually, Lady Lucan said, 'Just a driving licence would *do*.'

I finally got the case open and produced a letter that I had received that week, from the press office at Scotland Yard, headed: 'Re: The Lord Lucan Case'. She held this very close to her face and looked it up and down, squinting. Then she handed it back and said, 'All right, you'd better come in for a moment.' The door opened just a fraction more, to allow me in.

The front door opened straight into the sitting room. I paused in the entrance while Lady Lucan replaced the assortment of bolts and chains and then led the way through. She switched on a little table light and asked me, 'Where do you want to sit?' I gestured to the sofa, a small, two-seat couch in velvet, and Lady Lucan sat on a matching armchair opposite.

I had been told that the mews was a dim and scruffy place. The broadsheets spoke of Lady Lucan living in 'reduced circumstances'. To the tabloids she occupied a 'shabby little cottage'. It was certainly true that the place was gloomy. The décor was dull and muted; faded wallpaper and yellowed skirting boards. But it was not unkempt.

The drawing room where we sat was densely furnished. Behind Lady Lucan, one whole wall was filled from floor to ceiling with books, including Lucan's leather-bound family volumes and the old paperback thrillers that he loved. On each shelf there were many family portraits. There were several photographs of Lucan in his various guises: the sportsman at St Moritz, the flabby golfer, the declining Earl with his sullen face and his worn out ermine. There were photographs of the children with their parents and studio portraits of them. There was also a Lenare photograph of Veronica which had been taken just after the wedding, when she looked immensely elegant and happy.

To my left a door led into a second room, the converted garage, which had become a storage area, filled with family papers. Lucan's old upright piano, which had been in the basement at number 46 at the time of the murder, was also in there. A flight of stairs led up to the kitchen and bedroom. To my right, underneath the window, was a small table with a brown tablecloth which was furnished with Lucan's medals and old sporting trophies. It looked a sad collection, financially worthless but encapsulating memories of vanished glamour. The window itself was studded with locks and hung with thick grey mesh. The mesh, she later said, was to foil 'the net brigade'.

On the wall above Lady Lucan, on a partition that was weakly aimed at giving the room some semblance of being cut off from the front door, there was a long portrait of an 18th-century cavalier. He was leaning flirtatiously against a curved scabbard. The painting looked badly in need of a clean. It certainly added to the air of faded grandeur in the house. Upstairs, I later discovered, there was another portrait, just head and shoulders, of a 19th-century ancestor. This was positioned behind the guest's chair in the kitchen, and at one point in the conversation I turned my head sideways very quickly to make a point and banged my temple against the gilt frame. The painting shuddered momentarily.

Lady Lucan herself was a fascinating figure. She was dressed simply in a skirt and cardigan, with a knitted woollen shawl across her shoulders. She could not afford to heat the house except at the extreme end of winter, she said, and as we talked I noticed grey ghosts of breath evaporating into the air from our mouths. Her hair was still long, though far more grey than blonde now, and still parted in the centre, so that every few minutes she would reach round and pull it out of her eyes. I noticed she did this most often when it came to starting a new sentence or delivering an answer to a question. It was like a psychological trigger, before the words came. She sat with her legs together and her hands rooted between her knees. She would lean forward and then lean back, as though in meditation. She gave out an air of tension and irritability, and I felt that a wrong word, or a phrase loaded with sensitive connotations, would provoke an aggressive reaction. I thought of Susan Maxwell-Scott's description of her, from the days when Lucan and Ian Maxwell-Scott met for weekends, with the two wives as golfing widows. 'She's a very tense little person,' she had said. 'I can never remember her relaxed. Whenever we talked she would perch forward, knees together, head forward, and the palms of her hands flat together with the fingers pointing away from her – rather like a person praying.' It was an exact description.

I had expected Lady Lucan to be weary of talking about her husband or the murder, to have in fact a kind of jaded, cynical indifference to the gossip and the misrepresentations. But she was as quick and as intense as she had always been. She rarely smiled, except bitterly, and her opinions were immutable, on almost every issue, the result of years of intramural reflection. She was constantly defensive, which was not surprising in the light of the rumour and counter-rumour that had been whipped up. 'The fact is that all the people who should have been closest to me never bothered to take me out or get me seen around town so that all these disgusting stories could be quashed. I can't go out on my own. A woman on her own is a social liability. People only send me invitations so they can say they've met the notorious Lady Lucan. If I go to a club I can see them all staring at me and imagining that I must have loads of money, which is nonsense.'

I remembered James Fox's impression of her:

She is articulate, witty, quick to react. She sees herself as under attack, and is quick to reply. But, off the subject of the social milieu in which she found herself [after marrying Lucan], she is a woman who was obviously a great deal more intelligent and perceptive than

200

her husband. Lucan may have sensed this.

The overriding suspicion is that no one ever tried to conduct a sensible conversation with her . . .

Her qualities were never weighed in that marginal, socialite world, where appearance counts a little too much, and from which she was impatiently dismissed. She felt she was branded a social embarrassment, but once remarked that it was her husband and his friends who were the embarrassment: 'that is why they have to stay at the Clermont Club all the time'.

During that first meeting the atmosphere was charged with potential friction and hostility. I was acutely aware that there were no ground rules, no parameters, and that I really had no idea what I could or couldn't bring up for discussion. In due course, at later meetings, it was to become clear that everything in the story could be addressed, without exception, from the murder to her life as a Clermont widow. Lady Lucan was quite capable of fending off questions on difficult topics. But for the moment that was unclear and I treaded warily.

'So, what is this book?' she asked. I told her that it was an account of the case with an emphasis on the character of her husband, who, I felt, remained an enigma even after so long and so much inquiry. She told me that she had been approached herself many times to write something. 'Let's face it, I could have written a book myself at any time, couldn't I?' But she disliked the idea of creating more media attention. 'I did do a first draft of my life story and I *was* going to do a book right after the murder with someone. But I decided against it both times.' I asked her what she did with her time; how long had she been living in Eaton Row? She said that she spent most of her time reading or studying. She suffered with arthritis, both osteo and rheumatoid, and this made it difficult for her to go out. I mentioned a recent newspaper article about her that had been pursuing the theme that she was a recluse. She had not seen it, she said. 'I am *not* a recluse and I resent people saying that I am.' Did I have the item with me? I produced a handful of cuttings from my briefcase. 'This man is going to get a sore ear,' she said. 'I go out as much as I can but not as much as I would *like*. I sometimes find it difficult just to get around the house, and in *this* weather . . .' Later, she added, 'The last doctor who saw me said I might have to have my left foot amputated because the bone was in such a bad condition. I can only get relief from it by putting a hot-water bottle on it.' Then she said, 'How dare these people make up these stories about me being a recluse? They obviously don't know what arthritis is like. I had to go to the dentist on Tuesday and when the taxi pulled up outside I couldn't even walk to the door. It's monstrous.'

She longed for the summer, she said, when the warmer weather made things physically easier for her. 'Just usual things, like going to the shops.' A kindly man at the bottom of the drive brought her fruit and newspapers each day. Usually he came in and they would chat together. Sometimes she would go and have supper with the man and his wife or with other friends in London. If she went on holiday she generally signed in the hotel register under an assumed name. 'It just makes things much easier.' In the evenings she might have friends round, mostly those she had known before her marriage. Contact with the Shand Kydds was sporadic but there were other friends to see. The children were busy with their lives. She made sure she did not spend long periods alone. She had disliked being alone ever since she was a child.

She had been living in Eaton Row since 1976, she said. The trustees of the marriage settlement had sold the house in order to clear her husband's debts. Most of the furniture had been sold, too. The house had been sold by private auction and the exact figure had not been disclosed. Lady Lucan now said it had been sold for £42,000. She thought that was 'wicked'. 'It was worth far more than that,' she said, but, 'I was alone and there was really nothing I could do to fight them. When debts are being cleared they really have the law on their side totally.' Later she added, 'They don't care what happens to you, as long as they get their money. They didn't seem at all concerned that there I was with three young children and no husband and all the nightmare of the debts. But this is the law.' At one point in a later conversation, when we were discussing a recent murder in which the husband, the murderer, had received an absurdly lenient sentence for killing his wife, Lady Lucan said, 'This is exactly the way the law treats women in our society.'

I had expected to talk just generally about the murder. There were bound to be stock answers to questions, rehearsed over the years. But Lady Lucan was lively and animated. She did not try to dominate the agenda. She left the topics to me and spoke at great length, spontaneously. She always seemed quite prepared to confront the issues.

'The club life is an odd life,' she said, when I asked her about her views on the Clermont. 'It's so unreal. It's one of the few institutions where that kind of snobbery and that level of prejudice can still exist. John was much cleverer than these people [presumably journalists and writers] think, because he actually exploited all this snobbery for his own ends. He looked like a lord and he acted like a lord when so many others do not. He was the genuine article and he knew that Aspinall wanted to have him around for that reason. So he exploited it.' She didn't think that he was particularly gambling-mad, in the way that some people suggested. 'If you're an earl's son,' she said, 'you can't work in a merchant bank all your life. He had to do something more in keeping with his background. It was the *life* he liked really, not just the gambling.'

She said it was not right to say that the Clermont had destroyed her marriage or that she had tried to change her husband after they had married. 'I used to enjoy going to the club,' she said, 'it was a waking up time. But let's face it – it's not the sort of thing you want to do all the time if you've got children and you're running their lives. That was where there was a conflict.' She had supported her husband in his profession, she said, at least in their early days. 'I knew he was a gambler. I therefore did a gambler's moll act with him. We posed as a happy holiday couple but we were in these situations to make money. Making money was the principal objective and we were a team.

'After the children arrived things were different. They *had* to be different. We then had responsibilities and we had to think of the future. We had to consider their welfare. But John couldn't see that. He couldn't see that we needed financial security for the future. Well, of course he *could* see it but he didn't want to *acknowledge* it.'

She told me that she had tried to persuade him to go into politics. 'He had a great presence and he spoke beautifully.' She had heard Aspinall say that her husband was planning on speaking before his disappearance on immigration in the House of Lords. That wasn't right, she said. He felt strongly about it but during their marriage they had decided that, since a maiden speech was supposed to be non-controversial, he should speak on sheep farming in Ireland. She grinned at me as she told the story. 'I can't really think of anything less controversial than that, can you?'

As the conversation developed I was surprised to find her more rigorous in her attacks on the women at the Clermont than on the men. 'The men were not really a problem,' she had said at one point. I returned to the subject later and she added, 'I was resented by the women not by the men. I got on with most of the men. We were all there to try to make money and there was a kind of camaraderie that went along with that. But the women were a different matter. Most of the women were just girlfriends or loose acquaintances of the male gamblers and of course there was a great deal of jealousy. They resented me because I had married one of the gamblers and they couldn't get their boyfriends to marry them. Not only had I married one of the gamblers but I had married *the* most attractive man in the Clermont. I had a handle to my name. Most of the women subsequently wouldn't speak to me or went out of their way to be rude to me.'

Dominick Dunne, in his article on the case for *Vanity Fair*, had spoken of Veronica being dubbed an NOC by the women at the Clermont: 'Not Our Class, darling.' I remembered, too, Stephen Raphael's suggestion that she came gambling to see that Lucan didn't 'get off with any of the girls'. 'He doesn't even *look* at any of them,' someone had said to Veronica one night at the club. 'Ah,' she had apparently replied, 'but *they* look at him.'

'Yes, of course I was worried by that,' she said to me. 'Sex was a big preoccupation at the Clermont. It was like a schoolboy mentality. People slept around a lot. I know for a fact that some of the men wanted their girlfriends to sleep with John so that they could find out what Lucky was like in bed.' Lucan, she said, 'wouldn't descend to their level'. 'They tried to drag him down to their level with so many things. They didn't have his background or his breeding and they were constantly trying to pull him down to their position. Naturally, that included sex. He was a private person and secretive and they couldn't stand that. They tried to plant prostitutes on him and all sorts of things. But he was faithful to me. If he had ever slept around it would have got back to me. It would have filtered back. It never did.'

On my second visit we talked about the murder. I had already decided by that point to be as candid as the fragile situation allowed, and to ask outright as many of the key questions that troubled the police case as I could. Veronica described the day of the murder, when the children had gone out in the afternoon with Sandra Rivett to post some letters. When they came back the five of them had tea together in the basement, which was one of the family rituals that she had come to cherish. Sandra rang her parents at eight o'clock and told them that she would be home for Christmas. They watched television in Veronica's bedroom and then Sandra put the youngest to bed.

Veronica was sure of the times. Frances had not even been in the room when Sandra went down to make the tea, so she could not say exactly what time Sandra had set out. When she went downstairs to investigate she had a sudden sense of danger. Then it was too late, she said. He was rushing at her in the darkness and she was hit. When she screamed it wasn't because of the pain – that came later – it was because of the terror she felt at the moment of attack. She also wanted to alert Frances. She found it, she told me, 'utterly incredible' that Frances thought she had been attacked by the cat and could go on watching television. I asked her how she had been able to survive the attack and the physical struggle. Lucan was a foot taller and several stones heavier. It was a key point against the police case. 'I was as slippery as an eel,' she said, 'and every time he tried to grab me and strangle me I kept slipping out of his grip.' One woman could remember Veronica 'moving like lightning' when she crossed the room. I saw this myself once, when she went to get a document from upstairs and she seemed almost to glide across the sitting room. She was gone in a moment.

After the struggle, she said, they sat on the stairs, panting. Lucan was emotionally and psychologically wrecked. He was crying with the ordeal. She asked about Sandra. Sandra, he said, was dead. The basement 'was a ghastly mess'. She, Veronica, must *not* go and look. When she had first asked about Sandra, Lucan had said that she had gone out. Veronica had said, 'But she wouldn't go out without telling me.' And Lucan had then replied, 'All right, she's dead. She's down there.' They both peered down into the blackness of the basement, the stairs disappearing into a well of darkness.

'I knew then that I had to play for time,' she said. One of

the most striking moments of the account was when she described momentarily glancing behind her towards the front door. Her husband's head was bowed. He was trying to think about what to do next. Discreetly, she said, Veronica inched her head sideways and looked out of the corner of her eye at the front door. She wanted to establish whether it was close enough for her to risk running for it there and then. 'I remember,' she said, 'the door seemed miles away. The corridor was very dim. There was only the streetlight coming in through the glass over the door.' She remembered, she said, seeing the number 46 reversed on the glass. That memory had stayed with her all the years.

It was a constant concern to historians of the case that Veronica had never publicly disclosed what had happened between the attack and the moment when she fled the house. How had she persuaded her husband to stop attacking her, not to mount another assault when his strength returned? How had she tricked him into taking her upstairs? Didn't it suggest that, since Lucan gave his wife succour, he took her upstairs and tended to her wounds, that in fact he was innocent, that he had just stumbled in on the situation?

I brought the matter up. Would she say what had passed between the couple? It was no secret, she said, there was no mystery to it. She had simply calmed him, cajoled him even, in order to make her own getaway.

With some considerable ingenuity, she had told him that Sandra had no friends to speak of and her family lived miles away. She hadn't seen her husband for months. No one would make any fuss over her disappearance. They could get rid of the body together and then Lucan could go and meet his friends for dinner. Lucan thought about it for a moment. Veronica remembered thinking that she was going to pass out. Her neck was wrenched and she was bleeding badly from the forehead. If she passed out, she knew she would die. She struggled to keep alert while Lucan pondered. Sensing that she was slipping away, she said that, as an alternative, he could meet his friends for dinner and *she* would call the police and tell them that she had been attacked by a burglar. She would tell them that the attacker had killed Sandra, left Veronica for dead, and then vanished. Lucan need not even be brought into it.

Lucan said, 'I must make a decision.' Did that mean a choice between giving himself up or escaping? Or did it mean a decision about taking his own life? Before Veronica could discover what he meant he repeated, 'I must make a decision.' And then he asked her whether she had any sleeping tablets. That was the chance she had been waiting for. Some movement between the rooms would perhaps provide a chance to escape. Yes, of course she had sleeping pills, but they were upstairs. Lucan then asked her if she would take an overdose. He said they had to go away together and she must take an overdose. It was not clear, she said, whether Lucan would also kill himself, or whether it was merely Veronica who had to die. She placated him further. She would do anything he asked, she said, if only she could lie down somewhere. Would he let her lie down? Lucan heaved her to her feet. She could lie down upstairs. He would clean her up and then they must leave together and she must take her pills. She went into the cloakroom to get a drink of water. She knew that her chance was coming. He 'frog-marched' her upstairs and into the bedroom. The television was turned off. Frances went to bed. Veronica lay down. Her husband went into the bathroom. 'He was the one who said that he had to make a decision,' she said, 'but in the end *I* made the decision. I made it for both of us. I waited until I heard the taps running and then I got up. I had about four seconds to decide. I got up and crept out of the room. Then I ran like hell.'

The winter began to deepen. Snow slanted across London and ushered in what were, for Veronica Lucan, the most painful months of the year. The anniversary of November

7th had just gone, so had her husband's birthday and her own wedding anniversary. But the pain was physical. When I called round she was upstairs in the kitchen boiling two saucepans of water for a hot-water bottle. 'This *wretched* weather,' she said. 'It's enough to *make* you go abroad.'

Her temper was bad that day. She was in acute pain and I decided not to stay for very long. Anyone who called round and so forced you to adopt the attentive courtesy of the host made himself a nuisance if you were actually in physical pain and needed to rest. When I came to leave, I noticed that ice was beginning to snarl at the window. I told her to call me if she needed anything. 'Oh no,' she said, 'I'm quite all right. There's nothing I can do for the pain except wait until the weather gets better.'

A week later I returned. She was brighter; the pain was a little easier. We picked up the thread again and I got the impression now that she was enjoying the talk. It was not necessarily my company. She and I, after all, had nothing in common, and although I felt we got on, it was obviously much more that she enjoyed the process of going over the ground again with someone who knew the history of the case, who didn't have to have gaps filled in for them.

I asked her about the months preceding the murder, particularly the aftermath of the custody case. His state of mind in those last few months, I said, was fascinating to the outside observer. 'Complete devastation,' she said. 'He was shaken in a way that had never happened to him before.' On what had he based his confidence? 'He was an arrogant man,' she said. 'He was probably the most arrogant man I had ever met, even in the Clermont circuit. He hoped that I would crack under the strain of his campaign against me.' After a pause she said, 'You know he used to write his own solicitor's letters. That's how arrogant he was. He thought he knew the law better than the lawyers. He used to sit down and write the letters and then post them off to the solicitor with an instruction for him to sign them and send them on to me. I only found out about that later.' It was the same earlier in the marriage, with the doctors. 'The medical profession and the legal profession are complete scoundrels, you know. I had doctors basing their diagnosis of me entirely on what my husband told them. Instead of looking at the situation and saying, "He's a gambler, she's a housewife, therefore there are *bound* to be conflicts," all they could see was an English earl and they totally believed what he said. He didn't have an awful lot to occupy his mind so he became a sort of amateur psychologist and he used to tell the doctors what he thought was wrong with me. They had the attitude of awestruck guardsmen. For me it was an awful and depressing time.'

She said that Lucan had been 'deeply affronted' when he lost the custody case. It had been an affront to his ego and his pride. Worse than anything, she said, it had made him look a fool. 'He had gone around telling everyone that he was going to win and that the courts couldn't fail to see his argument, only to have to concede after two weeks. That took some explaining,' she said. 'It got back to me afterwards that he used all the usual excuses. He would say that things are always weighed in favour of the mother and against the father in these matters. He told people that no matter what you did as a husband it was always against you. He had to trot out the usual lines.'

How far had things degenerated between them before the murder? She thought that personal relations between them remained cool but not irreparably bad. 'Susan Maxwell-Scott said in her statement to the police that she was surprised to hear that we had split up because she had thought we had an established marriage. It was a stable marriage for a long time. Even after he left there was talk of reconciliation.' She resented the suggestion from journalists and writers that she and her husband had been on terms – to use one writer's expression – of 'cordial hatred'. 'It appalls me that people can write that,' she said, 'because it's so untrue. He didn't hate me and I certainly didn't hate him. He was my husband. There wasn't even an official separation between us and there was certainly no talk of divorce. There was a battle to get the children, of course, but I felt then and I have always felt that we were soul mates and the feelings we had for each other transcended those difficulties.'

Why hadn't there been a reconciliation, I asked. Why had things degenerated to the point of murder? 'The murder was about money,' she said. 'It was purely financial. He decided that he was about to go bankrupt and he had to save the reputation of the family. The only way he could do that was either to win a terrific amount at the tables – which obviously he couldn't – or to get hold of the house and sell it as fast as he could. Since I was firmly in place at the house he had to get rid of me. It was a calculated act. There was no personal feeling involved.'

I recalled Greville Howard's statement in which he and Lucan had discussed Lucan's financial problems. Lucan had said that getting rid of his wife and dumping her body in the Solent would enable him to clear his debts and rescue himself from bankruptcy. That statement certainly corroborated Veronica's own assertions about his motives.

Even towards the end, she went on, there was talk of reconciliation. Veronica would often ring him up to talk the prospect over with him. He had spent some nights away from the house even before he left for good in January 1973, and when he *did* finally leave, she said, she didn't believe that it would be permanent. 'I just thought he would come back again. He always used to come back. Sometimes he would spend a night away because it was very late when he finished gambling and he didn't want to disturb us. Sometimes he would spend the night away because we had had words. But always he would reappear in the morning and we would laugh about it over breakfast and start again. That's why it was an established marriage. Then, in January, he decided on a longer break away. The problem with that was that once

211

you have moved out and you've told everyone you've moved out then it's very difficult to go back. You lose face if you go back. And of course none of his friends *wanted* him to go back, so they would do everything they could to keep us apart. Some of them acted as *agents provocateurs*. There was a concerted effort in the Clermont Club to stop him coming back because they didn't much like me and they preferred him to remain single. Sometimes they would ring him up and tell him things about me and sometimes they would ring me up and tell me things about him. They were completely mischievous. He was more manipulated than me, though. He told me that he would like to be part of the family again but that it was difficult for him to lose face.'

That tied in with the recollections of Lucan's friends and family who had spoken to Sally Moore. Lilian Jenkins, the former nanny who became Lucan's housekeeper after the separation, said that Lucan told her that Veronica was often ringing him up to discuss the possibility of going back. His brother, Hugh, recalled how Veronica wanted a reconciliation but how Lucan felt unable to go through with it. His words to Hugh were, 'It cannot be.' Even on the night of the murder, Veronica had asked him why he never returned, and he had replied, 'It can never be now.'

When the spring came, late in April, the house seemed to shed its air of melancholy. The warm sunshine lifted away the dreariness that had hung about all winter. In May the air was sweet and dry, thick with the dust from the road and the smell of lilac from the garden of number 46. Veronica took to sitting at her top window, the lace curtains blowing around her like ghosts. She would sit there all afternoon, enjoying the sunshine, watching the comings and goings in the road below. She munched on apples and drank long tumblers of fruit juice.

Lucan was far from her mind. 'I got myself right,' she said, 'by eating decent food like this and by learning not to worry.'

The arthritis was still painful and she was perpetually sending off for books and magazines which described new treatments. She had developed another new friendship, she said, with a widow round the corner. They sometimes shopped together, and since the woman bought more or less all the newspapers each day she monitored the press on Veronica's behalf to see what was being said about her. Veronica was not hostile to the press. If a journalist called she was always cordial at the door. People expected certain standards and even if one was not going to give interviews you had to be polite. She did mind, however, when journalists were offensive about her or got it wrong. She did not like mistakes and was quick to draw people's attention to errors when they were made.

That spring she also produced the photograph albums and Lord Lucan's diaries. I had told her in a previous conversation that the Dowager Countess had lent Lucan £4,000 at the time of the custody hearing. She was not aware of that, she said. 'I didn't know that: you've put me on to something.' Later she told me that she had accounted for all his debts, but when she was going through his diaries she had come across an entry that perplexed her. The diary was produced. Lucan's handwriting was a tiny black scrawl, like a thin column of ants making their way over the page. The entries were, on the whole, brusque and businesslike. 'It's this entry here,' she said. 'Three hundred pounds. But no name.' I looked at the entry, repeated again a week later, and we pondered on whether it had been a fee for the private detective.

The photograph albums had all the careful cataloguing typical of the aristocracy. There were photographs of the most obscure relatives and domestic servants. 'That was the nanny who looked after him when he was a boy,' Veronica said, at one point, when I gestured to a faded black and white photograph of a woman in pre-war clothes. 'Her name was Elizabeth Coles. She was extremely right-wing and they used to call her Red Hot. That was her nickname. She was the kind of nanny you saw a great deal of in London forty or fifty years ago, but which you never see now.' There were photographs of the children in the United States, on Mrs Tucker's vast estate at Mount Kisco, Westchester. There was a photograph of Mrs Tucker herself, what Veronica called 'a rare photo of her', a small, bird-like woman under sunglasses and a wide-brimmed hat. The family's connections with Mrs Tucker had been maintained, Veronica said. George's education at Eton had been paid for by the family trust fund, but Camilla and Frances, who had both gone to St Swithun's, Veronica's old school, had had their fees paid by Mrs Tucker.

Shortly before the murder, Veronica went on, Lucan had flown to America to ask Mrs Tucker for a loan of £250,000. He wanted to try to 'buy' the children from Veronica. It was a 'monstrous' scheme, she said. He had already approached Jimmy Goldsmith, in Paris, and other friends in London. Goldsmith had said, 'I don't like loans. I'll *give* you the money.' But Lucan didn't want that. So Goldsmith guaranteed a £5,000 overdraft for him at the Midland Bank. Mrs Tucker, Veronica said, was less forthcoming, in spite of her huge wealth. According to her son, Luther, she thought Lucan's idea was 'crazy'. The correspondence from Lucan to Mrs Tucker read:

Although I have made my proposals in the bluntest possible way, as being a straight purchase of the children by you, on my behalf, the offer would naturally have to be dressed up in order to give Veronica the maximum amount of face-saving. It may seem incredible to you that she would entertain such a monstrous proposal, or that it should be necessary to go to such extreme lengths when a solution should be available in the courts. But I am reasonably confident that the offer would be considered by her. I regret having to involve you and your family in my domestic problems, but I did everything I possibly could in court.

If I could have afforded to battle on there would have been an appeal. But even if we were still successful in keeping the children there would be nothing to prevent Veronica from going back once a year to ask for their return.

The financial solution would have the advantage of Lady Lucan herself applying to the courts to return the children to me.

In a way, this would be more binding on her than a court order based on a relapse – alleged to have been temporary – in her mental health.

Luther had written back to ask what alternatives there were to this 'buy-off' plan. Lucan had replied, 'Only more court action. All the alternatives would involve legal struggles with a hostile and obstructive Lady Lucan.' Mrs Tucker quietly refused him the cash.

I thought the 'buy-off' plan was vital when one considered Lucan's motives. His friends and family argued that he would never have committed murder because, in the words of his brother, Hugh, 'he wanted a solution through the courts . . . he still hoped to gain custody of them legally'.

But the 'buy-off' plan disproved that. It showed that Lucan had given up on the idea of further court action; that, as early as November 1973, the date on his first letter to Mrs Tucker, he was considering extra-legal initiatives.

On my fourth visit, Lady Lucan invited me up to the kitchen, to share the sunshine. I had arrived on a sweltering day in July, just as she was throwing open the curtains and listening to the lunchtime news on the radio. In my estimation, I told her, I had lost about four stone on the train journey through London. I had a thumping headache, and I had been foolish enough to consume a glass of cold beer at the Plumbers

Arms, without stopping for lunch. 'Well, sit down and I'll find you something to eat.' She offered me 'a casserole thing that you can buy in these packets', which I declined, in deference to the heat. We settled for some toast and some fresh fruit.

I asked her about reported sightings of her husband and how she reacted to them. Veronica shrugged. She had 'no doubt' that he was dead. 'No doubt at all.' 'If he had access to a gun,' she had told Ranson, in 1974, 'he would have used it.'

At one stage, while we were flicking through the photograph albums, we came across a picture of him bobbing up and down in the Channel following the disintegration of his boat, *White Migrant*. Veronica tapped the photograph and said, 'That's how he went. I'm sure of it. Drowned himself . . .' She told me of an incident in the late 1960s when Lucan had got involved in a motor insurance deal which went badly wrong. 'The police were called in and there was a terrible fuss and he said to me then, "You do realize, Veronica, that if all this is made public I shall have no alternative but to kill myself." '

Later on she said, 'I know you *think* I think about this question an awful lot. But I don't. I used to. It was unbearable at first. But now I don't think about it at all. I suppose it *is* possible that he's still alive. No body has ever been washed up. But it's pointless for me to speculate, because things would never be the same even if he did come back.

'I think he went down to Newhaven and got on board his boat and sank it in the Channel.'

Finally, I asked her about her memories of Sandra Rivett. She had a photograph of Sandra, taken shortly before her death, sitting on a rug in the drawing room at Lower Belgrave Street. It was another 'rare photo'. 'Poor Sandra. What can one say? It's the most ghastly tragedy. We got on well together. It was not like the usual employer and employee relationship. We were friends. She was by far the best nanny we had had for a very long time. She had been working for this elderly couple in Paddington and she had been wanting to come for ages. She had originally come to see me months before, but there wasn't a vacancy. But I kept her name and rang her when a vacancy came up, because she seemed so nice. She jumped at the chance. We enjoyed each other's company and we laughed a lot.'

What, I asked, had Sandra thought of Veronica's situation, and of Lucan? 'She was very sensitive to my situation. She would call me on her day off if she went anywhere. She used to say I was vulnerable. She *did not* like my husband. She saw him far more than I did because she used to hand over the children when he came for them at access. Often I didn't want to face him. She would hand them over and then come and find me and tell me what he'd been wearing and how he'd seemed and what his manner was like. She was very loyal to me. But she thought he was a strange man. I used to tease her and say that he was looking for a girl and she was just his type. She was bright and friendly. We would laugh about that. She would say, "No fear".'

Then Veronica said, 'She told me once that he frightened her. I suppose that sounds melodramatic in hindsight, all these years later. But that was what she said. He called round one day and she dealt with him and afterwards she came into the kitchen and said that she found him frightening. He *could* be intimidating with that great height and bearing.

'I knew what she meant.'

Chapter Fourteen

'ALL MY DOING . . .'

Lucan had attacked Veronica. I felt sure of that. Or at least, I felt sure that *she* was sure of that. The description was so disturbingly graphic and vivid. And anyway, if she had been lying the truth would surely have emerged by now. She had been in and out of hospitals and had had psychiatric treatment. She had also been prescribed a variety of drugs. Somewhere along the line, when the conscious was diverted by inner psychiatric problems, the unconscious, the storehouse of truths, would surely have asserted itself. Whatever might have lain hidden would have emerged. But there had never been anything to throw doubt on her original story.

And yet, the evidence for Lucan's attack on Sandra Rivett still did not tally. The ferocity of the assault; the use of the bludgeon; the attack starting face-to-face. Consider, too, the difference in the nature of the injuries sustained by the two women. Sandra was hit in the face with a fist. She was then struck about eleven times with a length of lead piping. Her attacker was not concerned about the mess he was making. He seemed to have lost his nerve. And it was not an *accurate*

219

assault by any means, for he missed his target, which was the skull, more than half a dozen times. Blows were landed to the shoulders, the hands, the face and the arms.

Yet the attack on Veronica was very different. It was much more precise. There were five or six blows and they were staggered in an exact V-line across her forehead. They were so exact that the casualty officer at St George's was unable to tell where one blow started and the other ended. And yet, in spite of their precision, Veronica was able to survive this attack. She did not lose consciousness, even for a moment. She was able to scream and to fight back. So we might conclude that, although it was a more precise attack, it was not delivered with the same ferocity as the attack on Mrs Rivett. It was delivered by someone who was much more controlled – controlled enough to really *aim* their blows – but who also lacked the nerve to make those blows fatal.

For many years, those who knew John Lucan argued that the murder of Mrs Rivett did not suggest his hand, because it was a sloppy and imprecise attack, uncharacteristically inept and brutal. But if the attack on Sandra Rivett does *not* suggest the hand of John Lucan, the attack on Veronica Lucan surely *does*: it was exact and precise, but it also had the reluctance and reticence of someone innately squeamish.

Of course, this ostensibly serves to make things seem even more complicated than they already are. How could it be that Sandra Rivett was brutalized by one man, and Veronica by another? How could it be that, if Sandra was killed by one man, a twin bludgeon should be found in the boot of another man's car?

There have been many theories put forward over the years to account for the mysteries at Lower Belgrave Street. We remain in a vacuum of uncertainty and unknowing, and this situation is likely to persist indefinitely. It seems as if the murder will probably never be solved. But under the present circumstances, we can at least address all of the theories that have been advanced and draw a conclusion about which is the most probable.

Here, to my mind, is something that would fit.

Lucan, it was well-known, was desperate to regain the custody of his children. He also wanted to regain possession of the house where they lived. Having sought action through legal channels, and having failed to find a solution, he decided to act directly. He decided, in short, to kill his wife. But he was squeamish and unable to face doing the deed himself. His friends have testified, most notably in Sally Moore's book, about how he 'hated the sight of blood', 'couldn't stand violence', and that he would never have had the stomach for murder. Therefore, if the deed had to be done, and he had convinced himself that it did, then it needed the skill of a professional assassin.

So he resolved to hire a hitman, just as Veronica had feared that he would. But there was a flaw to Lucan's plan: his arrogance. Instead of letting the hitman choose the method, Lucan himself decided that the man must wield a bludgeon. It will be remembered that Lucan was adept at telling people how to conduct their business: from private detectives to solicitors and psychiatrists. As far as Lucan could see, the bludgeon was an ideal weapon for the murder of his wife. Silence was vital if the children were not to be disturbed, and, as Gerring said, Lucan believed that the killing would not produce an excessive amount of blood if it was done in a controlled fashion. He did not foresee that, for some reason, his killer would lose all control, perhaps through drunkenness, perhaps through nerves, and make a ghastly mess of the quick, neat job that Lucan wanted.

So, Lucan found a length of lead piping and wrapped it in surgical tape. The tape would have strengthened it and helped to soak up the little amount of blood that Lucan expected to be produced. Then he remembered that the ceiling of the breakfast room was rather low. Anyone over six feet tall would have difficulty in raising a sixteen-inch bludgeon over his head. So Lucan made a second piece, only nine inches, and kept both pieces in the boot of his car. He also looked out one of his old canvas sailing bags, which he'd used in his powerboat days to store boots and clothes when at sea. That would do for the body.

On the night of November 7th he met up with the hitman at his flat. He gave him the smaller of the two bludgeons (still leaving the original in the boot) and drove him round to Lower Belgrave Street for eight-thirty. He would have told him that his victim was a small, slight woman, who would be carrying a tea-tray. Once he had done the deed he was to place her body in the canvas sack and then leave through the front door, pulling it shut behind him.

Then he set off for the Clermont, to establish his alibi at the door, with the chat to Billy Egson.

When he returned to Lower Belgrave Street, Lucan would have let himself in through the front door. He would have expected to find the body of his wife, doubled up in the bag, perhaps a tray of broken crockery at the foot of the stairs. He would have expected a few splashes of blood on the parquet floor, which he would clear up with an ordinary cloth. Then he would put the body, the cloth and the lead piping into the family safe by the stairs. Of course, it might be asked why Lucan didn't simply give the hitman the code to the safe and allow him to stash the corpse away. But that would have entailed exposing the code of the safe. And besides, Lucan would want to be sure that everything had gone according to plan. He would want to be certain that there were no signs of the murder in the basement and that the three children were safe and unharmed. Allowing the hitman to put the body in the safe might have permitted him to establish a cast-iron alibi, but it would have prevented him reassuring himself that his master plan was progressing smoothly. So, he returned to the house, from the Clermont, expecting to find Veronica dead.

But it didn't work out like that. When Lucan came down the basement stairs he slipped in a pool of blood on the parquet floor. That would have alerted him at once. He would have pushed open the kitchen door and thrown a beam of light from the street outside on to the carnage in the breakfast room. He would have seen the blood across the furniture, the walls, the ceiling, the two huge pools leaking on to the floor from the mailbag. He might have gone over and looked at the contents of the bag, to check that his wife was dead, or he might simply have decided to begin cleaning up, perhaps thinking that no one could have survived such a violent attack.

Picking up the piping, he would have gone upstairs to start sponging the blood from his trousers. Perhaps he still intended to try to clean up the mess and conceal the crime. Perhaps he thought there was still a chance to rescue the situation, in spite of the carnage: the nanny was not due back for another couple of hours, after all. Alternatively, he could simply leave the house as it was, with Veronica dead in the basement, and wait for Sandra to get home and make the grisly discovery. If he took a few items of value from the house, and smashed a window in the basement, there would be the obvious deduction of a murder committed during burglary.

The answer to all these possibilities came as he stood in the cloakroom, sponging off the blood. It was then that he heard the sound of his wife's voice in the hall. His blood would have run cold. It would have dawned on him that the hitman had in fact got the wrong woman, that he had killed the nanny by mistake.

Suddenly cornered, Lucan would have leapt out of the cloakroom. Fired by panic, reacting instinctively, he would have attacked Veronica with the lead piping. But the piping was seriously distorted by the attack on Mrs Rivett. It was therefore ineffective as a weapon. Additionally, Lucan didn't have the stomach for murder. He was 'incredibly squeamish'.

He 'couldn't stand the sight of blood'. So when he leapt out of the cloakroom, his blows to Veronica's head lacked the ferocity that would have made them fatal. They were delivered with Lucan's customary precision but they did not have the kind of impact that was needed even to render her unconscious. Subsequently, she was able to stagger away and to scream for help.

In due course their fight ended and the couple agreed to talk things through. Lucan spoke about making a decision. They retired to the bedroom and Lucan laid a towel out on the bed. While he was in the bathroom, Veronica decided for both of them. She got off the bed, crept out of the house and escaped to the Plumbers Arms.

The hitman theory is not supported by any direct evidence. It is true that the police never found a blood-stained glove or any other concrete evidence of a third party at the house that night. But the theory is nonetheless the most persuasive of all those advanced since the murder. The idea of a second man, acting independently, surprised by Lucan, has been discounted. The police discredited Lucan's story of witnessing a fight. Similarly, the idea that Lucan *himself* carried out both crimes does not tally with the mess that was made in the basement or with the idea that Lucan would make a mistake over identity.

It can only be assumed that the killer, through inexperience or alcohol, lost control of himself, and, instead of making the neat job of the killing that Lucan had instructed, made the most appalling mess of it.

Afterwards, finding himself covered in blood, the hitman decided not to risk leaving via the front door. He went over to the french windows, unhooked them, and stepped out into the garden, looking for an alternative means of escape. In doing so, he trod heavily in the pools of blood, leaving the 'two or three large footprints' that Sergeant Baker would see when he arrived. He also dripped blood on to the leaves outside. Finding no way out, he came back in but he did not lock the back door. That is why Baker found it unlocked when he tried the handle (a fact that remains inexplicable if Lucan was the killer). He then left via the front door, never to be seen again.

It is for this reason that Lucan was able to speak so spontaneously about disturbing an intruder. The story came easily to him because, in a sense, there was a vein of truth in it. There *had* been a second man in the house. He *had* killed the nanny. Lucan *had* been falsely accused of murder. When he rang his mother, immediately after leaving the house, he was able to describe the horror of the basement in a completely convincing fashion. 'Oh, Mother, there was something dreadful in the corner, I couldn't bring myself to look.' This has the ring of truth to it.

Furthermore, Lucan wrote in his last letter to Shand Kydd: 'For George and Frances to go through life knowing their father had been in the dock for attempted murder would be too much.' The phrase 'attempted murder', not murder, is highly significant. Lucan was not guilty of the murder. But he already foresaw the charge of attempted murder being formed against him.

The hitman theory is the only theory that reconciles all the outstanding conflicts of evidence. It is supported by many of the findings at Lower Belgrave Street. It explains the discrepancies in the police case. And it is the only account of events which succeeds in reconciling Lucan's version of events with that given by his wife.

Chapter Fifteen

EVENS

As a gambler, I would give even odds on whether he is
dead or alive.

John Aspinall, 1975

Death is better than dishonour. And what of luck? Roy
Ranson's chief reason for his assertion that Lucan had killed
himself lay in his reading of the aristocratic mentality. 'If you
look at the last letters,' he said to me, 'you can see the tone is
very negative. I think he would rather have killed himself
than appear on a murder charge. I think he went off and
committed suicide, hoping never to be found again.'

That view certainly had its advocates. In the inner circle
there was almost a unanimity about what had happened. The
favourite term, reflecting the prevailing military culture, was
that Lucan had 'fallen on his sword'. Aspinall talked of him
meeting his death by drowning. Shand Kydd, asked if he
thought Lucan might be alive, said, 'Of course not.' And Sir
James Goldsmith, in Geoffrey Wansell's biography, *Tycoon*,
was quoted as saying, 'The reason why I'm convinced he is

dead is that he was so English the idea of him living anywhere else but England is absurd . . . He was a murderer because he went mad under the pressure, but I don't think his code would have allowed him to do anything except fall on his sword when he realized what he'd done.' The journalist James Fox thought that he would have been unwilling and unable to survive outside his narrow world of friends. Sally Moore inclined to the same belief. Lucan's mother also said she thought her son was dead. And the writer Norman Lucas, in his book on the case, said:

> The failure to find Lord Lucan's body is perhaps the strongest argument against the presumption of his death, but there is an equally strong objection to the assumption that he is still alive: how does he manage to maintain himself?
>
> He is fitted neither by training nor temperament to the rigours of workaday life. His tentative ventures into the business world were not very successful and he possesses few qualifications for earning a living. What could he do? Become a winter sports instructor, a rowing coach or boatman, a barman or croupier? None of these would bring him the sort of money he was accustomed to handling. Even on his income of £12,000 a year he ran hopelessly into debt and was obliged to take recourse to moneylenders. Because of his high standard of personal living he would not be likely to endure for very long the hardships and discomforts of a frugal existence. The one thing that would be left would be the gambling tables, but in spite of his soubriquet of Lucky he was neither very lucky nor very skilful in his adventures in the green baize jungle.

The theory that Lucan had killed himself rested on the key points that he had been morally and psychologically crushed by what had happened, and that, in the words of one friend, 'he would have found the murder on top of everything else just too much.' How valid was this? Certainly, he had been deteriorating for some time. He was obsessed with his children and obsessed about his finances. In the letter to Michael Stoop he talked about being 'destroyed'. He gave a last message to the children. There was no more talk of lying doggo. Later that day the Lucans' GP, Christopher Powell-Brett, was asked by the Dowager Countess why Lucan hadn't got in touch, as he promised, and Powell-Brett had said, 'Don't forget, he has been under the most fearful strain these past six or seven years.' Could Lucan, with his master plan awry, his last hopes of rescuing the old life finally gone, have simply picked himself up, brushed himself down, and then plunged straight into a plot to fool the police? Could he have faced all the trauma of escape and evasion, all the long-term problems of creating a new identity and living in some remote part of the world? It seemed unlikely.

But how had he died? Where was the body?

There were two clear possibilities. Lucan had drowned in the sea, or he had crawled into an animal trail and perished on the South Downs.

To the fishermen on the English South Coast, a body hauled into their nets and brought on board deck was the loss of a day's money. When they returned to shore the catch was destroyed and the boat was impounded because of the threat of disease and contamination. A fisherman would not be allowed to put out to sea again that day. The deck would have to be cleaned and inspected. A statement would have to be made to the police. There would be an insurance claim and all the nightmare of paperwork.

The alternative was much simpler and widely practised: when the nets were hauled in and the body flopped out on to the deck, the fishermen simply separated it from the catch and speared it with a bill hook. Once the gases had escaped they would sling it back overboard and it would sink to the bottom, where it would be consumed by crabs. In due course, only the bones would remain.

This was Ranson's theory about why Lucan's body was never found. He was convinced that 'the sea somehow holds the key to his death'. In his view, Lucan had crept on board an early morning ferry, weighed himself down, and then leapt overboard. Perhaps his body had gone straight to the bottom to be eaten by the fish. Perhaps it had been hauled in by a trawler and dispatched back down again. Either way, Lucan's remains would be gone for ever.

It was a fine old theory and it had many supporters. James Fox said:

> My certainty that Lucan drove the car to Newhaven persuades me to this day that he died near the port and in the sea, and that his body was consumed within 48 hours by crabs. I believe that . . . dulled with pills and whisky [he] threw himself into the sea. The fishermen pull up corpses with surprising frequency in their trawl nets, but instead of declaring the body . . . they spike it with a hook to let out the gases and send it below.
>
> The seawater crabs would have eaten the flesh from his bones within two or three days.

To check the point, I spoke to the staff at the ferry terminal at Newhaven, to ask about the formal security arrangements that might have existed in 1974. They confirmed that it would have been quite possible for someone to stow away on board twenty years ago. Now, they said, with the terrorism and drugs problems that existed, security was much tighter. But in the early 1970s the system was much less rigorous. A ferry had gone out at 7 a.m. that morning, and another at 11 a.m.: Newhaven to Dieppe crossings. It was quite conceivable that Lucan had boarded the ferry and thrown himself off once it was out at sea.

The other possibility was that Lucan had simply taken a

boat out from the Newhaven Marina. This seemed much less likely. There is no evidence that his own speedboat was moored there (he had planned to dump Veronica in the Solent, after all, which is much further up the coast). If he had stolen someone else's boat there would have been a reporting of the theft. And if he had simply taken a boat out into the Channel and then thrown himself overboard the boat would sooner or later have been found adrift.

But suicide by drowning was not the only option. All around Newhaven lies the dense area of the South Downs. The police had conducted extensive searches here. Gerring had coordinated a massive manhunt in the five-mile radius of the car. It was not as popular an explanation as the drowning theory, but it still had its advocates. Norman Lucas wrote:

> It may be months or even years before the peer's remains are discovered but I am convinced that one day they will be found. I believe that they are concealed somewhere on the South Downs, which, as the Sussex police say, could be searched every day for six months by a thousand policemen and still produce no evidence, so dense is the undergrowth.
>
> In recent years, the skeletons of three people for whom searches were organized on a major scale have been unearthed, but only when the activities of foxes or dogs have disclosed the whereabouts.
>
> It is a reasonable assumption that Lucan, having realized the enormity of his crime and the impossibility of escaping retribution, decided to seek oblivion in the almost inaccessible and impenetrable vastness of the South Downs.
>
> Having burrowed a way into the jungle-like overgrowth, he may have resorted to the four tranquillizers that Susan Maxwell-Scott gave him, or he may have taken a dose of easily available common aspirin

to induce a deep sleep. And, because of his own exhaustion and the exposure of a bitter winter night, it was a sleep from which he never recovered.

And Charles Benson, Lucan's old friend from Eton, a former golfing partner said:

The car was found abandoned on the South Coast. What happened then? Lucky had bungled the murder. What could he do? He had almost certainly found a means of disposing of [Veronica's] body. He had probably found a desolate spot up on the South Downs, a pot-hole in deep undergrowth. What options had he but to take his own life? If he had dumped himself in the sea he would have been washed up. So he [probably] shot himself in the very place he had earmarked for Veronica's body.

Chapter Sixteen

THE VIEW FROM THE DOWNS

The sun is sparkling on crystal waters. All night the rain has been lashing against the window of my hotel bedroom, swelling the gutters, pulling a thick silver veil across the sea. The ferries had braved it, as they usually do, but smaller vessels and fishermen had stayed at home. However, as I pulled back the curtains, the sea storm has given way to a beautifully clear morning. It is a typical morning in late summer on the English South Coast; a mild breeze; the sky a wide and spotless expanse of the deepest blue; the sea, now soothed after its rages the night before, glistening in the sun, studded with a thousand tiny laps and waves.

I am staying at the Solent, a large Georgian hotel on the sea-front at Portsmouth. Driving from the city centre towards Southsea, the hotel stands out on the sea-front as the smartest in a mélange of High Georgian buildings. By a curious coincidence, a little further up the front, I discover, there is the home of Florence Bravo, the woman at the centre of one of the great murder mysteries of the last century. Bravo was the next case I was intending to research, now that Lucan was nearly complete.

From here, there are all the pleasures of the South Coast of England. I had driven down from Oxfordshire on a fine, bright afternoon, taking the A34 on a leisurely route through Newbury and Winchester. I had deliberately avoided the motorway in order to catch a flavour of the sites and terrain which featured so strongly as a backdrop to the Lucan story. At lunchtime, I stopped in Winchester and found St Swithun's girls' school, a vast building that looked like an embassy or the government house in some fashionable colony. In gloomier times, with its heavy red brickwork and large square windows, it might have had an air of misery and confinement to it. Here, surrounded by lush playing fields in rural Hampshire, were the twin features that stayed in the memory of boarding-school pupils: a sense of grandeur, of being set apart, of a destiny assured, and the tough austerity of remote and cold imprisonment.

I detoured after lunch to go to North Waltham, the little village where Veronica had been brought up after returning from South Africa. The pub that her stepfather had run was still there. One of Lucan's friends had remembered it as 'that place on the way back from Ascot'. It was difficult to find, and seemed to have been encircled by highways and trunk roads. It was the kind of English village you would find dotted anywhere across the southern counties. My only memory, as I drove away, was of the vast spire of the church, St Michael's, which was cedar, and of the incongruity of the Victorian Church of England school, which was heavy red-brick with a slating roof.

By mid-afternoon all the central locations of the story were starting to feature on the squares of my road map and on the signs that I passed as I drove. I could feel the thrill and the tension as I moved across the chessboard between the key sites of the drama. There was Uckfield; roads to the Solent and Southampton and Seven-Mile Bottom. I passed a large white sign with an arrow pointing westwards that said, simply, 'The Hamble'. And now a flurry of boats appeared between the openings of the hedges that lined the road; quick flashes of water and all the excitements of boating in the summer – tall masts, the gay colours of the name plates, waterproofs flapping in the breeze. I turned off and ambled down a country lane that took me to the shores of the Hamble. It was here that Lucan had built and sailed *White Migrant*. The boat had been named after Mrs Tucker's ocean yacht, *Migrant*, which had been one of the biggest of its kind. *Migrant* had been requisitioned by the US Navy in 1941 and had done active service as a cargo vessel, but Mrs Tucker had taken Lucan on a tour of the Greek islands after the war, and periodically he would do the same journey as an adult in a hired yacht. Mrs Tucker had evidently awakened a genetic interest. Lucan's father, Patrick, had been a keen sailor and had owned a large canal boat, his one concession to luxury, called *Hesperus*. But it was Lucan who took the water seriously. He had designed *White Migrant* himself, with the advice of power-boat specialists, and had found the £10,000 to have it built. That year, 1964, he had competed in the race at Cowes and had even hired a helicopter to film the race. Lucan had led in first position for about five hours and then, unaccount-ably, the boat had disintegrated. This had caused a great furore at the time, since Lucan's boat had been widely championed in racing circles as a ground-breaking craft. The cameraman had missed the moment of disaster, too, which had irritated Lucan, because the pilot had had to fly back to refuel. Nonetheless, he and Veronica had dined out on the footage that he *did* have for several months.

Evidently, he didn't have much luck with his powerboats. Another boating friend I spoke to remembered a second craft being dropped and smashed on the Hamble just after Lucan had finished having it built.

As the evening shades began to draw in, I got back into

the car and drove on southwards, towards the Solent, Portsmouth and Southampton. I had decided to base myself at Portsmouth because it seemed like a central point on the map, between all the key locations; a good place for sorties and somewhere to write. Something had occurred to me as I drove away from the Hamble. If Lucan had had his speedboat moored there ready for the murder, as Taki Theodoracopoulos said, and as Greville Howard indicated in his statement, why had the car been parked at Newhaven? The Hamble was Lucan's territory. His boats had been built there. He knew the area well. Most of all, he knew the shipping and boating lanes around Southampton. He was familiar with the movements of the tide. It had been a hunting ground. But he had no such familiarity with Newhaven, which was a further sixty miles up the coast. Veronica herself had confirmed this to me. (And at the inquest, when the Coroner asked her if her husband had any connection with Newhaven that she knew of, she had replied, 'None that I know of.') If, therefore, Lucan had had his hearse moored at the Hamble, and had escaped from London when things went wrong with the intention of drowning himself, why was his car not found on the Hamble? Newhaven was the nearest Channel port to London. On November 21st, two weeks after Lucan disappeared, the MP and Postmaster-General John Stonehouse disappeared from his hotel in Miami. Stonehouse faked his own death by leaving a pile of his clothes on a deserted stretch of beach late at night.

The sunshine has transformed the sea-front. I drive up the esplanade and out of the city, on to the A27. I leave Portsea Island and follow the duel carriageway across the South Coast of England. Hampshire gives way to West Sussex, to Chichester, with its famous cathedral, and to Worthing. Then the road cuts into East Sussex, Uckfield and on, eventually, to Kent.

The excitement starts again. From Uckfield I go south, following the road Lucan would have taken if he parked the car at Newhaven. I reach Lewes, and the Sussex Downs begin to open out on either side of the road. The Downs are impressive but they are not wild in the way that some stretches of Cornwall or Dorset can be wild, nor are they oppressive to the senses, or claustrophobic, in the way that strikes you, if you are sensitive to such things, when you drive through Kent or the imposing hills of Berkshire. Several times I wanted to pull in and start taking photographs, but the flow of traffic and the design of the roads would not permit it.

I tried to imagine the same drive at night, in winter, with the rain beating down and the road empty of traffic. Then the Downs *would* start to close in around you, seeming to envelop your car. Your headlights would fail to penetrate the crevices and shadows of the landscape and you would suddenly start to feel isolated.

Had Lucan parked the car and then, taking alcohol and pills, stumbled on to the Downs? Gerring had said that when they opened the boot of the car they found two full bottles of vodka lying beside the spare tyre. There was nothing sinister to this. Probably Lucan had purchased them from a supermarket or off-licence in the days before the murder and then simply forgotten to unload the boot. But it did mean that there was alcohol to hand if he was seeking to destroy himself. He had asked Susan Maxwell-Scott for pills. Veronica said he had asked whether she had any sleeping tablets. Had he dumped the car and then followed one of the dirt tracks that led on to the Downs high over Newhaven? 'If he's dead,' Ranson had said, 'then I'm convinced that he's dead within a five-mile radius of the car.' Had he found a dense part of bracken, perhaps in a stretch of forest, and, after swallowing a bottle of pills and half a bottle of vodka, lain down in the foliage and waited for the same kind of oblivion that was to consume his friend, Dominick Elwes, ten months later?

Certainly the Sussex Downs was a notable place for suicide. Periodically, hikers and ramblers would unearth human bones, especially when the warmer weather came in late April or May, and the Downs gave up their dead from the previous winter. (If people go missing in the area from November to March, it is unlikely their bodies will be found until the walkers go out in the spring.) But how likely was it that *Lucan* had perished there? There are a number of problems.

First, he obviously didn't take a bottle of alcohol from the boot of the car because the moment he opened the boot he would have seen the bludgeon.

Secondly, it seems improbable that he would have had access to a fatal dose of sleeping tablets. The fact that he asked Susan Maxwell-Scott whether she had any tablets seems to indicate that there were none to be found at Lower Belgrave Street. She found him a couple of Valium, 'not a very strong dose'. And between leaving Uckfield and the parking of the car at Newhaven we know of no opportunity that would have presented itself for the acquisition of sleeping tablets. That doesn't mean, of course, that he *didn't* acquire them. Perhaps he saw someone else after leaving Uckfield. Perhaps he obtained a lethal dose of pills some other way. But it must remain unlikely.

Thirdly, if Lucan died on the Sussex Downs in 1974 it seems reasonable to suppose that his bones would have surfaced by the time of writing, twenty years later. Ranson had said that the landscape was too dense to fine comb and he appealed for locals to keep a look-out for a body when they went rambling. He said that it would take six months to search the whole area properly, 'and even then we might not find everything'. As if to illustrate his point, the police, as we have seen, found the body of another suicide, which had been there for three years. But there is considerable difference between a body lying concealed in bracken and foliage for two or three years, and one lying concealed for twenty years. It is not impossible that Lucan's body is still out there, somewhere, under a hedge, and that it has evaded everyone's attention for the last two decades. But given the thousands of people who go rambling on the South Downs every summer, often with dogs, and given the wild life that comes out when the ramblers and hikers go home, the foxes, badgers, ferrets and voles, sniffing into hedges and animal trails, it must be supposed that sooner or later, in a year or two, or maybe even three, the decaying remains of a human suicide would inadvertently be dragged out into the open.

Finally, Newhaven comes into view. In most respects it is as I imagined it to be, although considerably smaller. The streets are small and grey. Old people tootle around in foreign cars. A Sealink sign says 'Welcome to Newhaven' and blazons the company emblem at you. The A27 cuts right through the heart of the town and smaller networks of roads and estates lead off from it. But where is the ferry terminal, the quayside, the marina? Suddenly you are on a large bridge; the town has disappeared from around you and has been replaced by the sea. The bridge takes you across a wide expanse of water and you can now see, to your left, the whole painted set of the Lucan drama. There is the ferry terminal, a large jetty reaching out into the Channel, like a pier, to which a small white and blue Sealink ferry is already moored. On the other side of the expanse are the fishing vessels and pleasure boats. Many of them are moored up on vast mudbanks that shore up the landing bays. Some of them are empty, some are occupied by fishermen sweeping their decks or repairing motors. Between them, with the ferries on one side and the fishing boats on the other, there is the wide mouth of the harbour, full of debris and flotsam, which eventually, after two hundred yards, opens out into the great panorama of the English Channel.

Then suddenly the view is gone. The bridge has ended and

239

you are now in the second part of the town. The first part, as you come off the Downs and approach the harbour, has the ferry terminal as its central feature, and little else in the way of shops or commerce (just a number of streets and estates probably occupied by Sealink staff). But the second part of the town, which you meet once you have crossed the bridge, is another story. This is the town proper. From here you approach the other side of the harbour, where the fishing boats are moored. And this is the busy shopping centre. It is small, with all the roads seeming to lead back into each other, but bustling with shoppers. It is built on a hill, which slopes down towards the harbour. I stop the car and walk around, getting a feel of the place.

Here, written that night in my hotel, are my impressions of the town.

Impression: V. run down. V. grim. Occasional snatches of South Coast elegance, i.e.: Georgian or early Victorian façades; polished and gaudy mid-Victorian pub frontages; the wood is painted and shiny. The shops are small. But mainly it is ugly Victorian architecture. The church, probably, from its design, Methodist or other Non-conformist, is now a commercial building. It is exceedingly ugly. Stands on the hill overlooking the sea right in the centre [of the town]. The A27, which the locals call the Brighton road, cuts right through the town.

At the local pub, the Ship, the landlord and his customers are discussing the threat to the town from the Channel Tunnel. Sealink is virtually Newhaven's only link to the outside world. It has no potential as a tourist centre. The company is the town's biggest employer, and there are many small gift shops and restaurants which would go under if the Channel ferry service had to compete with the Tunnel. The air is thick with disenchantment and gloom.

240

The local feeling, says the landlord, is that Lucan is still alive and that he did not die in the sea.

Later, I wander out to the quayside, as the fishermen are sailing home, and speak to those cleaning their boats. There has never been any suggestion that one of them found Lucan, they maintain. In that tight-knit community, one assumes that such a story would have leaked out. I found myself wondering whether any fisherman, hauling Lucan's body on board his boat, presumably still with recognizable features, would really have sent it back down again. The heavy police presence at Newhaven would surely have deterred them. In 1974, the sea was briefly alive, with a flotilla of journalists and detectives, all watching the water for some sign of a body. Personally, though I had no strong feeling regarding Lucan's fate, I was disinclined to believe that he had been hauled into a trawler and stabbed with a bill-hook. I felt that explaining his disappearance by drowning was simply the easiest option when you were stumped by the discovery of the car at Newhaven and you looked out to sea. Additionally, I felt that if he *had* drowned his body would have been discovered in the underwater searches. A short while after Lucan's disappearance, the body of a man six feet two inches tall was found floating in the sea by trawlermen who brought it ashore, presumably thinking it was Lucan. The body was eventually identified and it was established that it had been in the water for almost six months. I discovered this when, moving up the coast to Brighton, I raked through the cuttings archives of the local paper, the *Brighton Evening Argus*, searching for contemporary reports about the Lucan hunt.

The article of June 9th, 1975 read:

Sussex police were inclined last night to discount a theory put forward that the body of a man found floating in the sea off Dungeness on Saturday might be that of the missing Lord Lucan, sought following the murder of a nursemaid at his London home last November.

The body was in an advanced state of decomposition and had apparently been in the sea for at least six months. The features were not recognisable.

The man was 6ft tall, aged between 40 and 60, and dressed in brown clothing.

Rye inshore lifeboat went out to the fishing boat which found the body, brought it ashore and it was transferred to the mortuary at the Royal East Sussex Hospital, Hastings.

Police are now checking the list of missing persons.

The more that I looked out at Newhaven, at the gun-metal grey water slapping the sea-wall, the less inclined I felt to believe that Lucan had perished here. At the Newhaven West Pier there is a careful log of all the boats going in and out of the harbour, even at night. The log-book of one of the local fishermen reveals that a force 8 gale was raging throughout the evening of November 7th and the morning of November 8th and that the sea was simply too choppy for a small boat to put out. 'Nothing moved,' the fisherman added.

Suicide seemed the most likely explanation for Lucan's disappearance when the car was found at a Channel port, as it did when the politician's clothes were found on the beach. But a closer examination of the circumstantial and practical problems associated with drowning here, together with the lack of a body (or even a sighting) shows that the *likely* explanation is not always the *real* explanation.

Chapter Seventeen

AN OPEN FILE

No one can be certain whether Lucan is dead or alive. One can examine the tangible evidence – the car at Newhaven, the tone of the letters, the asking for sleeping tablets – and be taken so far down the road of inquiry. But there is a point at which the road divides, and then it is merely psychological study, instinct and intuition which decide whether one goes down the avenue of escape or suicide.

Lucan behaved like a throwback. He was the genuine article. His family traces its roots back to the 13th century. There are descendants from Charles II. Lucans occupied a country seat in Ireland and had a seat in London. There is a long tradition of service in politics and in the military. Lucan himself went to Eton, served in the Guards, worked as a merchant banker. Most of his friends were old Etonians, and together they lived a furiously Anglophile life in a lavish London club. This was the culture that Ranson felt would have compelled Lucan's suicide, these the circumstances that Lucan would have been unwilling to exist outside. The argument is almost overpowering.

And yet, Gerring and others were quite able to proffer equally persuasive arguments that he was still alive. Several of his friends believed that he was 'not the suicide type', that the instinct to survive was more deeply rooted than any nurtured instinct about aristocratic culture. He was also a gambler. And whenever the two strains of his life came into conflict – gambling or upper-class honour – it was his gambler's instinct that triumphed. He had not hesitated to unshackle himself from the bank when gambling was legalized in 1960, even though that act brought him a mass of complaints and criticisms about honour from the more old-fashioned members of his family. Neither did Lucan behave with upper-class 'honour', when he kidnapped his children, nor when he plotted the murder of his wife. These were the acts of the desperate gambler, not of a man obsessed with ancient notions of aristocratic integrity.

Furthermore, Ranson's point about being seen in the dock was simply not valid. It presupposed that Lucan was actually going to be caught by the police. As Ranson himself later admitted, by the time they found the car their chances of catching Lucan had effectively been halved. The more time that elapsed, the slimmer those chances became. And even if he *had* been caught, and did not want his children to see him in court, there was still the option of suicide after his arrest. Why kill oneself to avoid being charged with a crime when the likelihood of actually being caught was apparently so slim?

It seemed to me that there were three other points to consider as well.

First, the car was parked in the centre of Newhaven, just off a main street. The spot is ideal if one wants one's car to be discovered by people who might be looking for it, but it is not very discreet for someone who is planning to disappear at the harbour. There are places much closer to the shore (in fact, the car was parked in the second part of the town, the more densely packed area, rather than the first part, which is the main ferry terminal), including numerous back streets very close to the ferries and the marina, from where the sea itself is only a few minutes' walk. Distance, of course, was vital if Lucan was not to be seen wandering around in the middle of the night in blood-stained clothes.

Secondly, there is the curious choice of Newhaven itself. It is the nearest Channel port to London. It is also one of the busiest. Presumably, when Lucan planned to motor out into the Channel with his wife's body in his speedboat he was intending to embark from a lonely beach somewhere. One would not choose to sail out into the sea, with a body on board, in the middle of the night, from a busy shipping lane. So why did Lucan choose to dispose of his own body at a busy sea-port? Why didn't *he* go to some remote little beach on the coast and fling himself into the sea? Newhaven has all the resonance of a stage suicide. That does not necessarily mean that Lucan did *not* die off the Newhaven coast, but it seems a curiously public place for someone who wished to meet his end in private.

Thirdly, there is the question of when the car was parked at Newhaven. If it had been parked there almost immediately after Lucan's departure from Uckfield, which was 1.15 a.m., it increases the possibility that he had committed suicide. Any delay between Uckfield and Newhaven is hard to explain using the suicide theory. Therefore I was amazed to discover that the Corsair had turned up in Norman Street between three and seven hours *after* Lucan had left Uckfield.

'I know,' said Gerring. 'Strange, isn't it? What the hell can you be doing for seven hours if it only takes twenty minutes to drive from Uckfield to Newhaven?'

'You see,' he went on, 'I found this chap who lived over the road from where the car was parked, and he had some eye trouble. His doctor had advised him to focus on something when he had a spare moment. Anyway, he got up at 5 a.m. to go to the toilet and he looked out of the window and focused on an empty space over the road. Then he went back

245

to bed. He got up at eight o'clock to go to work and when he looked out of the window at the spot where he'd been focusing, the Corsair was there.

'So it wasn't there at 5 a.m. And it was there at 8 a.m. Now this means, of course, that it could have been parked at one minute past five or one minute to eight. Somewhere in between. Either way, there are up to seven hours missing, totally unaccounted for. And, as you say, the 64,000-dollar question is what the hell happened in those seven hours? It's very disturbing.'

Those who believed that Lucan had killed himself could only explain this gap in the times by suggesting that he was sitting in the car, brooding. But seven hours is a very long time. It is the equivalent of a day at the office; a night out at dinner and a club; of watching almost five cinema films in a row. The idea of Lucan – an essentially impulsive person, whose ruminations about death or escape would have been made on the forty-minute drive from London to Uckfield straight after the crime – sitting in his car for seven hours, trying to pluck up courage to go and drown himself, is plainly ludicrous. It was therefore time for another lunch with Gerring. Gerring had always maintained that Lucan was at large, a belief he, like Ranson, based largely on a reading of Lucan's mentality. He agreed with Ranson that Lucan responded to certain psychological compulsions that were anchored to his upbringing and his aristocratic culture. But they disagreed about the extent to which that affected him.

'You're back,' he said, when I arrived. 'Have you found him yet?' He continued, 'I can argue Roy's position and he can argue mine, but at the end of it it's a gut feeling. As a police officer you're trained to respond to your instincts – where that's appropriate. My thinking that Lucan is alive is based on instinct, just as Roy's belief that he is dead is based on instinct.'

Gerring confirmed that Lucan's boat had not been moored

at Newhaven; they had checked through the marina registers, and he had heard himself that the boat was in reality moored on the Hamble. Again, however, there was no proof, since the boat was not on the Hamble by the time the police came to check (they had checked merely because *Migrant* had been previously moored there).

Gerring was unconvinced by the explanation that Lucan had jumped off a ferry. He agreed that he might have been able to stow on board but felt that such a distinguished-looking person would find it impossible to get to the deck without being seen and remembered. To stop his body being found, he said, Lucan would have had to weigh himself down before he jumped, and that was outside the realms of serious possibility. 'Can you see a six-foot-two-inch man tying great weights to his legs on the deck of a ferry and then jumping overboard? Personally, I think that's unlikely.'

In his book *Trail of Havoc*, Patrick Marnham said:

Many people are convinced that Lord Lucan is dead because his body has never been found. I do not agree with that deduction. If he had sunk his speedboat in some deep part of the Channel, having first chained himself on board, his body would still be at the bottom of the sea. The *Mary Rose*, a Tudor warship that sank in the Solent and was recently refloated, still contained the skeletons of many Tudor sailors. Alternatively, Lord Lucan could have killed himself in some other way, having arranged for a friend to dispose of his body. But did he kill himself? In the first place, he was a gambler. Gamblers believe in luck. Suicide leaves you with no chances. In the gambling world it is taken for granted that Lucan is alive.

Personally, I felt that it was curious indeed that Lucan should have gone to such extraordinary lengths to dispose of his own body. Why should he want to conceal his remains? What

247

advantage would that be to him? Indeed, it was actually a disadvantage to his stated concern of protecting the children, Lucan's first concern. Ranson's contention was that he killed himself to avoid the humiliating effect his appearance in the dock would have upon them. He feared for them in the blaze of publicity that would accompany his arrest and trial. But to kill himself and conceal his remains would be to keep alive exactly the kind of publicity that Lucan was trying to avoid.

If he was going to kill himself, surely it would have been open and quick. He could have taken an overdose in the car or hurled himself from the cliffs overlooking Newhaven. Whatever he did, the purpose would have been to kill stone dead any speculation about his fate: the kind of speculation that he feared would hurt his children.

'I don't think he's dead,' said his brother, Hugh Bingham. The Reverend Gibbs and his wife, Lady Sarah, agreed. 'I have always said that he is still alive, yes,' he told me. Stephen Raphael, Lucan's old stockbroker friend, also believed that Lucan was alive somewhere. Hugh said, 'I just hope he's managing to be comfortable somewhere.'

Gerring ended our discussion: 'He was a gambler. He was used to taking chances. People like that don't just throw the towel in. I don't think he'd have killed himself without some sort of a flourish, without an attempt at escape at least. He liked life too much.' I agreed but said that Lucan was a man of very limited resources, both psychologically and financially. Gerring merely said that Lucan had the kind of temperament that could adjust, provided the circumstances were lavish enough. 'I think he's probably still gambling out there, somewhere,' he said. He reminded me of what the Police Commissioner in 1974, Sir Ernie Bond, had said: that Lucan was still alive in his opinion and that some day, somewhere, an ordinary police patrol man would 'casually stumble upon him'.

Chapter Eighteen

CONCLUSIONS

In the autumn of 1989 I visited the Clermont Club.

This, in many ways, was the climax of the story, the place to which all doors led, the last few paces of the trail.

I had almost visited the club the previous year, when I had arrived in Berkeley Square for an interview with Mark Birley, the proprietor of Annabel's. I had hoped that when our talk came to an end he would offer to show me round. He did not. And in retrospect it was better that he didn't. It was more productive to visit the Clermont as simply the guest of a member, than to be shown round by the owner of the adjacent night club.

I arrived early on the night of my visit. Berkeley Square was starting to come alive as I walked towards the club, the street thronging with rich people going off for dinner. The doorman nodded and smiled, as though I came every night, and quietly ushered me inside. The entrance hall was large and square, with a sapphire-blue carpet and a vast log fire. Two beautiful young girls immediately appeared, their satin gowns rustling on the Wilton carpet. The first went to a large oak desk to produce the guest book, the second came over and took my coat. Her blonde hair was raised up in a high chignon at the back of her head, a few long wisps falling down the side of her face. She wore pearls, both round her neck, offsetting the gold of her gown, and on her ears. She also had a tiny green brooch, in diamonds and gold, on her left shoulder. When she smiled, which was often, she revealed a set of perfect white teeth. Her gown was cut so finely and so tightly that I felt I could enclose both my hands around her waist and watch as my fingertips met.

I resisted this temptation and walked through to the bar. Now, all at once, the magic of the place opened out, in a mélange of Georgian furniture, long oil paintings and large Chinese vases. I sat down on a high stool and surveyed the place.

The bar was clearly your starting point. To your right lay the entrance hall, to your left the staircase – fifteen feet wide and forty feet high, which opened out on to the second landing. Beneath the staircase lay the 'widows' bench', the waiting area for women who wanted to go home but whose happy husbands were gambling above. I could see Veronica sitting there, legs crossed, fingers anxiously tapping on the ornate arms of the sofa, one hand nervously curling around her emerald brooch. People would look at her on their way to the bar, and at the bar itself they would turn round while their drinks were being prepared and glance at her from the corner of the eye. She would feel their gaze, hear snatches of their whispered remarks. And soon she would start to feel like an outsider. For any member of the hoi poloi, the Clermont was a very easy place to despise.

And of course I could see Lucan himself, coming down those stairs, perhaps with Aspinall. Two tall and powerful men, striking to look at. At the foot of the stairs, here at the bar, there would be Elwes, Goldsmith and the Goldsmith cigar, Stoop, Benson and the portly Raphael. And now Veronica would come over, this single and tiny woman, her face fixed in ire. She would start to make a scene, the smiles would vanish, the bar staff would quickly, discreetly slip away, people would stare into their drinks. Lucan wouldn't turn and face her – there must be no arguing, not in front of his friends – and the more he ignored her the more furious she would become. Finally he would snap and grab her arm and haul her out of the club – 'See you tomorrow, John' – and climb into a taxi, and sit in a stinking silence all the way home and all the way to bed and all through the following morning, until at last he came back to the club that night. And then the whole cycle would be repeated. It would have been the humiliation that was the worst: the pitiful glances of his friends: the remarks after they had left – 'Bloody odd woman he's got there'.

'Pushy . . .'

'I only wanted a normal family life.'

The two sides of an impossible situation.

I left the bar and walked on; through the arch, into the drawing room. I picked up a copy of the *Guardian* and sat down near the fire, in one of the big leather armchairs. A waiter appeared in a green and gold uniform and asked what I wanted to drink. I shook my head. A man sitting opposite me coughed very quietly. The waiter went over.

'Scotch. Daniels. No ice.'

Then *The Times* was back in place and there was no sound except the flames licking and spitting in the Regency fireplace.

The colour scheme of the Clermont has always been green and gold. The walls are gold throughout, embroidered with white coving; the doors are green, embroidered with gold coving. It would have had much more of a Georgian feel in Aspinall's day, simply because of the grand, Regency Buck atmosphere that he was trying to cultivate. Then it had moved to the calmer, stilted air of the Edwardians. And now it was back to Aspinall's original design. Hugh Hefner, who had bought the club in 1973, had found that changing the style of the place hadn't worked – the fruit machines had

251

gone, the Kent fireplaces were back. The Heron Group had purchased the club from Hefner and had set about remodelling it, back to the 'golden days'.

I left the drawing room, where people were now starting up backgammon games, and walked through to the restaurant. This was an addition to the original William Kent house, which Aspinall had built in 1962 for a single function – a garden party, someone said. But he had been so pleased with the result that he had decided to keep the area open and furnish it as a dining room. Nothing had changed since Aspinall's time, I was told. Later someone pointed out 'Lucan's table'. The restaurant was lined with huge silk drapes, pink-tied with white velvet ribbons. The tables, no more than half a dozen, were set out in a semi-circle against the walls; Lucan's table was in the deepest part of the quarter-moon, right against the far wall. And since the restaurant opened out into the drawing room which I had just left, I noticed that this meant that whoever sat in Lucan's chair had – unlike any of the other seats – a totally unimpeded view of who was entering the club, who was in the bar and who was going upstairs.

I left the restaurant and went to the second floor.

'Lady Isabella [Finch] used to have mirrors on the landing,' said my host, 'so that she could look out from her bedroom and see who was waiting for her below.' The second floor was divided into different gambling rooms. I chose the roulette hall, to my left, where the croupiers were once again women, framed in satin gowns, perched on stools over eight or nine huge tables.

I sat down and bought some chips. An ashtray was produced. Someone asked for a free spin because they could hear the wheel creaking. But it made no difference. On five runs we lost a thousand between us.

I pulled myself away and went back downstairs. The place was starting to fill. Soon the big poker games would be under way.

In the cloakroom there were bottles of eau de cologne, combs and hairbrushes bearing the initials 'CC'; even toothbrushes 'impregnated with toothpaste'. I stole one of the latter items as a souvenir.

In the Clermont I found that people would quite freely chat about the 'good old days', as the Aspinall reign was known. There were many apocryphal stories about the celebrated figures who had been members or house-players in Lucan's day. A thread of truth undoubtedly ran through many of the stories, though some had clearly been embellished with perpetual recounting. All of them were laced with the flavour of style and social rebellion.

There was the time when, fresh out of Oxford, unemployed and drifting, the young John Aspinall found that his stepfather had secured him a 'proper job' as a salesman for a company in Nigeria. When the company sent him his tropical-kit allowance two weeks before he was due to sail, he took the chit round to a shop in Regent's Street and bribed one of the sales assistants into exchanging the chit for cash. He then took the cash to the nearest betting shop and laid it on three horses – all of which were outsiders and all of which came in first. From fifty pounds he now had over a thousand, enough to support himself until he had decided what he wanted to do with his life. The first thing, however, was to find Ian Maxwell-Scott, whom he had not seen since Oxford. Maxwell-Scott had been disowned by his parents because of his gambling. He had also been thrown out of a friend's flat because he had hocked his entire wardrobe in order to go to the races. When Aspinall finally tracked him down it was to a slum in south London, ripe for demolition, where Maxwell-Scott was lying on the floorboards. The room smelled badly. There was no furniture. The windows were boarded over. And Maxwell-Scott was asleep under two copies of the *Racing Times*.

'Ian,' said Aspinall, walking through the door, holding a silk handkerchief to his nose. 'Ian, things are looking up,

We've got a thousand pounds and we're going to stay at the Ritz.'

'Oh no, not the Ritz,' Maxwell-Scott replied. 'The food there is *quite* terrible.'

Later, Aspinall became a regular host in London for weekly gambling parties to which the young aristocracy of the city would loyally attend. But to entice them in the first instance, Aspinall had to prove himself as a host of some elegance and *bonhomie*. This was rather difficult on his limited budget. So, on one occasion, he visited an art gallery in London and showed interest in two magnificent Canalettos, each valued at a thousand pounds. He summoned the curator and told him that he was very interested in purchasing both paintings but he first of all needed to establish that they matched the décor of his apartment. Would the curator allow him to take the paintings home so that he could check this? Yes, of course, provided they were returned at once if Mr Aspinall did not wish to purchase them.

The Canalettos hung on the wall of his flat for several weeks, impressing all of his upper-class guests. It was nearly a month before the curator of the gallery realized what was happening. When the gallery's removal men arrived to snatch the paintings back, Aspinall, who was halfway through an afternoon gambling party, calmly told his guests that he was having the paintings sent away to be cleaned, and then assisted the removal men in heaving them from the wall.

'But he never looked back,' said one man, with a grin. 'My God, you've got to give it to him.' He remembered an evening at the Clermont when Aspinall had organized a vast backgammon tournament. The whole club had been transformed into an Indian palace. There were tigers and elephants strolling through the place. And when the gala opened, fifty Indian boys stood on the magnificent staircase, holding candles, as Aspinall appeared at the top and slowly walked down. The lights went out and the boys began to sing. 'Whatever you say about Aspers,' said my host, 'he's got bloody style.'

According to Brian Masters' biography, Aspinall made a habit of transforming the Clermont, particularly in the private upper quarters. Sometimes he would create the rooms of a sumptuous Egyptian palace, sometimes a medieval banqueting hall, on one occasion the Hanging Gardens of Babylon. Rooms would be built inside rooms. Decorators and designers would be flown in from abroad. Massive expense would be incurred in the use of rare and exotic materials. The guests would arrive appropriately attired, and the proceedings would quickly degenerate. There would be a great deal of drinking and, usually, the party would end with a vast food fight.

But those days were long-since over. Now the Clermont was strictly for gambling. The Clermontians had mostly gone their separate ways and met distinctly different fates. Maxwell-Scott suffered a serious decline after Aspinall sold the Clermont in 1973. He had been a director of the club and, though he stayed on for a while during the transition to Playboy, he was already in serious trouble with his drinking, which was eventually to get out of hand. In 1977 he was discovered living on Social Security in a council flat in north London, facing gaol for an unpaid rates bill. He died in 1993. Maxwell-Scott had been one of the most flamboyant figures in the inner circle. When he had started courting Susan Clark, in the 1950s, her father, a QC, had forbidden her to see him because he was a gambler. 'The fellow is not to my taste,' said Sir Andrew. 'He's a gambler. He has no proper job. I prefer a man who does a day's work to any amount of nobility or titles.' So the couple eloped, to Ireland. When they returned to England they married in secret at St Mary's Church, Cadogan Gardens, Chelsea. The priest who married them was Monsignor Valentine Elwes, an uncle of Dominick.

Maxwell-Scott then went on to enjoy some spectacular

gambling wins. He won £33,513 from an £80 investment with Ladbroke's, the turf accountants. He insured against his wife having twins in 1966 and when she had them he picked up a cheque for £100,000. (It was this win that enabled him to buy Grant's Hill House in Church Street, Uckfield, the seven-bedroomed Victorian rectory that Lucan drove to on the night of November 7th.) Other bets were less lucrative but more engaging. On one occasion, when the racing was over at White City dog track, he bet his companion, the million-aire Gerry Albertini, that he could win a private sprint around the track. Maxwell-Scott was ahead of the race when, to the disappointment of the crowd, who had made bets amongst themselves, they were ordered off by a steward. On another occasion, Maxwell-Scott attended a party in Gros-venor Square and, bored by the company, bet Sir Anthony Cope, a fellow guest, that he could win a race around the square. The guests watched from the balcony as they ran twice round the park, finishing neck and neck.

The undoubted triumph of the set was Jimmy Goldsmith, who, already prosperous in 1974, went on to become a billionaire. Goldsmith, too, had had a colourful existence. He was already a playboy of some renown in the 1950s when he eloped with Isabel Patino, the daughter of the Bolivian tin millionaire Don Antenor Patino. The couple went to Scot-land and married in Kelso. After Isabel became pregnant, her parents relented and accepted the marriage. But a few weeks before the baby was due Isabel died from a brain haemorrhage. The baby was saved, but several months later she was kidnapped by Isabel's mother, who took her back to Brazil. Goldsmith won back the child only after a protracted battle in the custody courts.

On several occasions, Goldsmith gambled everything he possessed in the business world in order to keep his fortune growing. He was saved from bankruptcy in 1957 by a sudden bank strike, which bought him a week in which to clear his debts. With uncanny intuition, he sold most of his British assets just before the property crash of 1974, and, even more spectacularly, he sold everything he owned only weeks before the huge stockmarket crash of 1987, which destroyed many of the world's biggest tycoons. 'In between,' said his biographer, 'he gambled everything on a single deal and made £500 million.' Today, Goldsmith is active in many disparate directions. He gave up business to create the Goldsmith Foundation, an international organization dedicated to saving the environment. His brother, Teddy, has been a lifelong exponent of environmental causes, starting magazines, writing books, campaigning politically. Aspinall, too, is passionate about the environment and about wildlife. On one occasion he hired the Albert Hall to make a speech about the plight of Indian tigers. On another occasion, he unveiled a ten-foot bronze statue of an endangered species of elephant at the Los Angeles home of Selim Zilkha. International celebrities, entrepreneurs and politicians heard him make 'an impassioned plea' for the protection of all endangered animals. Goldsmith also has an interest in European politics, and recently formed a new political party, on the right, to fight the European elections of 1994 in France. He had some considerable success. His main theme was an opposition to the Maastricht Treaty and to the growing concept of European federalism and integration.

Although he has homes in France, Britain and the United States, Goldsmith now spends most of his time, at least six months of the year, at his fiefdom in Latin America, called Cuixmala. Jacob Rothschild has been there. So has Richard Nixon, Kerry Packer, Mick Flick from Germany, and Henry Kissinger. The vast main house was designed by Richard Couturier, of New York, and Goldsmith regularly entertains up to a hundred guests at a time. There are swimming pools, beaches, tennis courts and stables. Last year, Goldsmith flew a jazz band down from New Orleans to entertain his guests at lunch and dinner.

John Aspinall prospers, too. He still owns two large zoos, Howletts and Port Lympe, which he manages personally.

It was easy, casting one's eyes around, to see how someone of Lucan's temperament could become addicted to the Clermont. It had the grandest staircase and the grandest drawing room of any 18th-century London house, the typical Kentian plaster easily rivalling those of the great European baroque architects. In the tunnel-vaulted saloon upstairs the walls were richly coffered with paintings of the Loves of Gods and Goddesses, while vast Ionic columns lined the landing and stairs.

By 10 p.m., the big games were in full swing: the club was warmed with dinner jackets and satin gowns, alive with the sound of exploding champagne corks, ice in cocktail shakers, the whoops and shrieks of women watching their lovers anticipating a Chemmy Nine. At 10 p.m. the Clermont Club looked like a *caricature grotesque* from *Punch*.

Looking back, I do not believe that Lucan had an overriding emotional dimension to his motive. He may have been maddened by his wife's ability to beat him in court. He may have been maddened by her ability to withstand his attempts to crush her psychologically. Many men who are separated from their wives find themselves in this situation, with these feelings. But they do not commit murder. They vent their feelings in a more socially acceptable manner. For Lucan, the exasperation he felt over his wife's triumph was, to use his mother's words, 'an obsession', but I do not believe that it was an obsession sufficient to drive him to plot her death. I believe that his motive was much more pragmatic, his purpose far more hard-headed.

In the final analysis, it was the fact that he was broke, and that he couldn't psychologically stand the horror of being broke, that drove him to act. All his adult life he had been used to the luxury and wealth that attended his position. From his childhood in America, his years at Eton, through to his days as a merchant banker and professional gambler, he had had the resources to underpin his way of life. It was a deeply-rooted addiction that could be traced all the way back to his boyhood with Marcia Tucker, to the plush estates of Penwood and Mount Kisco. But, by 1974, these things, which he cherished above everything, were under threat. And he was driven to act.

On that ghastly night in November, the Earl of Lucan gambled for the very last time. He gambled for the highest stakes. And, like most of the risks he had taken in his wasted life, it was a gamble that he lost.

Chapter Nineteen

TWENTY YEARS ON

This book first appeared on the twentieth anniversary, to the day, of Lord Lucan's disappearance. Naturally, a great deal of other Lucan material also appeared on the same date. When it became apparent that the sales of this book were going to warrant a paperback edition the following year, it seemed an appropriate opportunity for me to review what had occurred on the anniversary and to update the book by incorporating the more important developments in the case.

This proved harder than one would initially imagine. It would be fair to say that the twentieth anniversary was probably marked by more coverage than has been generally afforded to any *cause célèbre* – John Kennedy, Jack the Ripper, Marilyn Monroe – that occupies a comparable place in the canon of problematic unsolved crimes. Two books, including this one, were published, amid considerable publicity, whilst a third, by David Gerring, was reported to be on its way. The BBC broadcast a ninety-minute television documentary, presented by Ludovic Kennedy, and a ninety-minute radio play, based on this book, which caused immediate controversy. Channel 4 returned to the old question of whether Lucan was dead or alive for their programme *Dead Lucky*, and filmed Roy Ranson poking around the jungles in Africa. ITV, meanwhile, produced a major drama-documentary, *The Trial of Lord Lucan*, which rewrote history by having Lucan arrested at Newhaven and then put on trial at the Old Bailey. In the meantime, the press, of course, had their customary field day: whilst feigning weariness with the saga they simultaneously gave over yards of column space to all the old puzzles and speculations. The *Daily Mail* even advertised a £100,000 reward for anyone who led them to the missing man. In the middle of all this, George Bingham, who had hitherto been the Invisible Man of the British aristocracy, suddenly announced that he was seeking to have his father finally declared dead, a revelation that, given the already feverish state of things, could hardly have been timed to cool the public interest.

Indeed, there was one point, I vividly remember, when, as I hurried from one interview to another, it occurred to me that the appearance of the missing man *himself* could hardly have generated more publicity.

A few of the things that came out of the twentieth anniversary were of genuine historical value, which is why I felt compelled to update this book by setting them down. Most, of course, were worthless. Amid it all, one was perpetually conscious of the uncomfortable feeling that the past, on the whole, was being raked up out of the need to boost sales or improve ratings, rather than out of any sense of the value of a serious inquiry. But when I began my research there was no anniversary looming. I undertook it because of a strong desire, admittedly rooted partly in the ego, to solve an old and intractable mystery.

There were, as I have said, three major television programmes transmitted on the week of the murder. Each had a different theme and a different perspective. Probably the most engaging of them was Roy Ranson's excursion to Africa, in *Dead Lucky*, one of Channel 4's *True Stories* films. This started from the premise that Lucan had slipped through the police net in 1974 because Scotland Yard had refused to allow Ranson and Gerring to go abroad to check all the sightings. Subsequently, Ranson, following up (at the expense of Channel 4) many of the leads that he had originally been given, went out to Botswana, to the rich retreats of Gaborone and the Tuli Block, where he interviewed casino owners, hotel proprietors and indigenous policemen. The high point was probably a shot of Ranson in the Tuli Block desert, stopping a group of bemused Africans and showing them a photograph of Lucan that a make-up artist had touched up in order to artificially age him. 'Have you seen this man?' asked Ranson, with his Kentish burr, showing the assembled group what, thanks to the artist, looked like the victim of a bad fire. Sternly, the Africans shook their heads. And Maigret drove off again, empty-handed, into the jungle.

This was all good clean fun: it worked because it never attempted to take itself seriously. It was a charade of an investigation, done purely for the cameras, with no real resources put into proper research. Since Ranson had been retired for almost fifteen years, his original witnesses were now either dead or, in the words of a thrifty narrator, 'could not be found'. When Ranson went to a casino to interview a man who had reported seeing Lucan in the late 1970s, the man was not available; so Ranson, who had, after all, come a long way, found another chap at the same casino, plucked off the roulette table, who obligingly stood in with a 'sighting' of his own.

What was surprising was the way in which Ranson seemed ready to overturn everything that he had always steadfastly maintained about Lucan's fate. For twenty years he had been at the forefront of the suicide argument. He had ordered the sea searches and the hi-tech investigations on the Downs. He had concentrated the resources of the police on the search for a body not a living fugitive. After arguing for twenty years that Lucan was dead he suddenly announced a complete volte-face. He did not really believe that Lucan had killed himself. He had never believed it. The suicide theory was rubbish. He had always believed in fact that Lucan was alive and that he had escaped in 1974.

Amusing though it was, Ranson's programme was nonetheless the least successful of the three. By far the most popular (in spite of being screened after the others) was ITV's, *The Trial of Lord Lucan*, with Julian Wadham and Lynsey Baxter, a glossy ninety-minute drama-documentary. This started with the discovery of Lucan, ruminating in his car at Newhaven early on the Friday morning. Arrested and imprisoned, he was duly tried in front of a real jury, picked by Granada Television executives from the electoral roll. The evidence against him was tested within the legal framework applicable to 1974, and a practising High Court judge then summed up. The verdict, when it came, was a real verdict, not a scripted one, and for this reason it surprised some people and disappointed others.

I had been involved in *The Trial of Lord Lucan* from the outset. My enquiries into the case were well known in the media and I had anticipated being asked to cooperate with one production or another at an early stage. Although I had been approached by both ITV and the BBC, my instinct was always to go with the ITV project. ITV's efforts, I knew, were being handled by two of the most distinguished producers in British television. Ian McBride, a senior executive at Granada, had been responsible for *Who Bombed Birmingham?*, a drama-documentary instrumental in reopening the case of the Birmingham Six. Bill Jones, whose background was in the acclaimed series, *World in Action*, had produced several notable documentaries.

It soon became apparent that the Granada programme was

going to surpass anything done by the rival channels. Bill Jones had committed his team to more than just cosmetic research and, as a consequence, they became the only TV company to gain the support of the Rivett family. I agreed to join the team as Technical Adviser.

The most demanding moment in our efforts came after filming had actually begun. It was agreed that the jury would be unable to reach a verdict, based on hearing *all* the evidence, merely by watching ninety minutes of television. So, on a warm weekend in May, we assembled them at the Granada studios to hear sixteen hours of accumulated research. This was to be the basis on which they reached their verdict. For two days, from 9 a.m. on Saturday to 5 p.m. on Sunday, the technical crew at Granada Television acted out in a mock courtroom, in front of the jury, all the highlights of a full-blown trial. Technicians and crew members played the leading characters. Bill Jones and Ian McBride were, respectively, prosecution and defence counsel. I was asked to take the part of Lucan himself, and gave evidence for nearly three hours. A judge from the northern circuit summed up on the Sunday.

From my own point of view, sitting there in the dock, listening to the exchanges, I was struck by several things. First, how powerful Greville Howard's statement proved to be in the cold, microscopic atmosphere of a court. It quickly became clear that, in any real trial, this would be the strongest card in the prosecution case.

Secondly, it was also noticeable how plausible Lucan's story could be made to *seem* in the hands of a skilled counsel.

At the end of it all, after deliberating for two hours, the jury announced themselves unable to reach a verdict. They were split right down the middle. And so, when the jury told the judge that they could not agree, he had no choice but to order a retrial. This disappointed most viewers, who probably felt an inevitable sense of anticlimax. There was a

widespread feeling that the verdict had actually been manu-
factured for television in order to avoid prejudicing any
future trial. This, of course, was not so.

One of the most significant movements in November 1994,
was George Bingham's announcement that the family were
finally seeking to have Lucan declared dead. This was the
one genuine development in a mass of pseudo news stories. I
was immediately asked by radio producers and newspaper
editors to try to throw some light on the development. Why,
after all these years, was it happening now? What was the
position regarding the rents in Ireland? I cast my mind back
to my interviews with Lady Lucan and my exchanges with
other members of the family. There was no overriding
emotional or psychological reason why Lucan hadn't been
declared dead, Veronica had told me. It was purely because
of the complex legal position. Another member of the family
had told me that the death duties would ruin what little
remained of the family trust. There had therefore been
complex negotiations with the Inland Revenue on whether it
was possible to have Lucan declared dead without incurring
the customary tax duties. I replied, whenever asked, that
George's determination to have his father declared dead now
must presumably mean that an appropriate settlement had
been reached with the Inland Revenue.

And there was something else. Scotland Yard had, for
many years, resisted any attempt to have their suspect
declared dead. This was understandable. If Lucan was
declared dead and then turned up alive it would not prevent
the police from arresting him. But it would create confusion
and delays in the legal machinery. The problem would be
exacerbated if Lucan was unearthed abroad. The machinery
of extradition was complex enough: to have to extradite a
man who was officially dead would be bureaucratic torture.
So Scotland Yard had informed the courts that they wished
the present situation to remain static whenever the matter

was routinely explored at the request of the family. But, in the last twelve months, I had been told, Scotland Yard had reversed their position. They had told the family that they had decided not to stand in the way of a declaration of death. This effectively meant that they were finally acquiescing to the assertion that Lucan was dead; or at least that, if he were alive, they acknowledged that there was no chance of his being caught.

And so it was on this basis also that George Bingham presumably decided to proceed. Scotland Yard have since backtracked from that position. A statement issued on the anniversary insisted that sightings were still being checked and that the investigation would remain an active one.

In the event of Lucan's finally being declared dead, the real winners will probably be his tenants in Castlebar. It was in Castlebar, the town built and owned by the Lucans, that Charles Parnell and Michael Davitt launched the Land League more than a century ago, a movement that inspired rebellion against English landlords across the whole of Ireland. Indeed, their rallying cry, 'The land is for the people!' can still be seen booming from a poster above the fireplace in Castlebar's pub, the Hubert Inn. At one time, Castlebar was the Lucans' country retreat; they built a fine house (now a convent), a Presbyterian church (Lucan's name is still on his pew), and a large cricket pitch (now the town green). The estate was broken up after the death of the third Earl but the Lucans still owned much of the land around the town and most of the town itself. And the people of Castlebar remained liable to pay ground rents.

After Lucan's disappearance, the revolt began. Tenants tore up their rent books. The land agent, Michael Egan, a local solicitor, was turned away at the door. 'How can you pay rent,' one tenant asked a reporter, in 1975, 'to a man who *isn't*?' Since then, time has only hardened the resolve. The Lucan agent has not successfully prosecuted any of the rebels and general legal indifference has given the rebellion considerable momentum.

267

One resident, Mrs Brenda Parsons, the owner of a menswear business on Main Street, told a reporter on the anniversary: 'I stopped paying three years ago. I just decided that that was it. It was a negligible amount but I won't go along with an obsolete system.' Indeed, the figures were revealing. The rents, I was told, are between £25 and £100 a year. Furthermore, they have not risen since Lucan disappeared. The newspaper stories that appeared on the anniversary suggesting that George, on succession to the title, was owed £250,000 in rent arrears, if only he could grind it out of the unfortunate population, are plainly nonsense. One tenant told me that he had bought out the land from the trust. When Lucan disappeared he decided to burn the rent reminders as soon as they arrived. Then he decided it would be simpler just to buy out the property fee. He now owned his house. But there remained a strong resistance to paying, he said.

Dick Morrin, a local councillor, says: 'This system is a leftover from colonial days. De Valera told us not to pay ground rent to absentee landlords and they don't come much more absent that Lord Lucan.' The issue was taken up by the Fine Gael MP for West Mayo, Enda Kenny, who tried to persuade the British Prime Minister, John Major, to personally intervene to speed up the process of having Lucan declared dead. The townsfolk and their MP want what they call 'an end to uncertainty'. They want Lucan declared dead, they say, so that the estate can be given back to the people of Castlebar. They want 'the debts written off and the properties returned'.

They are not, of course, the only ones who seek such an end. However stoically they press on with their lives, the Lucan children are locked into the doubts and tensions of perpetual uncertainty. Sandra Rivett and her family are awaiting justice. Veronica Lucan remains in a limbo, drifting from one day to the next. The question that dominated events twenty years ago hangs over them still.

And the answer seems as far away as it ever was.

Index

MURDER AT WHITE HOUSE FARM

CLAIRE POWELL

In the early hours of 7 August 1985 Essex police received a telephone call from a distraught young man who told them that his sister had run amok with a rifle at the family farm. The young man was Jeremy Bamber. When police broke into White House Farm they found his parents, June and Nevill Bamber, his sister, Sheila Caffell, and her six-year-old twin sons shot dead amid scenes of mayhem.

The handsome Jeremy, who stood to inherit the family fortune, convinced the police that his unbalanced sister had murdered four times before turning the gun on herself. The house was cleaned, removing all forensic evidence, except for one vital clue. But Bamber's girlfriend knew more than she could live with and finally went to the police. After a sensational trial he received five life sentences for murder.

Murder at White House Farm is the inside story of the most notorious and fascinating murder case of the 1980s – a story of a charming but greedy and arrogant man who thought he could get away with murder.

NON-FICTION / TRUE CRIME 0 7472 4366 2

A selection of non-fiction from Headline

THE DRACULA SYNDROME	Richard Monaco & William Burt	£5.99 ☐
DEADLY JEALOUSY	Martin Fido	£5.99 ☐
WHITE COLLAR KILLERS	Frank Jones	£4.99 ☐
THE MURDER YEARBOOK 1994	Brian Lane	£5.99 ☐
THE PLAYFAIR CRICKET ANNUAL	Bill Findall	£3.99 ☐
ROD STEWART	Stafford Hildred & Tim Ewbank	£5.99 ☐
THE JACK THE RIPPER A–Z	Paul Begg, Martin Fido & Keith Skinner	£7.99 ☐
THE *DAILY EXPRESS* HOW TO WIN ON THE HORSES	Danny Hall	£4.99 ☐
COUPLE SEXUAL AWARENESS	Barry & Emily McCarthy	£5.99 ☐
GRAPEVINE; THE COMPLETE WINEBUYERS HANDBOOK	Anthony Rose & Tim Atkins	£5.99 ☐
ROBERT LOUIS STEVENSON; DREAMS OF EXILE	Ian Bell	£7.99 ☐

All Headline books are available at your local bookshop or newsagent, or can be ordered direct from the publisher. Just tick the titles you want and fill in the form below. Prices and availability subject to change without notice.

Headline Book Publishing, Cash Sales Department, Bookpoint, 39 Milton Park, Abingdon, OXON, OX14 4TD, UK. If you have a credit card you may order by telephone – 01235 400400.

Please enclose a cheque or postal order made payable to Bookpoint Ltd to the value of the cover price and allow the following for postage and packing:

UK & BFPO: £1.00 for the first book, 50p for the second book and 30p for each additional book ordered up to a maximum charge of £3.00.
OVERSEAS & EIRE: £2.00 for the first book, £1.00 for the second book and 50p for each additional book.

Name ....

Address ....

....

....

If you would prefer to pay by credit card, please complete:
Please debit my Visa/Access/Diner's Card/American Express (delete as applicable) card no:

Signature .... Expiry Date ....